RACISM

RACISM
An American Cauldron

Christopher Bates Doob

Southern Connecticut State University

■ HarperCollins*CollegePublishers*

To Carby

Acquisitions Editor: Alan McClare
Project Editor: Melonie Parnes
Design Supervisor and Cover Design: Stacey Agin
Production Manager/Assistant: Willie Lane/Sunaina Sehwani
Compositor: ComCom Division of Haddon Craftsmen, Inc.
Printer and Binder: R.R. Donnelley & Sons Company
Cover Printer: New England Book Components, Inc.

Racism: An American Cauldron

Library of Congress Cataloging-in-Publication Data
Doob, Christopher Bates.
     Racism : an American cauldron / Christopher Bates Doob.
       p.   cm.
     Includes bibliographical references and index.
     ISBN 0-06-041720-X
     1. United States—Race relations. 2. Racism—United States.
     I. Title.
     E184.A1D66   1993
     305.8'00973—dc20   92-2580
                                                         CIP

92 93 94 95   9 8 7 6 5 4 3 2 1

Brief Contents

Detailed Contents

Preface

Racism is deeply woven into our cultural fabric. One of the staunchest opponents of racism I have met told me of a recent incident where he approached a group of workers looking for the individual in charge. Without conscious thought he went directly to the only white member of the group. "Now why the hell did I do that?" he said to me. "Chris, it was racism, pure and simple."

Racism is a major social disease profoundly infecting our culture. But before we can implement cures, we must understand the nature of the disease. That is what this book attempts to accomplish. It focuses solely on racism to heighten awareness of its pervasiveness and deadly effects. The central issue here is racism as suffered by large racial groups in this society—African-Americans, Mexican-Americans, Puerto Ricans, Native Americans, Japanese-Americans, and Chinese-Americans—as well as by the majority group it ensnares.

The book's title suggests the tumultuous nature of American racism. The cauldron imagery is also consistent with the conflict perspective provided by the internal-colonialist theory introduced in the opening chapter and used throughout the text.

The focus is racism, not race relations. The book avoids lengthy and often discursive material about individual racial groups in order to hold readers' attention. In particular, I have provided studies and illustrations that demonstrate why institutional racism persists and how it affects people's lives. The use of internal colonialism helps keep students focused, guiding their analysis of material. I chose this theory because its application can make students keenly aware of the nature of racism and, in particular, of its economic and political sources.

The opening chapter introduces basic concepts and analyzes the significance of racism in American society. Chapter 2 examines theories of racism; Chapter 3 introduces the largest American racial minorities. Chapters 4 through 8 explore minorities' exposure to racism in politics, the criminal-justice system, violent situations, work, housing, education, the family, and the mass media. Chapter 9 analyzes racism in South Africa and Brazil; the final chapter discusses possible solutions to racism.

I have focused on producing a readable book. Vignettes introduce each chapter and within the text there are narratives of specific incidents or experiences to keep the presentation interesting and informative. However, the book also provides a substantial body of factual information, including historical sources, recent studies, and up-to-date statistical information.

A number of people have been critical to the project's effective development. The following colleagues in sociology have given invaluable commentary on the developing manuscript. The reviewers were Alvaro Nieves, Wheaton College; Donald Hayes, Sam Houston State University; Lynda Dickson, University of Colorado; Michael Pearson, University of North Carolina-Charlotte; Cynthia Chan Imanaka, Seattle Central Community College; Bilal Hashemi, Eastern Washington University; Karen Lynch Frederick, Saint Anselm College; Robert Miller, University of North Carolina-Wilmington; Bradley R. Hertel, Virginia Polytechnic Institute and State University; and Walter Cartwright, Texas Tech University. As acquisitions editor at HarperCollins, Alan McClare had the indisputable wisdom both to sign the book and to realize that what was originally conceived as a supplemental book for race-relations courses would prove more effective if developed as a text for a semester-long course. As project editor, Melonie Parnes ably guided the manuscript through the production process. I am grateful to the Sabbatical Committee at Southern Connecticut State University and President Michael J. Adanti for granting me a sabbatical for the fall semester of 1988—providing a valuable stretch of time in which to do background reading and thinking for this project. Eveline Bates Doob, Leonard W. Doob, and Gilbert M. Fagiani read the manuscript and gave helpful criticisms.

Teresa Carballal did extensive library research and was on hand to comment and criticize during the entire writing process. Her insightful, humane impact is apparent throughout the book.

Recognizing how interesting and valuable readers' input can be, I encourage any instructor or student with a comment or question about this book to write me at: Sociology Department, Southern Connecticut State University, 501 Crescent Street, New Haven, CT 06515. I promise to answer all letters.

Chris Doob

Chapter
1

Significance of Race and Racism

A light breeze stirred the assemblage of cypress, cedars, eucalyptus, and Monterey pines that stood in green relief against the sharp blue sky. In the ample space between the trees were many sets of sturdy wooden ladders, slides, stairs, and platforms, producing the general impression that trees and children's things were organically blended.

But attractive as it was, the physical environment was much less striking than the children who ranged between infancy and about twelve, spoke various languages, and represented a diversity of racial types. Smiles, laughter, and pleasure dominated the scene as children and parents enjoyed the idyllic setting. Was it the family version of the Garden of Eden, or, perhaps more appropriate for this generation of children, a moment from "Sesame Street"? Actually it was a real place—the children's playground in San Francisco's Golden Gate Park.

At the edge of the playground was a pavilion where refreshments were sold. Suddenly about a dozen eight- or nine-year-old African-Ameri-

1

can boys approached the pavilion. They started to line up, then broke out of line, and one reached into a relish container on a shelf next to the refreshment window, grabbed a handful of relish, and threw it point-blank at a companion's head. The victim retaliated, and several other boys joined in. A shout came from inside the window, and the boys quickly moved away from the refreshment area. A middle-aged white woman turned to her grandson and said deliberately, "Those are bad boys, Freddy, very bad boys. I want you to stay away from the likes of them." She looked at the relish container and ruefully shook her head.

Meanwhile a white man walked over to where the boys were now sitting. "That's no way to act," he said. "Food's to be eaten, not thrown." He started to walk away, then turned back to the boys and asked, "Have you kids got money for lunch?" The boys stared blankly at the man, and as his eyes traveled down the row, each, in turn, shook his head. The man looked at the list of items sold, shrugged his shoulders to suggest that buying lunch for the entire group would be too expensive, and then bought each boy a ticket for the nearby carousel.

This situation seems to epitomize the overall racial picture in this country. There are moving illustrations of racial cooperation and harmony; support exists from political and economic leaders as well as the majority of Americans for improving interracial relations. On the other hand, lurking in the shadows often unobserved, especially by white Americans, is the ever-present reality of poverty and racism. Most Americans don't consider themselves racists and do not believe that they encourage racism, but under pressure, like the grandmother, they often reject members of different races if they feel turmoil and violence about to descend. Many Americans manage to either keep racial issues out of their lives or to act interracially under easy conditions, such as in the children's playground at Golden Gate Park.

Before we leave that scene, one more point should be emphasized. Qualities about that situation are peculiar to the modern era. A century, even a half-century ago, such a rich racial assortment of children would not have occurred. In parts of the country, segregation laws would have prohibited children of different races from sharing the same facilities; in other areas, perhaps in San Francisco, informal standards maintained by both whites and racial minorities would have discouraged such a sharing.

This book focuses on racism toward large American racial minorities: African-Americans, Mexican-Americans, Puerto Ricans, Chinese-Americans, Japanese-Americans, and Native Americans.* By 1990 nearly one in four Americans had African, Hispanic, Asian, or Native-American ancestry, a sharp increase from 1980 when the proportion was about one in five.

---

*Currently several racial groups are referred to by more than a single term. My response to this ambiguity is to interchange the terms "blacks" and "African-Americans," and "Chicanos" and "Mexican-Americans."

The major reason for this increase was that during the 1980s the Hispanic population more than doubled (Barringer, 1991). The ratio may be even smaller as racial minorities' percentage of the population might be under-estimated. A prominent reason is that some minority groups are dispro-portionately represented among homeless and immigrant people, who often are not located by census takers.

A fundamental sociological concept in this text is "norms." A **norm** is a standard of desirable behavior. Norms are rules that people are expected to follow in relations with each other. Norms not only provide guidelines for appropriate behavior in a given situation but also supply people with expectations of how others will respond in a given situation.

Throughout this book we see that norms determine people's outlooks and behavior in interracial situations. Parents belonging to different racial groups are more likely to bring their children to a racially integrated playground than they would to a playground where local residents would oppose their presence. Most of the time nearly all of us follow the prevail-ing normative structure: We are creatures of current social custom.

ANALYSIS OF RACISM

Studying a sociological topic like racism requires an approach similar to building or bridge construction; in both cases tools are necessary. As befits an intellectual exercise, the tools used here are not physical but analytic, sociological concepts that examine certain key issues arising frequently throughout this work. In the pages ahead, we discuss two sets of concepts.

Minority Group, Prejudice, and Discrimination

A **minority group** is any category of people with recognizable racial or ethnic traits that place it in a position of restricted power and inferior status so that its members suffer limited opportunities and rewards. Minor-ity-group members are inevitably aware of their common oppression, and this awareness helps create a sense of belonging to the group. It is impor-tant to understand that minority status has no intrinsic relationship to group size. Sometimes a minority group has been many times larger than the dominant group in the society. Such a situation existed when the European countries established colonies in Africa, Asia, and the Americas. In other cases—African-Americans in the United States, for instance—the minority group is smaller in numbers than the dominant group. Minority status is the result of a subordinate position in society, not of the size of its membership.

Prejudice is a highly negative judgment toward a minority group, focusing on one or more characteristics that are supposedly uniformly shared by all group members. If a person rigidly believes that all members of a racial or ethnic group are innately lazy, stupid, stubborn, or violent, then that person is prejudiced toward the group in question. Racial, ethnic, and religious prejudice are the most prominently discussed types. In general, prejudice is not easily reversible. The fact that prejudice is not easily reversible distinguishes it from a "misconception," where someone supports an incorrect conclusion about a group but is willing, when confronted with facts, to change his or her opinion. While prejudice involves a negative judgment toward a minority group, discrimination focuses on the limitations imposed on a group. **Discrimination** is the behavior through which one group prevents or restricts a minority group's access to scarce resources.

The basic position throughout this book is that discrimination is more likely to cause prejudice than prejudice is to produce discrimination. Historically the majority group has discriminated against racial minorities for its own political, economic, and social advantage. Prejudice has been a rationalization for this exploitation. In fact, researchers have found that discrimination can occur without prejudice (Campbell and Pettigrew, 1959), and prejudice is neither necessary nor sufficient to produce discrimination (Kutner, Wilkins, and Yarrow, 1952; Warner and DeFleur, 1969).

Racism involves both discrimination and prejudice as the following analysis indicates.

Race, Racism, and Related Concepts

We begin with the distinction between social and biological definitions of race. *Social races* are categories of people that the majority group designates as sharing a membership that endures throughout members' life span, and that conveys certain rights and duties for them. At first glance this might seem like a straightforward designation, but it involves practical difficulties. While sometimes members of a given social race appear racially similar, in other cases they do not. So under the latter condition how is membership in a social race established? Generally there has been one way—descent: Regardless of racial appearances, individuals belong to a social race if they are at least partially descended from individuals who are confirmed members. But what if the particular society, such as in Brazil, does not use descent as a basis for establishing membership in a social group? Or what if an individual comes from mixed parentage? Then social-group membership is difficult or impossible to establish convincingly (Harris, 1968).

Biological race definitions have been equally confusing. While many criteria, including skin, hair, and eye color, hair texture, nasal index (the relationship between the nose's length and width), lip form, head shape, and genetic distribution have been used to distinguish racial types, none of the criteria taken singly has been able to establish distinct racial groups. For instance, skin color, widely considered the most obvious criterion for distinguishing races, is not an obvious indicator when analyzed thoroughly: There are wide variations within what are designated the major racial divisions of human beings, and considerable overlap among these racial divisions also exists (Molnar, 1975; Montagu, 1974).

Over the past several centuries, however, the danger of imprecision did not discourage efforts to develop racial classifications. In 1735 Carl von Linne produced an analysis of human varieties in which Native Americans were summarized as reddish in color, with thick black hair, and a personality that was considered "persevering, content, free;" Europeans were described as "light, active, ingenious" and "covered with tailored clothes;" Asians were labeled "severe, miserly, haughty;" and Africans as "crafty, lazy, negligent, anointed with oil" and "governed by whim" (Count, 1950: 359).

This schema was influential, and yet a rival outlook also developed during that era. The eighteenth century was a period in which leading scholars believed that the influence of education and the natural environment could have a powerful impact on human beings. A prominent European belief held that the great apes were actually human beings whose progress had been blocked by an unfavorable environment. In the United States, Samuel Stanhope Smith argued that dark skin color was a physical phenomenon like freckles and, with sufficient exposure to the sun, whites could become blacks. Smith contended that the reverse process occurred in the celebrated case of Henry Moss, a Virginia slave who appeared to have lost skin pigmentation after moving from the South to the North.

By the early nineteenth century, however, leading thinkers rejected the conclusion that short-term environmental factors affected people's racial type. Because of a growing comprehension of geology, it was understood that the human species had evolved over a much vaster length of time than previously recognized, and thus while scientists still accepted the idea that savages could become English gentry, whites or Caucasoids were considered to be thousands of years more advanced than the other races (Harris, 1968). In the middle and late nineteenth century, in fact, prominent leaders supported social Darwinism, which, as we will see in Chapter 3, claimed that a white elite's uncompromising pursuit of its self-interest would promote the most universally beneficial social evolution.

Whether social or biological criteria are used, the designation of people's racial membership is an imprecise process. Most frequently **race** refers to a classification of people into categories falsely claimed to be derived from a distinct set of biological traits. While racial classification is imprecise, it proves useful to the majority group. Once people are divided by race, the likelihood exists that membership will be the basis determining people's access to political, economic, and social rewards. Racism then develops.

Racism is the ideology contending that actual or alleged differences between different racial groups assert the superiority of one racial group. Like any ideology, racism serves the interest of the group endorsing it—in this case the majority group—which becomes the chief beneficiary of political, economic, and social discrimination. Throughout the book we see that racist ideologies serve a variety of interests for those who support them. Recognition of racism is widespread. In a national survey, 55 percent indicated that overall American society is racist while 37 percent said that it was not (Media General-Associated Press Poll, August 1988).

Two types of racism exist: individual racism and institutional racism. Whether practiced by one person or a group, **individual racism** is an action performed by one person or a group that produces racial abuse— for example, verbal or physical mistreatment. Frequently this type of racism is intentional, but it need not be. One might argue, for instance, that individual racism occurs when a white customer seeking information approaches a group of five store employees and addresses the only white member, the customer assuming that this individual is better informed than the others.

Currently individual racism remains common. In lengthy interviews with 37 middle-class blacks, 24 respondents reported incidents in the previous two years concerning individual racism in workplaces, schools, restaurants, and retail stores, and 15 research subjects revealed incidents of individual racism on the street (Feagin, 1991).

Institutional racism involves discriminatory racial practices built into such prominent structures as the political, economic, and education systems. The idea of institutional racism is distinctly sociological, emphasizing that social structures establish norms guiding people's behavior. By accepting the norms maintained in racist structures, individuals invariably perpetuate discriminatory conditions. Institutional racism is the prime factor maintaining racism.

It seems useful to examine institutional racism in detail since many people find this important concept difficult to grasp. One must realize that within many structures of American society—for instance, schools, work organizations, prison systems, and government agencies—the impact of institutional racism has dramatically limited many citizens' chances for success.

Inner-city schools with students who tend to belong to racial minorities often suffer institutional racism. Local and national spending for these schools tends to be modest. Court orders requiring legislators to equalize tax allotments in neighboring school districts are likely to encounter foot-dragging from the representatives of wealthier districts reluctant to lose their funding advantage; a 20-year-old lawsuit in San Antonio, Texas, is a case in point. In such a situation, opponents of equalization of tax allotments are likely to assert that they are not racists, that their resistance is motivated strictly by financial considerations. While this claim might be true, opponents' actions help perpetuate racial discrimination.

Different groups associated with inner-city schools—administrators, teachers, parents, and the students themselves—go through the educational motions but recognize that inner-city students are casualties of society, with bleak futures. A writer, summarizing the feelings of a mother sending her children to an inner-city school with 98 percent African-American students, observed that the woman felt that such schools "were hardly schools at all . . . more like warehouses where the kids were stored for a few years, sorted, labeled, and packed for shipment to the menial, low-paying jobs at which they would be doomed to labor the rest of their lives" (Lukas, 1985: 104). Institutional racism, in short, involves a discriminatory legacy of structures and practices carried over from eras when racist actions were widely and openly supported.

Institutional racism can spread from one institutional structure to another—for instance from the educational to the economic area. Minority-group members attending the kind of mediocre schools just described are less likely than whites, who generally attend better schools, to have educational credentials making them eligible for many jobs. For instance, if a custodial job requires a high-school certificate, minority-group members are more likely than whites to be excluded.

While institutional racism is more concerned with discrimination than with prejudice, other important concepts are focused on the meaning and significance of prejudice. A **stereotype** is an exaggerated, oversimplified image, maintained by prejudiced people, of the characteristics of the group members against whom they are prejudiced. In an early study of stereotypes, blacks were considered superstitious, lazy, happy-go-lucky, ignorant, and musical while Jews were designated shrewd, industrious, grasping, mercenary, intelligent, and ambitious (Katz and Braly, 1933).

Stereotypes often prove useful to those who maintain them. These oversimplified conclusions offer a more orderly, straightforward analysis of a minority group than a nonstereotyped evaluation would provide. Furthermore stereotypes help to either confirm that a downtrodden group should remain in its lowly position or encourage members of the dominant group to push down minority-group individuals who are starting to achieve some economic and political success (Simpson and Yinger, 1985: 100–101).

One of the disturbing, potentially tragic qualities of stereotypes is their self-fulfilling nature. A **self-fulfilling prophecy** is an incorrect definition of a situation that comes to pass because people accept the incorrect definition and act on it to make it become true. For instance, if white teachers believe that black children are superstitious, lazy, happy-go-lucky, and ignorant, then they are unlikely to make a serious effort to help them learn. The students, in turn, will recognize their teachers' disinterest or contempt and will probably exert little effort in school. The teachers see "confirmation" of what they already "know"—that their black students are inferior. In reality what the teachers confirmed was the process performed by the self-fulfilling prophecy. This concept vividly illustrates how prejudice serves as a rationalization for discriminatory behavior.

SIGNIFICANCE OF RACISM IN THE UNITED STATES

While such prominent social theorists as Émile Durkheim, Karl Marx, and Max Weber disagreed on many issues, they agreed that ethnicity and race were relatively unimportant concepts. Analyzing the development of industrialization, they felt that both social bonds and conflicts created by people's ethnic or racial status were characteristics of preindustrial times and would disappear in the industrial world, where discriminatory tendencies associated with those narrow, prejudice-laden ties would give way to more rational relationships that would transcend ethnicity and race and help accomplish the practical goals of modern life (Blauner, 1972: 3–4).

The tendency to dismiss or deemphasize the importance of race and racism is not limited to the past. In *The Declining Significance of Race*, William Julius Wilson (1978) used a class analysis of American race relations to conclude that while modern American capitalism has maintained an underclass of poor people, the process leading to that result has been largely color blind (Wilson, 1978; Wilson, 1987).

According to Wilson, there have been three stages of American race relations. The first stage was blatantly racist, with African-Americans exploited as slave workers on plantations and farms. The second stage occurred with the emancipation of slaves; during the next half-century, industrial expansion was accompanied by both class conflict and racial oppression. The third stage currently exists and involves the transition from racial inequalities to class inequalities.

Wilson concluded that for modern African-Americans barriers no longer concern legalized racial inequality. The passage of equal-employment and affirmative-action legislation has made it possible for blacks with appropriate educational and training credentials to get good jobs and move comfortably into the middle class. In contrast, African-Americans, other racial minorities, and, in fact, whites who do not have the credentials making them eligible to move into the industrial and government sectors find job possibilities increasingly limited. Wilson contended that affirmative-action programs, set up with the best of intentions, have increased opportunities for privileged African-Americans but have not improved chances for poor blacks, thus producing growing economic class divisions among blacks (Wilson, 1978: 19).

Wilson's conclusion that a variety of current economic factors diminish opportunities for poor people, regardless of color, is widely supported. However, two limitations to his central conclusion about the declining significance of race seem apparent, one involving the continuing objective significance of racism and the other its current subjective importance.

First, racism persists objectively in both individual and institutional form. In the chapters on politics and the criminal-justice system, work and housing, education, the family, and mass media, there are studies showing that while racism might often be more subtle than in the past, it remains alive and healthy. Particularly significant is the continuation of institutional racism. Because racism permeates the structures and culture of modern society, policies can perpetuate racist conditions even though those who initiate and carry them out claim to be free of racism, and, in fact, express no prejudices. For instance, hiring practices for blue-collar jobs, which rely heavily on written test scores, are likely to disportionately screen out minority candidates whose more limited schooling means that they are less effectively prepared than whites for these tests. This discriminatory practice can be implemented with no direct reference to the issue of race.

Second, there is the subjective dimension of racism. A recent investigation compared blacks and whites of similar socioeconomic status in their reports of their own psychological well-being and quality of life over a fourteen-year time span from 1972 to 1985. Differences between whites' and blacks' reported feelings remained stable over the time period. The overall result was that blacks reported lower life satisfaction, less general happiness, less trust in people, less marital happiness, and lower physical health than whites. The researchers concluded that being black means "a less positive life experience than being white" (Thomas and Hughes, 1986: 839).

It is clear that race and racism are important realities in modern American life. We need to consider perspectives for analyzing them.

In a provocative article, Troy Duster (1987) suggested that when two distinctive social groups, such as whites and African-Americans, are in contact, and the members of one group plan to study the other, the most fundamental issue involves what questions are posed and answered. For instance, whites, who have comprised the majority of race-relations researchers, have often begun an investigation of blacks focusing on a question similar to this one: Which group is more likely to have members living in poverty? The answer, Duster indicated, is that African-Americans are about three times more likely than whites to be living in poverty. From this information researchers are likely to pursue studies of welfare and its apparently debilitating effect on black communities, as well as the absence of a strong work ethic. Recommendations emerging from such research might emphasize the necessity of workfare programs that force "the lazy parasites" to support themselves and to stop living off productive tax payers.

On the other hand, Duster indicated, researchers studying black citizens might begin with this question: Between blacks and whites in America, which group is more likely to earn their income by working? The answer is that while blacks obtain 80 percent of their total income from wages and salaries, whites receive only 75 percent of their total income from that source. While blacks receive about $1.2 billion from private property or investment sources, whites obtain $87 billion. From this perspective it seems that whites, not blacks, are more inclined to live off "the fat of the land." Investigators primed with the answer to this second

question are then likely to initiate an investigation that is distinctly different from the first one. They might be particularly interested in discover-
ing why the once highly regarded American work ethic seems less apparent among whites than among blacks.

Thus the questions asked are fundamental, structuring both the results
of research and the recommendations investigators make. Coming back
to the present work, we need to find a question broad and incisive enough
to guide our inquiry. Duster suggested the following question: "How and
why has race been the persistent category of advantage throughout every
generation of the nation's history?" (Duster, 1987: 12)

Starting with Duster's question, analysts recognize that American society has consistently practiced racism, with racial minorities invariably
losing out in the process. One possible reservation about Duster's question
involves the *the* in the phrase "the persistent category of advantage."
Many sociologists would argue that social class has been equally "persistent," and it seems impossible to determine whether race or social class
wins the persistence contest.

Duster's question suggests a conflict-theory approach. **Conflict theory**
contends that the struggle for power and wealth in society should be the
central concern of sociology. Over the past half-century, this perspective
has been widely applied to racism. For instance, John Dollard (1937) and
W. Lloyd Warner and Leo Srole (1945) indicated that when slavery was
abolished, white Southerners established a caste system maintaining segregation in all private and public facilities, thus ensuring blacks' economic,
political, and social disadvantage.

More recently such conflict theorists as Mario Barrera (1979) and Robert Blauner (1972) have described **internal colonialism,** where the control
imposed on indigenous racial minorities passes from whites in the home
country to whites living within a newly independent nation. This approach appears in the next section and throughout the book.

INTERNAL COLONIALISM

The ideas of "control" and "exploitation" are central to internal-colonialist
theory. Like colonial subjects, members of American racial minorities are
subjected to a battery of extreme political, economic, and social discrimi-
nations. They receive minimal representation in the political process, and
they are restricted on where they can live and work. They work long and
hard for low wages, and they receive inferior food, housing, education, and
medical care.

Four conditions of internal colonialism, all of which have been present
in American society, are (1) control over a minority group's governance,
(2) restriction of its freedom of movement, (3) the colonial-labor principle,
and (4) belief in the inferiority of racial minorities' culture and social
organization (Blauner, 1972: 53–70). As we briefly examine these four

conditions, it might be useful to remember that they involve situations in which institutional racism readily develops.

Control Over a Minority Group's Governance

Historically whites imposed government control on racial minorities, making the decisions that determine major outcomes in their lives. A recent study found that on the Fort Yuma Reservation in California, where Quechan tribespeople are permitted to elect their leaders, U.S. government officials still impose a great deal of control—for instance, by not providing federal funding for business development unless their favored governing style is maintained. Quechan leaders indicated that while their approach supports more argument and leadership turnover than U.S. officials wanted, the Quechan style represents a modern application of their traditional approach, improving people and practices by a process of continuous criticism. Government officials were unimpressed and threatened to cut funding (Bee, 1990).

Restriction of a Racial Minority's Freedom of Movement

Whites stringently limited Native Americans' and blacks' freedom of movement. Native Americans had their native land invaded, and for over 400 years were systematically deprived of their land and freedom and eventually forced to settle on reservations. Blacks, on the other hand, were transported against their will from Africa to the United States, where they were enslaved until the end of the Civil War and then, while technically free, have continued to encounter limitations on their physical freedom. In modern times ghettos house many African-Americans, who are more systematically denied opportunities to leave such areas than are Hispanic-American and Asian-American groups (Feigelman and Gorman, 1990). As a result higher-income white groups are able to stay distant from poor blacks and their problems, and those who are oppressed and confined to the ghettos are more likely to vent their frustrations and rages within their own locales. We will see that other racial minorities have also encountered various controls over physical activity.

The Colonial-Labor Principle

The colonial-labor principle indicates that racial minorities must serve white controllers' interests and needs. While capitalist theory emphasizes a free market and free labor, these privileges have been restricted primarily to whites. Historically racial minorities have been required to serve at the pleasure of those who owned or employed them. They have been expected to "know their place," appreciating the necessity to be resigned to a less-than-full participation in society—denied the rights and privileges reserved for whites. A recent study indicated, for example, that while most

Table 1.1 DISCRIMINATION, PREJUDICE, AND RELATED ISSUES

Discrimination ——————————————→	Prejudice

Racism: a form of discrimination
    a. Individual racism
    b. Institutional racism
Internal colonialism: a theory analyzing the
    oppression of American racism, with more
    emphasis on discrimination than on prejudice
	Stereotype: image maintained by
	    prejudiced people
	Can support self-fulfilling prophecy

Asian-Americans are better educated than whites, only Japanese-Americans approach income equity with them (Barringer, Takeuchi, and Xenos, 1990).

Belief in the Inferiority of a Minority Group's Culture and Social Organization

Finally a basic tenet in the internal-colonialist scheme has been the prejudiced position that racial minorities' culture and social organization are inferior to whites' and that, therefore, they should readily discard their traditional culture and embrace that of the dominant white culture. Thus traditional cultures have been undermined or destroyed, and racial minorities wishing to obtain at least some of the privileges of the dominant culture have had to master its knowledge and skills. From the seventeenth century to the present, Europeans and later white Americans have attempted to educate Native Americans so that they will reject their "inferior ways" and adopt whites' "superior standards" (Feest, 1990).

Table 1.1 demonstrates the relationship among some issues we have just analyzed. In Chapter 2 we will examine prominent theories of racism.

REFERENCES

Barrera, Mario. 1979. *Race and Class in the Southwest.* Notre Dame, IN: University of Notre Dame Press.

Barringer, Felicity. 1991. "Census Shows Profound Change in Racial Makeup of the Nation." *New York Times* (March 11): A1ff.

Barringer, Herbert B., David T. Takeuchi, and Peter Xenos. 1990. "Education, Occupational Prestige, and Income of Asian Americans." *Sociology of Education* 63 (January): 27–43.

Bee, Robert L. 1990. "The Predicament of the Native American Leader: A Second Look." *Human Organization* 49 (Spring): 56–63.

Blauner, Robert. 1972. *Racial Oppression in America.* New York: Harper & Row.

Campbell, Ernest Q., and Thomas Pettigrew. 1959. *Christians in Racial Crisis.* Washington, DC: Public Affairs Press.

Count, Earl. W. (ed.). 1950. *This Is Race: An Anthology Selected from the International Literature on the Races of Man.* New York: Schuman.

Dollard, John. 1937. *Caste and Class in a Southern Town.* New Haven, CT: Yale University Press.

Duster, Troy. 1987. "Purpose and Bias." *Society* 24 (January/February): 8–12.

Feagin, Joe R. 1991. "The Continuing Significance of Race: Antiblack Discrimination in Public Places." *American Sociological Review* 56 (February): 101–116.

Feest, Christian F. 1990. "Europe's Indians." *Society* 27 (May/June): 46–51.

Feigelman, William, and Bernard S. Gorman. 1990. "Blacks Who Live near Whites: 1982 and 1987." *Sociology and Social Research* 74 (July): 202–203.

Harris, Marvin. 1968. "Race." *International Encyclopedia of the Social Sciences* 13: 263–269.

Katz, David, and Kenneth Braly. 1933. "Racial Stereotypes of One Hundred College Students." *Journal of Abnormal and Social Psychology* 28 (October): 280–290.

Kutner, Bernard, Carol Wilkins, and P. R. Yarrow. 1952. "Verbal Attitudes and Overt Behavior Involving Racial Prejudice." *Journal of Abnormal and Social Psychology* 47 (July): 649–652.

Lukas, J. Anthony. 1985. *Common Ground.* New York: Alfred A. Knopf.

Media General-Association Press Poll. August 1988.

Molnar, Stephen. 1975. *Races, Types, and Ethnic Groups.* Englewood Cliffs, NJ: Prentice-Hall.

Montagu, Ashley. 1974. *Man's Most Dangerous Myth: The Fallacy of Race.* New York: Oxford University Press. Fifth edition.

Simpson, George E., and J. Milton Yinger. 1985. *Racial and Cultural Minorities.* New York: Plenum Press. Fifth edition.

Thomas, Melvin E., and Michael Hughes. 1986. "The Continuing Significance of Race: A Study of Race, Class, and Quality of Life in America, 1972–1985." *American Sociological Review* 51 (December): 830–841.

Warner, Lyle G., and Melvin L. DeFleur. 1969. "Attitudes as an Interactional Concept." *American Sociological Review* 34 (April): 153–169.

Warner, W. Lloyd, and Leo Srole. 1945. *The Social Systems of American Ethnic Groups.* New Haven, CT: Yale University Press.

Wilson, William Julius. 1978. *The Declining Significance of Race: Blacks and Changing American Institutions.* Chicago: University of Chicago Press.

Wilson, William Julius. 1987. *The Truly Disadvantaged: The Inner City, the Underclass, and Public Policy.* Chicago: University of Chicago Press.

Chapter

2

Racism Theories: Perspectives on Intergroup Oppression

*A*t the age of 13, I was living with my family in Durban, on the east coast of the Union of South Africa. One morning while at the docks, we watched the unloading of a fishing boat.

I left the spot where I'd stood and walked over to speak to one of my brothers. Suddenly a voice behind me said, "So you're moving because it sickens you to stand next to a dirty Indian." Surprised I turned around to see a young Indian man, probably in his middle 20s, frowning at me intently.

I started walking away but then stopped and moved back toward him. "I didn't even see you there," I said.

Instantly the frown was gone. "You're an American!" he shouted. "I've never met an American! Tell me," he continued, signaling to come closer, "have you ever been to Chicago?" I shook my head. "No matter. Perhaps just living in the States, you'll know enough. I've got an absolute obsession about Chicago, especially Chicago of the Prohibition era. Tell me. Do shoot-outs between crime families still take place on the streets there?"

We talked for 10 or 15 minutes, and then it was time for us to leave. The rest of the day and for many days to come I thought about the encounter. I was old enough to have a general sense of the virulent racism that dominated South Africa. But this encounter had been personal, graphically demonstrating the potent impact of racially linked symbols: A white skin could instantly create anger and frustration for a minority-group member, and yet when it became apparent that the white skin covered an American, the sense of oppression could be immediately washed away. Following that incident I was left with the shadowy outlines of questions which I have pondered ever since: Why does racism develop? Who benefits from it and how? Just what damage does racism produce for the members of both the minority and dominant groups? And, above all, how can racism be eliminated?

In the intervening years, I've found that while sociological theories analyzing racism have not provided complete answers to these questions, they do address them. To combat and ultimately eliminate racism, we must first understand it. Theories are a major source of understanding. Theories, in short, are not simply abstract, formal statements: They can be practical steps toward comprehension and change.

Many theories analyze either the macro level or the micro level. The **macro level** involves the large-scale structures and activities that exist within societies and even between one society and another. The **micro level** concerns the structure and activities of small groups. Table 2.1 lists the theories included in this chapter.

Table 2.1   THEORIES INCLUDED IN CHAPTER 2

Macro-Level Theories

1. *Structural-Functional Theories of Race Relations*
   Park's assimilation theory
   Gordon's seven-level assimilation theory
   Glazer and Moynihan's pluralism theory

2. *Conflict Theories of Racism*
   Davis, Gardner, and Gardner's caste theory
   Dollard's caste theory
   Cox's theory of racism
   Wilhelm's theory of racism
   Internal-colonialist theory

Micro-Level Theories

Allport's social-psychological theory of prejudice
Frustration-aggression theory

MACRO-LEVEL THEORIES OF RACISM

As we noted in the opening chapter, conflict theory contends that the struggle for power and wealth in society should be the central concern of sociology. Many people are restricted or controlled by limits that powerful members of society impose, and such restrictions create or at least encourage conflict. According to the proponents of this theory, conflict inevitably produces change.

Structural-functional theory is less concerned with conflict and change. **Structural-functional theory** suggests that interacting groups tend to influence and adjust to each other in a fairly stable, conflict-free pattern. According to this theory, these groups are mutually supportive and interdependent, and each group contributes to the overall stability of the society. Since World War II, most advocates of structural-functional theory, notably Robert Merton (1968), have acknowledged the roles conflict and change play in social relations, but those factors are less prominent than in conflict theory. In this section we see that there remains a distinct difference between structural-functional theory and conflict theory when applied to the conflict-laden issue of race. One might argue that structural-functional theories center on race relations and that conflict theories focus on racism.

In this discussion we examine prominent examples of both theoretical types.

Structural-Functional Theories of Racism

In the opening decades of the twentieth century, one of the most prominent American sociologists was Robert Ezra Park. Park recognized the existence of racism, but he believed that in the course of relations between different racial groups, it would eventually be eliminated. He wrote: "The race relations cycle which takes the form . . . of contacts, competition, accommodation and eventual assimilation, is apparently progressive and irreversible" (Park, 1950: 150). We consider Park's four steps.

Park indicated that contacts between different racial groups occur when explorers from one group discover new areas that can serve as sites for economic gain. Then, according to Park, competition develops. But it is not uncontrolled competition; rather members of the different racial groups must act within established customs and laws. They adapt to the new environment, finding work that, while not necessarily what they would choose to do, contributes to the developing economy. Eventually a new division of labor develops, incorporating the different racial groups.

With the division of labor in place, accommodation begins. Park asserted that within any established economic system, even one which is as oppressive as slavery, intimate and personal relations among members of different racial groups develop, undermining the more sinister elements within the system. According to Park, one sign of such accommodation during Southern slavery was that in spite of legislation and custom strongly supporting the system, the number of slaves given freedom by their masters steadily increased (Park, 1950: 150).

Assimilation—the elimination of separate racial interests and the development of a common identity involving all racial groups within a society—is the final step. Park suggested that invariably some racial groups would assimilate more rapidly than others, and writing in 1950, he conceded that African-Americans had still not fully assimilated: "though the white man and the Negro have lived and worked together in the United States for three hundred years and more, the two races are still in a certain sense strangers to one another" (Park, 1950: 76).

Park was vague in analyzing the precise nature of African-Americans' incomplete assimilation, indicating that while they were not fully assimilated "in just what sense this is true is difficult to say" (Park, 1950: 77).

Milton M. Gordon (1964) sought to be more precise than Park, developing a seven-level framework for analyzing different types of assimilation. To illustrate his scheme, he suggested the existence of two hypothetical ethnic groups—the Sylvanians and the Mundovians. Originally they had separate homelands, but at one point the Mundovians started moving to Sylvania. By the second generation, the Mundovians were completely assimilated. What precisely did this mean?

First, it meant cultural assimilation, by which Mundovians adopted all the patterns of the host culture—the language, educational system, religion, beliefs, values, and norms—and put aside their own previous cultural standards.

Second, the second-generation Mundovians achieved structural assimilation, making friends by joining cliques, clubs, and other Sylvanian organizations and thereby receiving full acceptance in their residential communities.

Third, the new arrivals obtained marital assimilation, intermarrying in large numbers with native Sylvanians.

Fourth, in order to achieve complete assimilation, second-generation Mundovians had developed identificational assimilation, meaning that their sense of themselves as a people was linked to the host culture; in short, they now considered themselves Sylvanians, not Mundovians.

Fifth, second-generation Mundovians enjoyed a prejudice-free assimilation; the Sylvanians did not feel and thus did not convey a sense of inherent superiority.

Sixth, the Mundovians also benefited from a discrimination-free assimilation; in no manner were they treated as second-class citizens by the Sylvanians.

Seventh, the final step is civic assimilation, in which the group seeking assimilation, in this case the Mundovians, did not make any significant demands on the host culture requiring a change in its established ways of thinking and acting.

Gordon seemed to be less confident than Park about complete assimilation in the United States. When he examined Americans' friendship patterns and club memberships, it was readily apparent that most preferred to relate to their fellow racial- and ethnic-group members. On the other hand, Gordon noted that by choice some people reached out beyond their own groups and sought the friendship and stimulation of those with diverse racial and ethnic backgrounds. Furthermore contacts among Americans of varied heritages occurred because of the racial and ethnic mixing produced in the industrial work world and in higher education systems. Gordon wrote:

> Ethnic communality will not disappear in the foreseeable future and its legitimacy and rationale should be recognized and respected. By the same token, the bonds that bind human beings together across the lines of ethnicity and the pathways on which people of diverse ethnic origin meet and mingle should be cherished and strengthened. (Gordon, 1964: 265)

In later years Gordon acknowledged conflict theory's perspective, admitting that groups with greater wealth and power are able to use those scarce resources to exploit groups that are less well situated. His use of conflict theory, however, was brief and unsystematic, failing to analyze in detail the sources and effects of the unequal distribution of wealth and power (Gordon, 1978).

Pluralism is another structural-functional theory concerned with race and ethnicity. **Pluralism** is a theory emphasizing that a dispersion of power exists in government or other structures within American society. Unlike assimilation theory pluralism does not contend that all cultural differences will ultimately fade away. In fact, a supporter of the theory has argued that in modern times racial and ethnic identities have become stronger than in the past (Scott, 1990).

Nathan Glazer and Daniel Patrick Moynihan (1963), proponents of pluralism, produced a well-known book with a decidedly nonassimilationist title. *Beyond the Melting Pot* was a clear statement that the nineteenth-century idea emphasizing that all ethnic and racial groups simply would disappear in the great "American melting pot" has been proved inaccurate. Analyzing the major ethnic and racial groups in New York City, Glazer and Moynihan concluded that common history, community ties, organizational linkages, and often religion and language have united members of a given racial or ethnic group, making it likely that the group will serve as an interest group and provide the most efficient means for members to achieve full participatory rights in the political and economic systems.

When a racial or ethnic group lacked those rights, members of the group needed to be mobilized to function as an interest group. For example, Glazer and Moynihan contended that in order for blacks to achieve equitable participation in modern society, new, effective African-American leaders capable of organizing a movement to demand full rights for their people had to emerge. Glazer and Moynihan suggested that while there had been some promising signs of the emergence of such a leadership over the past quarter-century, black leaders had recently proved ineffective. This failure, the authors argued, was significant, because only African-Americans could lead their own people in certain problem areas. They wrote:

> It is probable that no investment of public and private agencies on delinquency and crime-prevention programs will equal the return from an investment by Negro-led and Negro-financed agencies. It is probable that no offensive on the public school system to improve the educational results among Negroes will equal what may be gained from an equivalent investment by Negro-led and Negro-financed groups. (Glazer and Moynihan, 1963: 84)

It might be noted that solutions to such pervasive problems will prove formidable and expensive. To expect the emerging leadership of any minority group, in fact the leadership of any single ethnic or racial group, to play a major role in its solution is unfair and unrealistic, particularly in the financial area.

A decade later Glazer and Moynihan reasserted the earlier thesis, emphasizing two points: first, that by the middle 1970s, there were more interracial struggles for prestige, respect, political power, and access to economic opportunity than in the past; second, the use of ethnic groups as interest groups had become a more persistent trend in recent years (Glazer and Moynihan, 1975: 5–7).

Once more, in 1990, Glazer and Moynihan reevaluated their thesis during a panel discussion that occurred at the time of the trials for two white men accused of participating in the killing of a black man in the Bensonhurst section of Queens, New York (to be discussed in Chapter 4). They suggested that the racial unrest and hatred the killing had produced underlined the relevance of their thesis and invalidated an assimilationist perspective—that, as a reporter cryptically phrased it, "the melting pot metaphor was a crock" (Roberts, 1990: B1). Mr. Moynihan, now Senator Moynihan, took the opportunity to criticize Marxist thought, suggesting that the beyond-the-melting-pot thesis, which emphasizes the prominent role of race and ethnicity, has refuted Marx's claim that industrial forces would annihilate the significance of race and ethnicity by creating a united working force committed to overthrowing capitalism. Giving his colleague major credit, Moynihan said, "What Karl Marx proposed in the British Museum, Nat Glazer disproved in the New York Public Library" (Roberts, 1990: B1).

As we noted in the first chapter, it is true that Marx was one of several prominent social scientists—Durkheim and Weber were others—who discounted the significance of race and ethnicity as major forces in the industrial world. In that regard Moynihan was correct: Undeniably ethnicity and race play important roles in affecting political, economic, and social events in modern society.

On the other hand, the Moynihan and Glazer thesis, which emphasizes that racial and ethnic groups serve as effective interest groups for their members, often has not proved accurate. For instance, Glazer, who wrote the original chapter on African-Americans in *Beyond the Melting Pot,* conceded his claim that blacks would manage to be as economically and politically mobile as white groups proved to be naive (Roberts, 1990: B1).

Whether assimilationist or pluralist, structural-functional theories fail to address harsh realities of wealth and power inequalities. They simply assume that different racial and ethnic groups have essentially equal access to these scarce commodities and that therefore they will have similar opportunities to receive the prized benefits of society. If, as in the case of African-Americans in the early 1960s, the majority of group members have not been successful economically and politically, then, according to Glazer and Moynihan, responsibility rests with the group's leadership. These leaders are largely on their own to learn to resolve their group's enormous difficulties. Since such structural-functional theorists never directly address issues of unequal distribution of wealth and power, it is hardly surprising that they do not assess the massive mobilization of funds and personnel needed to eliminate such problems.

In contrast, conflict theories focus on topics of wealth and power as well as racial minorities' historically unequal access to these prized commodities.

Conflict Theories of Racism

One of the prominent conflict theories of racism is the caste analysis. A **caste system** is a socially legitimate arrangement of groups in which the ranking of the different groups is clearly designated, members' expected behavior is specified, and movement of individuals from one group to another is prohibited. In the 1930s and 1940s, social scientists first applied the concept to American race relations, and in recent years researchers have continued to analyze the concept of caste (Forbes, 1990).

In *Deep South* Allison Davis, Burleigh B. Gardner, and Mary R. Gardner (1941) studied a small Southern city with nearly 10,000 inhabitants, about half of whom were black, as well as the caste system maintained in that city. One feature of the caste system was the established set of beliefs subordinating blacks. Whites generally felt that African-Americans were inherently inferior—that they were a lower form of organism which was mentally inferior and emotionally undeveloped. Whites believed that in some general sense, blacks were "unclean," and thus it was unfitting for whites to eat from dishes or wear clothes that African-Americans had used. The researchers also found that local whites felt that the caste system was the "will of God." A physician explained:

> The way I look at it is this way: God didn't put the different races here to mix and mingle so you wouldn't know them apart. He put them here as separate

races and He meant for them to stay that way. . . . I don't think God meant for a superior race like the whites to blend with an inferior race and become mediocre. I think God put all the different races here for a purpose, and He didn't mean for them to mix. I think I am right in saying that, and my attitude is Christian-like. (Davis, Gardner, and Gardner, 1941: 17)

In addition, whites contended that blacks were "childlike" and would never grow up, living entirely in the present with no regrets for the past nor fears about the future. Finally, since Southern whites believed that blacks were childlike and thus irresponsible, whites considered themselves responsible for blacks. Invariably, whites were convinced, black servants would steal from them. It was in their nature, and thus blacks could not be held responsible. Whites, in fact, bore the responsibility since they were the ones capable of such preventative actions as locking liquor cabinets or keeping a check on stockings, handkerchiefs, and food (Davis, Gardner, and Gardner, 1941: 20).

Davis, Gardner, and Gardner also indicated that certain social practices, which they called "rituals of subordination," maintained the caste system. These rituals included spatial separation, with Southern blacks and whites always knowing that public facilities were segregated; and deferential behavior, which meant that blacks were always expected to respond respectfully to whites, using titles of respect and letting whites be served ahead of them in stores and offices.

Essential for maintaining the caste system was endogamy, the prohibition of interracial marriage. Had African-Americans and whites been permitted to intermarry, it would have been much more likely that individuals could pass from the black to the white caste. Such a prospect represented a frontal attack on the caste system.

Blacks, the system dictated, needed to be kept in their place. When this occurred, whites received a variety of benefits. In a study conducted in another Southern town during the 1930s, John Dollard (1937) suggested that local middle-class whites received three principal gains from their dominant position in the caste system. First, there was an economic benefit. Middle-class whites were able to avoid menial, often physically demanding jobs. Generally they did not mow their own lawns, cook their own food, nor clean their own houses. In what was largely an agricultural area, most of the farming, including the backbreaking work of cotton picking, was blacks' responsibility. Furthermore, while blacks' work was more physically taxing than whites', it also paid considerably less. Thus many whites could use advantages they obtained from blacks' low-paid employment to maintain a luxurious life-style.

Second, Dollard discussed whites' sexual gain, meaning that because of their superior position in the caste structure, white men had unchallenged sexual access to both African-American and white women. Dollard suggested that Southern white men's traditional outlook toward white women increased the significance of this issue. Southern white men were expected to idealize white women, celebrating their beauty and chastity and restraining erotic feelings and behavior. While sexual activity with their wives was necessary to produce children, Southern white men felt guilt-ridden about it. For uninhibited, passionate sex, freed from "cares, threats, and duties" (Dollard, 1937: 144), they often turned to black women, many of them prostitutes.

Third, Southern whites received a prestige gain. Simply because people were white, they were able to demand forms of deference from blacks that would enhance their self-esteem. For whites, Dollard suggested, the prestige gain created an illusion of greatness similar to alcohol's intoxicating effect. The difference was that this benefit was not an illusion but "a steadily repeated fact." Dollard wrote:

> From the standpoint of the white man the crucial thing may be that his aggressive demands are passively received; this gives the gratification of mastering the other person. Still more important perhaps is to receive the deference in advance of demanding it, a submissive affection which is freely and automatically yielded. (Dollard, 1937: 174)

The prestige gain, in short, provided whites gratification on the spot, and it also served to emphasize the legitimacy of the caste system, in which blacks were classified distinctly inferior to whites and controlled by them.

During the same era, Oliver Cromwell Cox (1959), an African-American Marxist sociologist, analyzed the relations between African-Americans and whites. As a supporter of Marxist thought, Cox accepted Marx's claim that under capitalism, modern societies would be divided into two basic classes—the ruling class, whose members owned the factories and farms that were sources of wealth, and the working class, whose members depended on wages. Capitalism, Marx emphasized, was exploitative, paying workers barely enough to survive and forcing most of them to do assembly-line work that was repetitive and boring. Eventually, Marx indicated, workers would recognize that as a class they shared common grievances against the ruling class and the capitalist economic system. Organizing themselves into an army, workers would overthrow the ruling class and establish a new economic system—socialism—in which all citizens would own the means of producing wealth (Marx and Engels, 1959).

Writing in the 1940s, Cox extended the Marxist analysis to include blacks' oppression. He suggested that as members of the working class, blacks in capitalist society faced all the limitations and problems imposed on white wage earners. In addition, they were racially exploited, designated inferior to whites and denied many of the modest rights available to members of the white working class. In Richard H. Thompson's phrase, blacks faced "double exploitation" (Thompson, 1989: 151).

Cox concluded that the core of the American racial problem was that blacks wanted to assimilate, to obtain equitable opportunities in modern society and reduce greater exposure to disease, unemployment, poverty, and illiteracy. The white ruling class, however, opposed blacks' assimilation. Its members felt that it was to their advantage to keep blacks and other racial minorities economically, politically, and socially under-privileged.

While whites used various techniques to keep blacks in an oppressed state, Cox believed that lynching was the "fundamental reliance" of the white ruling class. Although the practice occurred more frequently in the South than in the North, Cox contended that support for the practice—what he called "the lynching attitude"—existed among whites throughout the country.

Cox defined **lynching** as one group's use of mob action to kill a member of an oppressed group, thereby warning members of that oppressed group either to accept an even more lowly status or to forsake any developing plans to rise above their subordinated position (Cox, 1959: 549).

Because of the purpose lynching served for whites, the actual victim was unimportant: What was necessary was that some black person's violent death conveyed a warning. Cox believed that sending a warning to local blacks was a central element in the cycle producing lynchings. The process involved the following steps. First, a growing belief developed among local whites that in some respects, such as gaining wealth or acting assertively, local African-Americans were getting out of hand. Second, discussing the issue among themselves, whites reached the conclusion that blacks in the area represented a distinct, immediate threat. Third, there was a rumored or actual occurrence of some outrage committed by a black person against a white individual. If tensions among whites were extreme, some of them simply created an incident. For instance, they falsely accused a black man of making sexual advances toward a white woman or of stealing from his employer. Fourth, once the alleged incident took place, the white mob mobilized, and a black victim was burned, hanged, or shot in public, preferably before the court house to emphasize the legitimacy of the savage act; then the victim's remains were dragged through the black section of town. In the fury of mob violence, other African-Americans were often killed or beaten, and considerable property belonging to blacks was destroyed. Fifth, within two or three days, the mob had achieved its emotional release, and a movement for judicial investigation occurred. Sometimes on the Sunday following the violence, courageous local ministers preached that lynching was barbarous and un-Christian. Eventually a grand jury returned the finding that the deceased individual met death by burning, hanging, or shooting at the hands of unknown parties. Sixth, a new racial adjustment developed, with blacks becoming very cautious in dealing with whites and accepting even more oppressive relations and conditions than previously. If, at this time, some black people dared to defend their rights against whites, most local blacks were much more likely to be critical than supportive. For most black citizens, the major task at hand was to get on with life and to convey to whites a sense of normalcy—that they, the blacks, bore whites no malice. Cox wrote, "The lynching had accomplished its purpose . . . and the cycle . . . [was] again on its way" (Cox, 1959: 551).

Cox suggested that the extraordinary violence whites inflicted on blacks might have been necessary to overcome "possible inhibitions of conscience" occurring because of black and white workers' common plight as exploited wage earners within industrial capitalism. Cox asserted that one of the significant effects of racism was that it prevented black and white workers from appreciating that under capitalism they shared common grievances that 'could have served as the basis for an organized interracial effort to overthrow the ruling class and the capitalist system. Were Cox alive today, he might conclude that modern outbreaks of violence against racial minorities have produced a similar divisive effect.

In order to encourage structural changes that would eliminate violence against them and permit them to seek a full share of the rights and privileges of modern society, African-Americans needed effective leadership. Cox indicated that although many blacks lamented the fact that no great leader had emerged among them, the absence of such leadership was inevitable. Why? The key, Cox claimed, was blacks' position in society: "The destiny of Negroes is cultural and biological integration and fusion with the larger American society" (Cox, 1959: 572). Like other Americans, blacks were pursuing their individual destinies, seeking assimilation into the economic, political, and social structures of modern American life. A leader who either promised to carry the entire race to glory or who negatively represented whites and white-dominated society would work against individual blacks' efforts to obtain success and satisfaction.

According to Cox, Marxist analysts of race relations needed to appreciate that blacks were only a small part of American workers' struggle for political and economic power. Cox believed that for blacks and whites alike, the most effective leadership would undoubtedly come from white leaders who sought to improve downtrodden poor people's lives, regardless of color. Without any undue concern for "the Negro problem," President Franklin D. Roosevelt did more to elevate blacks' status than any other leader of the first half of the twentieth century (Cox, 1959: 582).

A recent study of Cox noted that in his later years, he became more willing to make concessions about American society, moderating his earlier position about the necessity to overthrow capitalism and declaring that racial equality would most readily be produced by reforming current political and economic systems (Snedeker, 1988).

Sidney Wilhelm (1983) is a modern proponent of a conflict theory of racism. He has developed an idea similar to one already mentioned twice in this book: Like Marx before them, modern Marxist thinkers have failed to recognize that racism exists independently of economic forces. Marx believed that as capitalism advanced, narrow allegiances that produced racism would disappear. Modern Marxist theorists have tended to conclude that socialism would provide that benefit. According to Wilhelm these theorists believe that "the destruction of capitalism will immediately eliminate any economic necessity for the continuation of racism" (Wilhelm, 1983: 129). But Wilhelm suggested that racism is also the product of noneconomic factors. Currently racism cuts across all social classes, with middle-class members of various minority groups who are spared oppressive economic conditions nonetheless vulnerable to racism. Certainly ample evidence in this book supports that claim.

Wilhelm's second principal conclusion is that many African-Americans represent a special category of disadvantaged people—those who are permanently unemployed. Historically blacks have had uniquely restricted educational and occupational opportunities, and as a result many of them have been much less prepared than other groups to prosper in the computerized, automated postindustrial world. Wilhelm indicated that African-Americans "are not so much oppressed as unwanted; not so much unwanted as unnecessary; not so much abused as ignored" (Wilhelm, 1983: 233). Both past and present Marxist theory, Wilhelm claimed, have failed to appreciate how historical conditions have placed poor modern African-Americans in a position of unique economic exploitation.

Some commentary on conflict theories of race relations seems appropriate. To begin, it should be emphasized that some of the observations about racism offered here are dated; for instance, the Southern caste system with associated lynching and other horrors has been largely dismantled. Nonetheless we might consider the possibility that some oppressive social patterns described in this section are still applicable; for instance, while lynching no longer occurs, perhaps a similar process of terror and intimidation occurs in modern situations in which whites initiate violence against African-Americans and other racial minorities.

Modern conflict theorists, perhaps the Marxist theorists in particular, need to address the respective impacts of race and social class on racial minority-group members' lives. For example, evaluating Wilhelm's conclusion about modern blacks' high level of unemployment, Richard H. Thompson indicated that one can dispute his claim that Marxist theory fails to provide conceptual analysis of blacks' high level of unemployment in modern capitalism. Thompson contended that traditional Marxist theory contains the concept of surplus labor that addresses such an issue (Thompson, 1989: 166–167). On the other hand, Thompson and many other conflict theorists would agree that Wilhelm is correct in asserting that more than traditional, class-oriented Marxist concepts must be used to analyze the causes of modern American racism. A major challenge for the advancement of conflict theories of race is to sort out the respective impacts of race and social class on racial minorities' lives and on modern society itself.

Analyzing racism, some conflict theorists would include a third factor—gender. They have argued that poor women of color are most effectively understood if their three minority statuses are considered simultaneously. Several scholars are developing a unified theory of class, race, and gender that considers diverse combinations of these three factors (Collins, 1989; Sacks, 1989).

Many conflict-theoretical analyses of American racism, such as Oliver

Cox's work, are compatible with internal-colonialist theory, emphasizing that racial minorities have been systematically controlled and exploited by whites, and focusing on minorities' governance, freedom of movement, work, and supposed cultural inferiority. In this section devoted to conflict theory, it seems appropriate to evaluate internal colonialism, which was introduced in the previous chapter and is used throughout the book. If you wish to review the theory's content, turn to pp. 10–12.

It appears that three criticisms most frequently directed against internal colonialism are doubts about the accuracy of the analogy between colonialism and internal colonialism; concerns about who actually benefits from the exploitation of racial minorities (Feagin, 1989: 37–38); and underestimations of minorities' ability to determine their own destiny.

First, we consider the criticism of the analogy between colonialism and internal colonialism. Supporters of internal colonialism concede that the situation faced by American racial minorities is different than that confronted by the indigenous African, Asian, and American peoples who were subjected to ruthless exploitation by European colonialists. No longer can American whites enslave or systematically kill members of racial minorities, but the proponents of the theory emphasize that the analogy remains particularly potent in the four areas of governance, freedom of movement, work, and culture.

Second, critics claim that internal-colonialist theorists fail to identify the benefactors of minorities' exploitation. Is it simply a white ruling class; is it middle- and upper-class whites; or what? The question is difficult to answer. Over two decades ago, Herbert Gans (1971) wrote an article about the uses of poverty, specifying thirteen of them. Many of these uses—such as providing personnel for the dirty work that must be performed in restaurants, hospitals, and on farms, or subsidizing more affluent people's careers by releasing them from most domestic tasks—do not distinctly link to one social class; a number of social classes benefit. Since a disproportionate number of the poor are members of racial minorities, this analysis applies to them. While this is a less exact conclusion than we might wish, it nonetheless suggests that racism has served many whites' interest. In the chapters ahead, we encounter little information to dispute this conclusion.

Third, critics of internal colonialism have indicated that the theory underestimates racial minorities' ability to control their own destiny. While analysts must consider the harsh realities of racism, they should not overstate their case, failing to evaluate minority individuals' capacity to confront or surmount these harsh realities and obtain various successes. This is an important, complicated issue, and it seems that the modern observer of racism must steer a narrow course—on the one hand, one must thoroughly examine the devastating impact of racism and, on the other hand, acknowledge minority-group members' successful efforts to control their own lives. While internal colonialism provides the dominant theoretical perspective in this book, the other position receives considerable attention: Discussion and analysis of minorities' successful activities will occur throughout this book.

Let me conclude the commentary on conflict theories of racism with a personal observation. Frequently sociologists find that both structural-functional and conflict theories offer useful analyses of major sociological topics. For instance, in my own introductory sociology text (Doob, 1991), the two theories complemented each other effectively in examining the functions of religion, the impact of education in modern society, and the concentration of political authority. But while structural-functional theory can prove useful, its focus on stability and harmony and failure to address wealth and power inequities are glaring deficiencies in the area of race. Or, to phrase it differently, the only way this author could comfortably write this book is if a conflict perspective were to permeate it.

We now shift from the macro level to the micro level and examine social-psychological theories of racism.

MICRO-LEVEL THEORIES OF RACISM

Theories in this section examine the small-group context encouraging prejudice and discrimination. In *The Nature of Prejudice,* Gordon W. Allport (1954: 307–310) suggested that prejudice is a three-stage learning process to which children in American culture are exposed. The following situation illustrates the first stage: Janet, a six-year-old girl, comes running home and asks, "Mother, what is the name of the children I am supposed to hate?" In Allport's apt phrase, Janet "is stumbling at the threshold of some abstraction" (Allport, 1954: 307). She identifies with her mother, seeks her approval, and wishes to fuse her obedience to her mother with appropriate feelings toward her own social contacts. The girl, Allport contended, engages in *pregeneralized* learning, having accepted the information that a certain African-American boy is dirty or a particular Native-American woman is not to be trusted, but generalizations involving prejudice toward entire racial or ethnic groups still elude her. Language is the key to the development of racist thought. Listening to her mother, father, other adults, and older children express their prejudices toward different groups, Janet will gradually be able to grasp which racial and ethnic groups are the culturally approved objects of prejudice.

In Janet's case the second stage in learning prejudice begins with her mother's response to the question about the children Janet is expected to hate. The mother might reply, "I told you not to play with black children. They are dirty; they have diseases; and they will hurt you. Now don't let me catch you playing with them." Such a directive can initiate the period of *total rejection:* Prompted by parental order, the child vigorously rejects all members of a certain racial or ethnic group—in this case African-Americans. For Janet and other six-year-olds, total rejection of a particular group might prove unsystematic since, according to research, until children are eight, they do not have a clear, stable sense of people's race and ethnicity (Aboud, 1984). By ten or eleven, when white children subjected to a prejudiced upbringing answered a series of questions comparing blacks' and whites' qualities, the whites were scored higher on every question. Allport concluded that these children "had learned to reject the Negro category *totally*" (Allport, 1954: 309).

The third stage involves *differentiation.* Now the child has become more sophisticated, learning to make gracious exceptions when it seems appropriate: "Some of my best friends are Puerto Rican." Or: "How could I be prejudiced against Asians? The woman who took care of me when I was a kid was Chinese, and I loved her dearly." By about age 15, young people have become sophisticated enough to turn the racism faucet on and off at will. As part of the package, they have learned what Allport called "the peculiar double-talk appropriate to prejudice in a democracy"—speak in favor of individual rights and equality and simultaneously support prejudice and discrimination (Allport, 1954: 310).

Recent research has examined the impact produced by this process. Preschool and young school-age children of all major racial groups generally demonstrate more positive attitudes toward whites and greater identification with them. For adolescents the pattern is not as distinct. More independent than young children, they appear much more capable of combating the impact of racial stereotypes imposed either on their own racial group or on other groups (Aboud, 1988; Spencer and Markstrom-Adams, 1990).

Another social-psychological perspective is the frustration-aggression theory. Consider the following situation. A four-year-old is scolded by an angry father. The child, in turn, is angry and frustrated and glances up at her dad, momentarily wondering whether she might risk kicking him in the shins. But Dad, his towering height convinces her, is much too formidable, and so taking a less though somewhat satisfying action, she slugs her innocent two-year-old brother. The **frustration-aggression theory** emphasizes that people blocked from achieving a goal are sometimes unable or unwilling to focus their frustration on the true source, and so they direct the aggression produced by frustration toward an accessible individual or group. The displacement of hostility from the true source of frustration to this substitute—a so-called "scapegoat"—permits a release of tension called "catharsis."

Three conditions make it likely that a racial or ethnic group will become a scapegoat. First, the group must be easy to identify, whether by skin color, a tattoo, or some insignia such as the Star of David that Nazis forced Jews to wear. Second, the group selected must be weak enough so that it is unlikely to retaliate. Third, to qualify as a scapegoat, a group must be physically accessible (Simpson and Yinger, 1972: 66–69).

For racist individuals scapegoating is often an emotionally charged process. In his study of poor Southern whites in the 1930s, Leonard W. Doob indicated that at least half-a-dozen white men informed him that when farmers for whom they were working forced them to leave the cabins in which they were living and replaced them with blacks, their immediate impulse was to kill the blacks. Before pursuing the impulse, however, each concluded that "killing the nigger wouldn't get me anywhere, since there are plenty of other nigger families for the place" (Doob, 1937: 471). The quotation is notable because it suggests that even though the frustrated poor whites eventually toned down their initial aggressive reaction toward blacks, they were still in the grips of the frustration-aggression perspective, which protected them from facing the painful truth that the real source of their frustration was the powerful, inaccessible farmers.

A recent review of this theory basically supported it with one major modification: that frustrations generate aggressive responses only when negative emotions are aroused. Thus if whites fail unexpectedly, they are likely to become angry and frustrated and vent their aggression on minority scapegoats. In contrast, if they expect to fail, negative emotion will be minimal, and little or no aggression will occur (Berkowitz, 1989).

For the first time in this book, we examine a concrete situation involving racist oppression. These brief sections are scattered throughout the book and represent good opportunities to see how norms governing racism develop in micro-level contexts. Internal colonialism, as well as other theoretical perspectives and concepts, contribute to each analysis and demonstrate the utility of a given theory or concept.

Ishi, the Last Surviving Yahi

Early in the morning of August 29, 1911, in a small northern California town, the sharp barking of dogs made workers at a slaughterhouse aware of a man crouching against a nearby fence. He was emaciated, close to starvation, and his hair was closely shaved—a sign that he was in mourning. In the months that followed, it became apparent why Ishi was in mourning. He was the last surviving member of the Yahi tribe, whose other members had been mercilessly hunted down. Ishi's story is a stark account of what can happen to a highly oppressed group whose members are brutalized victims of internal colonialism.

With the discovery of gold in northern California in 1848, whites began coming to the area by the thousands. Some were law-abiding citizens and others were not, but the new settlers shared a sense of racial and cultural superiority: Native Americans were inferior beings who should be exploited as servants, slaves, or sex objects. Any white man who actually married a Native American was viewed with contempt. Thus early white settlers drew caste distinctions. Native Americans, even so-called "good Indians" who lived on or near white homesteads, were always classified as lower caste members.

Inevitably the stereotypes accompanying this classification process proved deadly for northern California Native Americans. White immigrants had come across the plains where they had encountered Native Americans who were mounted on horses and were often armed with rifles. These were formidable opponents, and the whites adopted the convenient rationalization that the Yahi and other northern California Native Americans would be equally dangerous. Significant differences—that the Yahis were on foot and without guns—apparently escaped the recent settlers. Many whites made little or no effort to distinguish different Native Americans' abilities and motivations, and some killed Native Americans with little or no discretion. No saying more clearly demonstrates Native Americans' stigmatized status than the well-known, nineteenth-century phrase, "The only good Indian is a dead Indian."

With such an outlook, no Native Americans were safe. The Yahi and other northern California tribesmen sometimes responded to being tracked and killed by turning against whites and robbing or killing them. Following such acts, trigger-happy whites were likely to murder any Native Americans, including "good Indians". Because of their inability to fight back and their accessibility, these Native Americans served as scapegoats for the whites.

Until the 1880s, however, the Yahi had few encounters with whites. Certainly the members of this tribe were aware of the invaders and viewed them as an oppressive force. However, their nomadic life, which entailed gathering fruits, nuts, and berries, and hunting game, confined them to hilly country, far from the new settlements. Eventually whites' livestock began roaming the hills, destroying many plants that were a major source of the Yahi's food. At the same time, settlers began to pollute the streams, which provided salmon and other fish. For the Yahi, survival had always been precarious, but now it became even more so. Using all the skills developed by living close to nature, they fought back. They raided whites' homesteads and stole livestock and other food. When whites began killing them, they too killed in return. Theodora Kroeber indicated that the Yahi image "of the white man became fixed during those days when it was a careless boast that 'You can't tell one Indian from another.'" The Yahi "found themselves, too, indifferent to making distinctions between one white person and another" (Kroeber, 1969: 49–50). This situation illustrates how stereotypes can create a self-fulfilling prophecy. When whites and Native Americans began to stereotype each other as indiscriminate murderers, they created a situation in which it was believed necessary to kill or be killed. As a result members of each group felt compelled to become even more committed to indiscriminate murder.

Ishi was probably born in 1862. By that time the surviving Yahi had grasped one of the central ideas of internal colonialism—that their freedom of movement was highly restricted and that they could only survive if they used all their skills to avoid whites. But avoidance sometimes was impossible. When Ishi was about three, a raiding party attacked the Yahi camp. Most of the Yahi were killed, but he and his mother escaped. As Ishi grew up, he learned to hunt and fish and to live on the run, hiding from whites. Always threatened by starvation, the diminishing band sometimes raided white farms and stole food. Such a difficult life took its toll. By 1870 only about sixteen Yahi tribespeople survived, and by 1906 just four remained. At that point a surveying party discovered the hidden Yahi camp close to a stream. Three members fled, and the fourth, Ishi's crippled mother, was discovered by the whites. They took the Yahi's food and weapons but left the old woman unharmed. Shortly afterwards Ishi returned and carried his mother to a secluded spot, where she soon died. Ishi never again saw the other two tribal members. He was convinced that they must have died, or otherwise he would have encountered them. For the last three years in the wild, Ishi was entirely alone—the sole survivor of a tribe that had been systematically reduced to a single person by whites' genocidal efforts.

This is hardly an inspiring account with which to conclude the chapter. Unfortunately as we examine the history of American racism in the next chapter and then move on to consider current racism in later chapters, we will see considerably more evidence of racial oppression. The role of theory for analyzing racism will also be apparent.

REFERENCES

Aboud, Frances E. 1984. "Social and Cognitive Bases of Ethnic Identity Constancy." *Journal of Genetic Psychology* 145 (December): 217–230.

Aboud, Frances E. 1988. *Children and Prejudice.* New York: Basil Blackwell.

Allport, Gordon W. 1954. *The Nature of Prejudice.* Cambridge, MA: Addison-Wesley.

Berkowitz, Leonard. 1989. "Frustration-Aggression Hypothesis: Examination and Reformulation." *Psychological Bulletin* 106 (July): 59–73.

Blauner, Robert. 1972. *Racial Oppression in America.* New York: Harper & Row.

Collins, Patricia Hill. 1989. "The Social Construction of Black Feminist Thought." *Signs* 14 (Summer): 745–773.

Cox, Oliver Cromwell. 1959. *Caste, Class & Race: A Study in Social Dynamics.* New York: Monthly Review Press.

Davis, Allison, Burleigh B. Gardner, and Mary R. Gardner. 1941. *Deep South: A Social Anthropological Study of Caste and Class.* Chicago: University of Chicago Press.

Dollard, John. 1937. *Caste and Class in a Southern Town.* New Haven, CT: Yale University Press.

Doob, Christopher Bates. 1991. *Sociology: An Introduction.* Fort Worth: Holt, Rinehart and Winston. Third edition.

Doob, Leonard W. 1937. "Poor Whites: A Frustrated Class," pp. 445–484 in John Dollard, *Caste and Class in a Southern Town.* New Haven, CT: Yale University Press.

Feagin, Joe R. 1989. *Racial & Ethnic Relations.* Englewood Cliffs, NJ: Prentice-Hall. Third edition.

Forbes, J. D. 1990. "The Manipulation of Race, Caste, and Identity: Classify Afroamericans, Native Americans and Red-black People." *Journal of Ethnic Studies* 18 (Winter): 1–51.

Gans, Herbert. 1971. "The Uses of Poverty: The Poor Pay All." *Social Policy* 1 (July/August): 20–24.

Glazer, Nathan, and Daniel Patrick Moynihan. 1963. *Beyond the Melting Pot.* Cambridge, MA: M.I.T. Press and Harvard University Press.

Glazer, Nathan, and Daniel Patrick Moynihan. 1975. "Introduction," pp. 1–26 in Nathan Glazer and Daniel Patrick Moynihan (eds.), *Ethnicity: Theory and Experience.* Cambridge, MA: Harvard University Press.

Gordon, Milton M. 1964. *Assimilation in American Life: The Role of Race, Religion, and National Origins.* New York: Oxford University Press.

Gordon, Milton M. 1978. *Human Nature, Class, and Ethnicity.* New York: Oxford University Press.

Kroeber, Theodora. 1969. *Ishi in Two Worlds: A Biography of the Last Wild Indian in North America.* Berkeley and Los Angeles: University of California Press.

Marx, Karl, and Friedrich Engels. 1959. "Manifesto of the Communist Party," pp. 1–41 in Lewis S. Feuer (ed.), *Marx & Engels: Basic Writings on Politics & Philosophy.* Garden City, NY: Anchor Books. Originally published in 1848.

Mead, George Herbert. 1934. *Mind, Self and Society.* Chicago: University of Chicago Press.

Merton, Robert K. 1968. *Social Theory and Social Structure.* New York: Free Press. Third edition.

Park, Robert Ezra. 1950. *Race and Culture.* Glencoe, IL: Free Press.

Roberts, Sam. 1990. "Moving Beyond the Melting Pot 25 Years Later." *New York Times* (May 17): B1.

Sacks, Karen Brodkin. 1989. "Toward a Unified Theory of Class, Race, and Gender." *American Ethnologist* 16 (August): 534–550.

Scott, George M., Jr. 1990. "A Resynthesis of the Primordial and Circumstantial Approaches to Ethnic Group Solidarity: Towards an Explanatory Model." *Ethnic and Racial Studies* 13 (April): 147–171.

Simpson, George Eaton, and J. Milton Yinger. 1972. *Racial and Cultural Minorities: An Analysis of Prejudice and Discrimination.* New York: Harper & Row. Fourth edition.

Snedeker, George. 1988. "Capitalism, Racism, and the Struggle for Democracy: The Political Sociology of Oliver Cox." *Socialism and Democracy* 7 (Fall/Winter): 75–95.

Spencer, Margaret Beale, and Carol Markstrom-Adams. 1990. "Identity Processes among Racial and Ethnic Minority Children in America." *Child Development* 61 (April): 290–310.

Thompson, Richard H. 1989. *Theories of Ethnicity: A Critical Appraisal.* Westport, CT: Greenwood Press.

Wilhelm, Sidney M. 1983. *Black in a White Society.* Cambridge, MA: Schenkman.

Chapter
3

Passage to Racism

*T*he best-known estimates of the number of slaves brought to the New World range between 9 and 15 million, with perhaps half dying during the infamous "middle passage" from Africa to the Americas. Is it surprising that so many died? Consider the prevailing conditions.

After being branded and chained, the captured Africans were rowed out to slave ships, where they were packed into areas sometimes no more than 18 inches high. One captain said, "They had not so much room as a man in his coffin, either in length or breadth." Here they lived from six to ten weeks, in conditions horrible enough to drive people mad and often worsened when epidemics of dysentery, smallpox, or the flux, an illness which spared whites, swept the ships.

Suffocation in the unbearably close quarters was frequent, and in the frenzy to obtain more air, some men strangled those next to them. So many dead slaves were thrown overboard that reports indicated sharks would pick up a ship off the coast of Africa and follow it for its entire journey (Bennett, 1982: 49).

How could one group of people treat another so savagely? To analyze the historical development of racism, we can use a final theoretical framework. It is Donald L. Noel's (1968) theory of ethnic stratification, which concerns how ethnicity and race become central factors for determining people's access to valued political, economic, and social rewards of their society. This theory represents an additional conflict-theoretical perspective. While the theory can apply to diverse ethnicities, including different white ethnic groups, our focus in on race.

According to Noel, three conditions permit racial stratification to develop. First, there must be **ethnocentrism,** which is the automatic tendency to evaluate other cultures by outsiders' cultural standards. Ethnocentric individuals believe that their way is the correct or most appropriate way, and if other cultures have different standards, they invariably are inferior. The more one culture differs from another, the more likely people's ethnocentric tendencies appear. Nineteenth-century white Americans were ethnocentric toward African slaves, because slaves differed from them in many ways—language, clothing and appearance, norms, religion, and other cultural standards.

Second, competition for scarce resources is a necessary factor. Competition can be between or among different racial groups or simply within the dominant group. Two conditions affecting the extent to which competition produces racial exploitation are (a) whether or not custom or law puts limits on how much the minority can be oppressed and (b) whether the dominant group's opportunities are static or expanding. Both conditions favored extensive exploitation of slaves. Owners' treatment of slaves was almost completely unrestricted, and during the first half of the nineteenth century, use of slaves in the South greatly increased agricultural production and profit.

Third, as we have noted in the case of internal colonialism, for racism to occur, one racial group must possess superior power. Without it there will be intergroup relations ranging from peaceful coexistence to frequent conflict, but one group cannot consistently impose its will on the other. Frequently when one group possesses superior power, it is likely to try to establish structures and practices that permit it to keep long-term control. When blacks were brought to America, they were at the mercy of their masters, who went to great lengths to establish a slavery system that would last indefinitely.

In analyzing the process by which whites subordinated racial minorities, Noel's scheme proves useful. Internal colonialism seems a more appropriate perspective once the minority group's subordinate status has been established.

THE PREINDUSTRIAL ERA OF RACE RELATIONS

Whether Dutch, English, Portuguese, or Spanish, Europeans who encountered racial minorities used their superior power to deprive them of two precious resources—their material wealth or labor. Physical conditions determined the most efficient means of exploitation. When inhabitants were fairly sparsely settled, as in the Americas, they were either driven back, as in the North-American technique, or exterminated, the approach used in the West Indies and the South American lowlands. When the population was densely settled, a more practical or efficient policy was to enslave the local people, the approach used widely in Africa and in Indonesia (Cox, 1976: 9–10).

With the opportunity to exploit the minority members of technologically simple cultures, Europeans used ethnocentric stereotypes as rationalizations. By the middle of the sixteenth century, the Spanish declared that they enslaved local Native Americans to work in tropical mines "because, among other things, of their 'barbarous natures,' 'their sins,' their need of religious instruction, and because their labor was naturally due to a people of such 'elevated natures' as the Spainards" (Cox, 1976: 26).

During the preindustrial era, European explorers and settlers of what is now the United States dealt primarily with two minority groups, Native Americans and African-Americans, originally slaves from Africa.

The Art of Making Breakable Treaties

Members of the Tainos tribe who received Columbus on the island of San Salvador made a very favorable impression on the explorer. Writing to the King and Queen of Spain, he enthusiastically noted how peaceful they appeared, observing, "They love their neighbors as themselves, and their discourse is ever sweet and gentle, and accompanied with a smile; and though it is true they are naked, yet their manners are decorous and praiseworthy" (Brown, 1972: 1).

To Columbus, like the European hoards that followed, these positive qualities were clear signs of weakness. Native Americans were sweet, pliable, but definitely savage children, who, Columbus believed, should be "made to work, sow and do all that is necessary and to *adopt our ways*" (Brown, 1972: 2). While not known as the father of Western racism, Columbus might have laid claim to this dubious title: He initiated a broad policy where white explorers, colonists, and settlers followed a system of racist exploitation that incorporated the three factors in Noel's scheme: They used their greater power to seize what they considered the Native Americans' most precious commodity—land. This land permitted whites to expand their economic activity steadily, and neither law nor custom imposed much regulation on land takeover and other dealings with Native

Americans. In addition, ethnocentrism helped rationalize the takeover: Native Americans benefitted greatly, the ethnocentric argument went, because they were now recipients of whites' supposedly superior cultural offerings.

For the millions of European settlers arriving in what was to become the United States, obtaining land was the basic necessity. To facilitate this process, Europeans and later Americans began establishing treaties with Native Americans and then invariably breaking them.

The first treaty between Native Americans and Europeans occurred in Massachusetts. When English settlers landed in Plymouth in 1620, they received aid from several Native Americans who gave them corn and taught them where and how to fish. Without this help the Pilgrims undoubtedly would have perished. Five years later the colonists asked one of these Native Americans, a Pemaquid chief named Samoset, if they could have an additional 12,000 acres of Pemaquid land for accommodating the steady stream of English settlers. Like other Native Americans, Samoset believed that people could no more own land than they could the sky, but he was willing to humor the colonists, with whom relations had been good, and so he put his mark on a piece of paper.

In the following half-century, most arriving colonists did not bother with treaties, simply appropriating land to meet their needs. Metacom, the chief of the Wampanoags and the son of one of the four men who aided the original Plymouth settlers, realized that Native Americans would be pushed relentlessly westward unless they resisted, and so even though the colonists flattered him by crowning him King Philip of Pokanoket, he dedicated himself to establishing military alliances with the Narragansetts and other local tribes. In 1675 under Metacom's leadership, Native Americans attacked 52 English communities, completely destroying 12 of them and suffering substantial losses themselves. After being captured, Metacom was drawn and quartered and, as a warning against further rebellion, his skull was displayed on a pole in Plymouth for the next quarter-century. Meanwhile European settlement in the new land expanded, and many tribes continued to resist (Brown, 1972: 3–4).

During the seventeenth century, some tribes allied themselves with the French, who were more inclined to hunt and trap than settle the land. When the British defeated the French after a ten-year war, the British had to confront an array of hostile tribes. In 1763 these uprisings encouraged a Royal Proclamation in which the King of England declared that exploration and settlement of all lands west of the western slope of the Appalachian Mountains would cease until negotiations with all tribes involved were complete.

More than 20 years later, in 1787, the U.S. Congress was also conciliatory, offering the following solemn pledge:

> The utmost good faith shall always be observed toward the Indians; their land and property shall never be taken from them without their consent; and in

their property, rights, and liberty, they shall never be invaded or disturbed, unless in justified and lawful wars authorized by Congress; but laws founded in justice and humanity shall from time to time be made, for preventing wrongs being done to them, and for preserving peace and friendship with them. (Quoted in Deloria, 1972: iii)

In the early 1800s, Supreme Court decisions established the principle that Native-American societies were self-governing nations with a right to their land and that the American government must abide by the treaties it made with them. But the steady influx of settlers to the frontier undermined that position. Congress passed what became known as "Pre-emption Acts," which validated settlers' claim to lands that treaties had assigned to Native Americans. In 1824 the Bureau of Indian Affairs was established to coordinate relations between the tribes and the federal government. Its major task became the relocation of Native Americans. The "utmost good faith" expressed in the lofty statement of 1787 was discarded under what Noel's theory described as pressures of an expanding, competitive society.

In 1829 Andrew Jackson became president. Known as "Old Hickory" by whites and "Sharp Knife" by Native Americans, Jackson exhibited a tough, adversarial approach to Native Americans, whom he had fought throughout the Southern states and considered incapable of living peaceably with whites. Jackson claimed that the best solution for all concerned was to move all Native Americans west of the Mississippi, where, he promised them,

> your white brothers will not trouble you; they will have no claim to the land, and you can live upon it, you and all your children, as long as the grass grows or the water runs, in peace and plenty. It will be yours forever. (Quoted in Bailyn et al., 1976: 441)

To any Native Americans who were students of diplomatic relations with whites, this message must have seemed ominously familiar and must have provided little consolation or sense of security. Though phrased in peaceful terms, its author was an enthusiastic advocate of whites' superior military power against Native Americans. Certainly it was realistic to be pessimistic, because within a few years settlers were streaming into territories west of the Mississippi, and what had once been considered "the permanent Indian frontier" was steadily shifted westward.

Reading this material, you might begin to wonder if racism is the central issue. After all, you might say, the primary motive for removing the Native Americans was economic—the settlers' need for land. A critical point is that if settlers and officials had not classified Native Americans as inferior, they could not have so easily exploited them economically. Racist and ethnocentric assessments were apparent from colonial times. The first settlers' written records indicated that they considered Native Americans "depraved, savage brutes, as impious rascals who lived in filth and ate nasty food" (Jacobs, 1985: 110). A major element in the eighteenth- and nineteenth-century stereotype of Native Americans was the idea that they were all nomadic hunting people wandering free-as-the-wind over thousands of acres of virgin wilderness. While this image simply ignored the obvious fact that many of the eastern tribes lived in stable towns and villages, such prominent individuals as presidents John Adams and Theodore Roosevelt found it a fine rationalization for depriving Native Americans of their land (Jacobs, 1985: 111).

The most famous racist rationalization was the concept of "manifest destiny," which described Indians' culture as inferior to whites', and then suggested that this supposed inferiority should serve as the basis for their exploitation. According to manifest destiny, God ordained that white Americans should liberate the continental territory and direct native people's movement toward participation in modern political and technological life. The idea proved convenient when gold was discovered in California in 1848, and many thousands of fortune seekers once again violated treaties and annihilated the idea of "the permanent Indian frontier" as they pushed nearly to the Pacific.

So it was clear that no treaties would stop the whites' advance. During the second half of the nineteenth century, the Sioux, Cheyenne, Arapaho, Kiowa, and Apache, under such leaders as Sitting Bull, Crazy Horse, Cochise, and Geronimo, fought soldiers and settlers in a vain effort to retain their land and way of life. Eventually they were killed or pacified and placed on reservations. Ethnocentrism was apparent in systematic efforts to destroy Native-American cultures. Officials compelled many Native-American children to attend boarding schools, where they had to abandon their native languages and customs. In 1892 the Commissioner of Indian Affairs issued a directive requiring all male Native Americans to keep their hair short; he also banned wearing paint and holding tribal dances and feasts and discouraged wearing blankets (Nichols, 1986: 133–134). Native-American cultures were inferior, the whites argued, and so such measures were believed to be beneficial for everyone, including Native Americans.

The preceding discussion has outlined some of the major historical developments in early contacts between whites and Native Americans. Shifting from the macro level to the micro level, we now examine racism in the life of a Native-American chief and his people.

Little Crow Goes to War

In 1862 Little Crow was a 60-year-old warrior whose people, the Santee Sioux, steadily lost their homelands as 150,000 settlers extended the "permanent Indian frontier." Furthermore local traders and Indian agents were constantly cheating the Santee Sioux out of most of the annuities they received as compensation for their land loss.

Little Crow's position was difficult. He had adopted some aspects of white culture, exchanging breechcloths and blankets for trousers and brass-buttoned jackets, joining the Episcopol Church, building a house, and starting to farm. At the same time, he realized that as a chief he had signed two treaties that had not only led to the Santee Sioux losing their land but also to their being tricked out of most of the financial compensation owed them.

In July 1862 several thousand Santees gathered at two Indian agencies seeking money that the government owed them—money they needed in order to buy food. Realizing that their people were approaching starvation, Little Crow and several other chiefs rode to one of the agencies and asked the agent to issue food that was in the warehouse. Eventually the agent complied, and the Santee Sioux left quietly.

In the second agency, however, the agent refused to pass out food until the Santee Sioux paid for it. Angered, Little Crow said that his people had waited a long time for money owed to them and that it was the only way they could pay for food. He continued, "We have to get it. We have no food, but here are these stores, filled with food. We ask that you, the agent, make some arrangement by which we can get food from the stores, or else we may take our own way to keep ourselves from starving."

Instead of answering Little Crow, the agent turned to another white man, a trader, and asked him what he should do. "So far as I am concerned, if they are hungry let them eat grass or their own dung," the trader replied (Brown, 1972: 40). For a moment the Santee Sioux were silent, and then in unison they stood up and left.

Little Crow went home, and the following Sunday he was in church where he listened to a sermon, shook hands with other worshipers, and then returned home. It was an unhappy time for him. Earlier that summer his people relieved him of some of his duties, showing that they had lost confidence in him because of the two treaties he had signed. Had Little Crow been able to convince the agent to give them food, his prestige probably would have been restored, but the trader's insult eliminated that possibility. Before the arrival of the white man, Little Crow would have been able to win back his honor by leading his people to battle, but the treaties prohibited him from going to war.

Little Crow's predicament was a distinct illustration of internal colonialism: He and his people were controlled and exploited by whites, who systematically deprived them of their land and made them dependent on whites for their survival. In spite of his oppressed status, Little Crow tried to get along with whites, adopting some of their cultural standards.

But it was a situation that Noel's scheme would analyze as possessing increasingly rigid racial stratification because the whites' drive for more land was very strong, and because their custom and law placed few if any restrictions on their treatment of Native Americans. Many encounters could set off incidents in which whites' greater power, coupled with their sense of caste superiority, illustrated here by the trader's comment, permitted them to tyrannize the Native Americans. Little Crow and his people were placed in a life-threatening situation where their limited power meant little or no opportunity to produce a favorable outcome.

In this context the final event is hardly surprising. Late that same Sunday night, Little Crow awoke to hear many voices outside his house and a group of Santee Sioux entering his bedroom. Several young tribesmen had raided a farm and killed three white men and two white women. No Santee Sioux would be safe from whites now, the men claimed, and reluctantly Little Crow agreed to their demands. Yes, he would lead them to war. About ten months later he was killed in a gun battle (Brown, 1972: 42–65).

In the upcoming discussion of African-Americans during preindustrial times, it is apparent that whites' oppression was equally systematic.

Behind the Cotton Curtain

As we noted earlier in the chapter, the American slavery system is a clear illustration of Noel's theory of racial stratification. Whites used their power to establish a system of nearly complete control, which thrived in an expanding economy and existed with almost no limits on owners' conduct toward slaves. Whites' ethnocentric attitudes about blacks also contributed.

For the first 40 years of American settlement, there was little slavery. Instead of slaves early colonists were more likely to have indentured servants, whose passage to the New World and room and board were financed in exchange for a specified number of years of unpaid employment.

But eventually settlers became convinced that because of several problems, white servants were unsatisfactory. First, since slaves were owned, they could be forced to accept whatever living conditions would be most advantageous to their owners. Second, even though settlers could recruit a fair supply of servants, there simply were not enough of them to work on the steadily growing number of tobacco, rice, and indigo plantations in the South. These first two points are consistent with the Noel theory's analysis of conditions promoting competition: The absence of regulation, and the need for a vast supply of laborers in an expanding economy encouraged the development of slavery. Third, indentured servants' contracts were often a source of dispute, with servants either suing their masters or simply running away. In contrast, slaves could be purchased outright and did not need to be replaced at the end of a contract. Finally maintaining slaves was cheaper than hiring indentured servants (Franklin and Moss, 1988: 32).

Slavery existed through the seventeenth and eighteenth centuries and was always most widely practiced in the South, which, unlike the New England and Middle Atlantic states, had large agricultural crops that could effectively use a large slave population; by the early nineteenth century, the Northern states had outlawed slavery. Until the end of the War of 1812, in fact, the growth of slavery was relatively slow, even in the South. Then with the virtual elimination of war in the Western world, trade with

Europe flourished, and a great demand for cotton developed. Massive cotton production required large numbers of unskilled laborers, and with the growing demand, slavery expanded. In 1790 there were fewer than 700,000 slaves; by 1830 the number had reached two million; at the last census before the Civil War, the slave population had nearly doubled to 3,953,760 (Franklin and Moss, 1988: 112–113).

According to one historian, the American slavery system developed into "a social system as coercive as any yet known." Most slaves served on farms and plantations, and about two-thirds of them worked on cotton plantations. These plantations varied considerably in size. In 1860 about 88 percent of slaveowners possessed fewer than 20 slaves, and evidence suggests that the most profitable economic unit contained between 30 and 60 slaves. While not maximally efficient, large plantations were enormously productive, especially in the states where "King Cotton" prevailed—Mississippi, Alabama, Louisiana, and Georgia (Bennett, 1982: 86–87).

Slavery was an economic system which permitted owners to use fellow human beings brutally to maximize profits, and the cotton plantation, which was a totalitarian system established with this economic goal in mind, controlled slaves' lives from birth to death. Generally there was a nursery, where a slave, often designated an "aunty," cared for young black children while their mothers worked in the fields. At about the age of six or seven, slave children started working, and when they reached ten or twelve, they received a full set of adult tasks.

One ever-present danger slaves faced was the possibility that the owner would find it economically productive to sell or hire out a family member, and thus many children were torn from their parents and often never saw them again. Frederick Douglass, who later became a prominent opponent of slavery, recalled seeing his mother only four or five times. She lived 12 miles away and had to receive permission to walk the distance on foot after a full day's work in the fields; she faced a whipping if not back before sunrise. Douglass wrote:

> I do not recollect of ever seeing my mother by the light of day. She was with me in the night. She would lie down with me, and get me to sleep, but long before I waked she was gone. Very little communication ever took place between us. Death soon ended what little we could have while she lived, and with it her hardships and suffering. (Douglass, 1968: 22)

Like Douglass's mother most slaves on large plantations were field hands. The cultivation of crops was a demanding undertaking, and planters felt that the system proved most successful when slaves were scrupulously supervised by the owner or a hired overseer and were permitted little or no initiative. Planting, cultivation, and harvesting of cotton, tobacco, rice, and sugar cane required minimal skill but considerable time and effort. For slaves the most demanding time of the year came during the harvest season. Worried about inclement weather destroying crops, planters sometimes forced slaves to work 18 to 20 hours a day (Franklin and Moss, 1988: 116–117).

Most owners managed plantations themselves, but overseers were necessary if a plantation possessed more than 20 slaves or the owner was frequently absent. Overseers, also known as drivers, tended to be poor whites, who often despised and resented the slavery system. These whites considered the system responsible for their own poverty and that slaves, in particular, bore major guilt. Setting high production quotas for their overseers, planters placed few limits on their authority as long as slaves, admittedly valuable property, were not permanently damaged. Sometimes, however, drivers exceeded even these liberal limits as Frederick Douglass noted in the case of his own master's cruel overseer.

> The overseer's name was Plummer. Mr. Plummer was a miserable drunkard, a profane swearer, and a savage monster. He always went armed with a cowskin and a heavy cudgel [club]. I have known him to cut and slash the women's heads so horribly, that even master would be enraged at his cruelty, and would threaten to whip him if he did not mind himself. (Douglass, 1968: 24)

Slaves experienced different degrees of misery. It was generally considered preferable to live on a small plantation rather than on a large one because the slave would work directly with the master who tended to be less ferocious than overseers. Masters also differed markedly, ranging from cruel and sadistic to, if one might use the words loosely, kindly and caring. Yet we should remember that simply by owning fellow human beings, even the most benevolent masters were committed to the slavery system, and when faced with a situation where they had to choose between their economic welfare and their slaves' well-being, they seldom opted for the latter (Bennett, 1982: 94).

Besides work, other daily issues affecting slaves' lives were food, clothes, and housing. Slaves' food was often a problem for planters, who were preoccupied with producing their staple crops and frequently had to purchase food both for themselves and their slaves. Food for slaves was carefully rationed—a week's supply was about a peck of cornmeal, three to four pounds of bacon or salt pork, and sometimes supplements of sweet potatoes, peas, rice, syrup, and fruit. Some slaves maintained their own gardens but risked possible punishment if they spent too much time at them. On most plantations slaves were fed fairly well because owners recognized that decent food was necessary for efficient work. They reached no such conclusion about clothes, and most slaves wore crude, homespun garments known as "Negro clothes" and poorly made, skimpy shoes called "Negro brogans." Housing too was poor, with slaves generally living in small, crudely made huts that had no windows, little furniture, and usually no beds. Worse than the absence of comforts, however, was the crowding. A Mississippi planter kept 150 slaves in 24 tiny huts that were only 16 by 14 feet each. An ex-slave noted, "Everything happened in that one room—birth, sickness, death—everything" (Bennett, 1982: 89–90; Franklin and Moss, 1988: 120–121).

Like whites in their dealing with Native Americans, slaveowners used racist rationalizations to justify the oppression. Slaveowners claimed that blacks were inferior and destined to occupy subordinate positions, and that Southern whites, far from being corrupted by the practice, had developed a uniquely refined culture which would not have evolved without slaves performing the menial tasks (Franklin and Moss, 1988: 174–175).

To legitimate slavery, legislators in each Southern state enacted what became known as Slave Codes, a body of laws covering every aspect of slaves' lives. While the Slave Codes differed from state to state, the general point of view was that slaves were property, not people. The laws were supposed to protect ownership of that property and to ensure that slaves were maintained under repressive conditions for a maximum level of production. Thus most of the laws focused on exclusion, indicating activities slaves were not permitted to do—for instance, leave their plantations without authorization, possess firearms, hire themselves out without their owners' permission, buy or sell goods, or visit the homes of whites or free blacks. Most of the petty offenses were punished with whippings while the more serious ones incurred branding, imprisonment, or death. Arson and conspiracy to rebel were capital crimes in all slave-owning states (Franklin and Moss, 1988: 114–115). The Slave Codes solidified racial segregation: Owners' rights were carefully protected, but blacks' rights were scrupulously denied.

In the early-industrial stage, new economic and political conditions produced some changes in racial minority-group members' lives.

THE EARLY-INDUSTRIAL STAGE

According to Oliver Cox (1976: 14–15), industrial leaders have always been willing to accept racist outlooks and practices. Their dominant motivation has been to expand their economic enterprises, and racism within a given culture has certainly not hampered that expansion.

Soon after the Civil War, Herbert Spencer thrilled most prominent Americans with the doctrine of social Darwinism, which loosely built upon Charles Darwin's research with plants and animals. Spencer declared that as a fundamental scientific principle, the most intelligent and capable people would invariably rise to dominant economic and political positions and that society would evolve most rapidly and efficiently if citizens recognized that this "survival of the fittest" was the natural and proper order of things. Those who failed to rise to the top—including some whites and all racial minority-group members—were simply proving their inherent inferiority. The timing of social Darwinism was perfect for wealthy and powerful whites, appearing just when American industry was rapidly expanding and justifying its leaders' success and prominence. We wouldn't be at the top if we didn't deserve it, they triumphantly declared, and John D. Rockefeller enthusiastically lectured about social Darwinism to children in Sunday school, and industrialist Andrew Carnegie felt privileged to consider Herbert Spencer a close friend (Hofstadter, 1955).

Spencer and the other social Darwinists, of course, had never heard of the "self-fulfilling prophecy" and, if they had, undoubtedly would have dismissed it as the muddled thinking of sentimental, unscientific minds. There is little doubt, however, that what social Darwinism did was to offer a giant boost to those already well located and, conversely, a shove toward the bottom for those who were not.

It was not just the leaders who subscribed to this doctrine. Members of various social classes read and applauded Spencer's work (Hofstadter, 1955: 34), and it seems likely that the racist position inherent in social Darwinism must have readily blended with racist views already firmly fixed in American culture. Whether one had recently arrived or already been settled, it was not a good time to belong to a racial minority in America.

We consider experiences for Native Americans, African-Americans, Chinese-Americans, Japanese-Americans, Mexican-Americans, and Puerto Ricans during the early-industrial era.

Native Americans' Reservation Life

Throughout this period Native Americans continued to experience the racist treatment inflicted on them since Columbus's time: In their passion for what they considered the Native Americans' one precious resource—land—white Americans used their superior power to subdue the native inhabitants and relocate them on reservations, where they fell under the control of the Bureau of Indian Affairs. At the same time, whites' ethnocentric outlook drove them to provide their victims a new and "better" culture and way of life.

In 1887 the passage of the Dawes Act mandated the end of common land holdings on reservations; instead each single Native-American adult or family was supposed to receive a 160-acre plot. One immediate effect of the Dawes Act was that millions of acres of so-called surplus reservation land not included in the allotments was taken from Native Americans and sold to white farmers, miners, and corporations.

For many Native Americans, the 160-acre allotment provided inferior land, which was inadequate for crops or grazing animals. In other instances, however, land quality was good, and Native Americans were able to lease it to farmers and ranchers for substantial income. While many Native Americans were pleased with this arrangement, white reformers obsessed with the work ethic were disturbed, feeling that such a system made Native Americans unproductive and lazy. These people reasoned that if Native Americans could sell at least some of their land, then they could buy machinery and homes that would allow them to become effective, hard-working farmers in the best American tradition.

The reformers convinced Congressional members of the righteousness of such an approach, and between 1902 and 1910 Congress passed legislation permitting the sale of all Native-American owned land. Within a decade over half the Native Americans who had received allotments under the Dawes Act had sold their land at far below market value and were both landless and penniless. Landless Native Americans were in a much more economically deprived state than landless whites, because they were unprepared educationally and culturally to face the white work world, whose members tended to respond violently to Native Americans venturing outside of reservations (Berthrong, 1986: 204–209).

During this era missionaries, officials of the Bureau of Indian Affairs, reservation teachers, and personnel at federally funded boarding schools stressed the importance of dropping traditional ways and learning white people's culture. Native-American boys and young men were supposed to receive training as farmers or laborers while girls and young women were prepared for housekeeping and domestic tasks.

In the late nineteenth century, boarding schools, which supposedly trained young Native Americans for jobs in the industrial world, reached their highest level of recruitment, with 25 schools containing over 6000 students. The schools proved unsuccessful, however. The young people were lonely living in a culturally alien atmosphere, and they were repelled by the inevitable emphasis on military organization: By the middle 1890s, both girls and boys were placed in drill companies on the first day of school, were required to wear uniforms, and were led by student officers following army drill regulations. Ethnocentric in outlook, most school officials praised the military structure, contending that it

> served to develop a work ethic; it broke the students' sense of "Indian time" and ordered their life. The merits of military organization, drill, and routine . . . were explained by one official who stated that "it teaches patriotism, obedience, courage, courtesy, promptness, and constancy." (Trennert, 1986: 225)

Teachers frequently humiliated their students. In an autobiographical account, one Native American indicated that in class a teacher asked him to read a paragraph, and he did so without error. The teacher, however, questioned the reading and demanded that he read it again, and again, and again. After the eleventh reading "everything before me went black and I sat down thoroughly cowed and humiliated for the first time in my life and in front of the whole class" (Luther Standing Bear, 1978: 146).

By the early 1920s, Native-American boarding schools ceased to operate. Gradually educational officials recognized that while government officials might have established the schools with the intention of preparing Native Americans for work in the white world, actual training occurred in an atmosphere conveying a sense that they were racially and culturally inferior beings. Furthermore jobs for which they were trained were rarely available, and Native Americans' criticisms of the boarding schools was growing (Trennert, 1986: 229–230).

During the late nineteenth and early twentieth centuries, blacks, who were now nominally free, faced new forms of oppression.

African-Americans' Survival in the "Survival-of-the-Fittest" Era

While the end of slavery meant that blacks were technically free, an oppressive system of racial stratification continued. Whites were still much more powerful than blacks, using them to financial advantage in the expanding, early-industrial economy.

After the Civil War, most ex-slaves found little reason to celebrate their recent freedom. The land had been devastated, with many blacks and some whites suffering from disease and starvation. Furthermore Southern whites, determined to retain as much power as possible over the newly freed blacks, passed the infamous Black Codes, which provided blacks scarcely more rights and opportunities than under slavery. In addition, President Andrew Johnson was sympathetic to white Southerners, declaring that African-Americans were not ready for the privileges of citizenship and vetoing Congressional legislation in their behalf. A fight between Congress and the president broke out, and, in spite of Johnson's strenuous campaign for his program, the people sided with Congress, providing an overwhelming mandate to Thaddeus Stevens and other Congressional supporters of blacks' rights.

For blacks it appeared to be a great moment. Historian Lerone Bennett, Jr., concluded, "Never before had the sun shone so bright" (Bennett, 1982: 214). The Reconstruction Act of 1867 passed, and all Southern states had to convene racially mixed constitutional conventions, which outlawed slavery, eliminated race as a criterion for determining a person's right to possess and inherit property, and extended the vote to all black males. Suddenly whites' overwhelming political power was threatened. In the next few years, blacks were elected lieutenant governors in Mississippi, South Carolina, Louisiana, served as secretary of state in Florida, sat on the state supreme court in South Carolina, were a majority in the South Carolina House of Representatives, and held a host of less influential but important posts in Southern state and municipal governments (Franklin and Moss, 1988: 206–220).

Change was social as well as political. In South Carolina, probably the most racially liberal Southern state, dramatic developments were occurring. One account noted:

> The social life was gay, glittering and interracial. A dashing militia captain gave a ball, and blacks and whites—some of them native South Carolinians— glided across the polished floor. At official balls, receptions and dinners, blacks and whites sat down together and got up in peace. (Bennett, 1982: 216)

But it was no more than a quick burst of sunshine. American public opinion was turning against people of non-Anglo-Saxon background in what was to become the heyday of social Darwinism. The Supreme Court adopted the tone of the times, emasculating the Fourteenth Amendment, which ensured that African-Americans were citizens with full rights and privileges, by ruling that the amendment prohibited states but not individuals from discriminating. Many whites expressed their racism less elegantly. A group of South Carolina whites, whose state we already noted had the most liberal racial policies, appeared before Congress in 1868, protesting African-Americans' participation in politics and vowing to carry on the fight until blacks were once more subordinated. Expressing their racism proudly, they declared:

> That is a duty we owe to the land that is ours, to the graves that it contains, and to the race of which you and we alike are members—the proud Caucasian race, whose sovereignty on earth God has ordained. (Bailyn et al., 1977: 766)

For blacks, Reconstruction had seemed to be an era of great hope and promise, but by the middle 1870s, it was clear that no significant economic, political, or social reforms would emerge from it—no guaranteed 40 acres of land and a mule (as one Congressional supporter had promised), no guaranteed citizens' rights, no guaranteed boost in social position, but only a full share of racism and terror.

The terror struck with full force at the turn of the century, primarily in the South. Two general factors seemed to lie behind the beatings, shootings, and lynchings—the desire to drive blacks out of political activity initiated during Reconstruction and into terrorized submission; and a general sense of social crisis generated by economic depression, with blacks serving as scapegoats for fearful, frustrated whites. Between 1882 and 1901, 1914 African-Americans were lynched. While still alive, victims often had limbs or sexual organs amputated or were roasted slowly over fires. After death pieces of the victim were distributed routinely to onlookers who wanted souvenirs of the notable event (Shapiro, 1988: 30–31).

During that era most whites believed that most of the lynch victims had raped white women. Records, however, do not support this conclusion. In the first 14 years of the twentieth century, just 315 lynch victims were accused of rape or attempted rape while over 500 were accused of homicide and others of robbery, insulting whites, and a variety of nebulous "offenses" (Franklin and Moss, 1988: 282).

How did the people of that era feel about lynching? Unfortunately systematic survey research did not start for several decades. In 1905 one writer, however, did have the initiative to record the following data: In the trial of white men accused of burning two black men to death, 76 of 110 prospective jurors (69 percent) indicated that even if evidence clearly demonstrated that the defendants had taken part in the murders, the prospective jurors would not have favored their conviction (Baker, 1973). Such sentiment was consistent with the Slave Codes and other norms for whites' unregulated treatment of blacks established during slavery.

Even more threatening to blacks than lynchings were race riots, which were not directed at individuals but ranged across large areas and could victimize any African-Americans unlucky enough to be in the vicinity. In the early 1900s, while the number of lynchings slowly decreased, the number of riots rose in both Southern and Northern cities. As black immigration to the North increased, hostilities toward blacks grew proportionately, and in 1908 the riot that occurred in Springfield, Illinois, during which two black men were killed within a half-mile of the only home Abraham Lincoln ever owned, was as ferocious as any that occurred in the South (Franklin and Moss, 1988: 282–286).

Violence against African-Americans was the most vicious example of the racism they encountered. In 1908 a writer asked blacks in both the North and South to summarize their chief complaints. In the South the first problem cited was almost always the separate and inferior railroad cars or facilities in railroad stations, followed by references to injustice in the courts, the low quality of schooling, and the prospect of physical violence. In contrast, in the North, overwhelmingly the most frequent complaint involved discrimination in the work place, even though job opportunities were much more extensive than in the South. To the Southern black man, the North proved to be a shock. He was seeking work where he would be "judged at his worth as a man, not as a Negro: this he came North to find, and he . . . [met] difficulties of which he had not dreamed in the South" (Baker, 1973a: 279).

Until World War I, most African-Americans were in the South, earning about 40 percent of what counterparts in the North received. But the situation changed rapidly with the outbreak of World War I. A sudden sharp decline in the supply of European laborers, along with a severe labor depression in the Southern states causing wages to plummet, encouraged black laborers to respond to industrial recruiters who came south seeking workers.

Southern whites were alarmed by African-Americans' flight and took measures to limit it. In Jacksonville, Florida, a local ordinance declared that all labor recruiters needed to pay a license fee of $1000. In many Southern towns and cities, whites threatened departing blacks, and the local newspapers urged that they remain. But blacks recognized that this was their chance to participate, if modestly, in the bounty of the industrial age. Northern employers appreciated the influx of African-Americans at a time when they would have otherwise remained understaffed. Furthermore patriotic Americans realized that without blacks the labor shortage would have significantly hampered the country's war effort. In the decade of 1910–1920, the black population in the Northern and Western states increased by about 330,000 people (Franklin and Moss, 1988: 251–252, 305–306).

We now move from the macro level of analysis to the micro level, considering one young African-American's struggle during the early twentieth century.

Perils of Being Black in the Early Twentieth-Century South

When famed author Richard Wright was growing up in the South, the Civil War had been over for about half a century. For those 50 years, African-Americans had been technically free, but, in the well-known phrase, they were expected "to know their place"—to accept that they would be deprived of full rights and privileges in society.

As the introduction to a book of short stories entitled *Uncle Tom's Children*, Wright wrote an autobiographical essay that showed how perilous the lives of young black people could be. One tenet of internal colonialism is the colonial-labor principle, stressing that racial minorities are expected to perform tasks that primarily benefit majority-group members. But what if a young black man ignored this principle and considered work a personal growth experience? Such an approach represents a direct challenge to the current racial order. It illustrates what Erving Goffman called **normification**—behavior that gives the impression that an individual widely considered inferior is trying to deny being different (Goffman, 1974: 115).

Wright applied for a job at an optical company in Jackson, Mississippi. The interview went well, with Wright careful to show the expected deference by pronouncing his "sirs" very distinctly. He was hired, and the new boss indicated that Wright would be able to learn the business. As a result the new employee had visions of working his way up. The first month went well enough, but while cleaning the shop and polishing lenses, Wright gradually realized that he had no opportunity to learn anything, in spite of the boss's claim.

So one day Wright approached Morrie, a young white colleague about his own age, and asked about his work. Morrie grew red and asked, "Whut yuh tryin' t' do, nigger, git smart?" No, Wright replied, he wasn't trying to get smart. "Well, don't, if yuh know what's good for yuh!" Morrie replied.

Puzzled, Wright concluded that Morrie simply did not want to help him, and so he went to Pease, the other employee, and asked him about his work.

> "Say, are you crazy, you black bastard?" Pease asked me, his gray eyes growing hard.
>
> I spoke out, reminding him that the boss had said I was to be given a chance to learn something.
>
> "Nigger, you think you're *white*, don't you?"
>
> "Naw, sir!"
>
> "Well, you're acting mighty like it!" (Wright, 1938: xv)

Pease went on to warn Wright to stay away from "white man's work."

From then on both Pease and Morrie treated Wright differently. They ignored him unless he was a bit slow performing some task. Then they called him "a lazy black son-of-a-bitch" and told him to hurry up.

Wright indicated that early twentieth-century African-Americans faced the constant danger of being perceived as seeking normification. One day as he entered an elevator along with some white men, Wright had an armload of packages. Because of the packages, he could not remove his hat—as whites always expected of African-Americans in their presence. After staring at him coldly, one of the white men removed Wright's hat and stuck it under his arm.

Had Wright thanked the white man, he would have risked a punch in the mouth, since such a response would have suggested normification— implying a situation of racial equality in which the white man had done him a favor. The safe course of action would have been to look at the white man out of the corner of his eye and grin. Wright refused to demean himself by taking the easy way out, but he also wanted to avoid the punch in the mouth. So as soon as the hat was placed under his arm, he used another strategy—acting as though the packages were slipping and making a highly concentrated effort to prevent them from falling (Wright, 1938: xxx).

In his youth Richard Wright had several painful experiences indicating that when dealing with whites, black people put their physical safety on the line if they even hinted at normification. In the early twentieth-century South, African-Americans were safe only if their words and actions constantly reassured whites that they, the blacks, accepted the caste system and its rituals of subordination (discussed in Chapter 2).

During the preindustrial era, other racial minorities began arriving in the United States.

Chinese, Japanese, Mexican, and Puerto Rican Pioneers

In the late nineteenth and early twentieth centuries, the four groups to be examined in this section started arriving in the United States. The factor in Noel's scheme most saliently affecting their situation is the issue of competition. Workers from these countries were welcomed when it proved beneficial to businesses to obtain cheap labor. On the other hand, white workers frequently found themselves in competition with these immigrants for jobs, and as a result resentment, even violence against them developed. The law provided minority groups with little protection. Noel's two other factors also are relevant: At times whites' ethnocentrism helped make it acceptable to oppress a particular racial minority, and whites' superior power allowed them to establish policies and pass laws limiting newly arrived minorities' opportunities.

Chinese immigrants, who were escaping the ravages of the Taiping Rebellion in southern China, reached the West coast when gold was being discovered in California. At first, relations between the races were amiable because the Chinese were willing to work the areas already abandoned by whites who had moved on to more profitable sites. Eventually, however, the Chinese workers' willingness to put in long, arduous, but productive days proved abrasive to whites; even though the recent arrivals were restricted from the richest areas, they simply were too successful. The remedy was to pass a special foreign mining license tax imposed once a month almost exclusively on the Chinese. Still they kept coming to California and in 1860 represented nearly 10 percent of its population.

By the early 1860s, the gold supply had started to dwindle, and most Chinese had little to do. White leaders wanted to exploit this eager, hard-working labor source. Would the seemingly puny Chinese be strong enough to lay track for the transcontinental railroad? Widespread debate developed, and eventually Charles Crocker, a contractor for the Central Pacific Railroad, decided to give them a try. Although scornfully called "Crocker's pets," 1200 Chinese were hired for construction and between 1864 and 1869 proved to be excellent workers. But then the job was done, and along with about an equal number of non-Chinese, they were out of work. Meanwhile about a million people had moved to California on the transcontinental railroad, and the result was a distinct labor surplus.

In the context of racist, late-nineteenth-century America, it was not surprising that the Chinese became scapegoats for white workers' economic plight. At a miners' meeting, the participants concluded that any means necessary should be used to stop the "Asiatic inundation" and that the ruling class and the Chinese shared responsibility for job scarcity. The miners produced a fierce, racist statement flatly declaring that

> the Capitalists, ship-owners and merchants and others who are encouraging or engaged in the importation of these burlesques on humanity would crowd their ships with the long-tailed, horned, and cloven-hoofed inhabitants of the infernal regions. (Daniels and Kitano, 1970: 36)

In the 1870s and 1880s, hostility toward the Chinese was more than verbal. Violence started in the mining districts and surged into the cities. Chinese were robbed, beaten, and sometimes killed, but because of the laxity of law enforcement and a statute prohibiting Chinese from testifying against whites, almost no criminal prosecution occurred. Mark Twain wrote:

> I have seen Chinamen abused and maltreated in all the mean, cowardly ways possible to the invention of a degraded nature, but I never saw a Chinaman righted in a court of justice for wrongs thus done him. (Twain, 1868)

One analyst suggested that supporters of the Chinese were "the rich, the good, and the wise"—merchants seeking trade with the Far East, ranchers and farmers looking for cheap laborers, most Protestant clergy, and individuals searching for low-paid, docile servants. The anti-Chinese forces were composed of white working-class people competing against Chinese immigrants for jobs and two groups who needed support from working-class whites to survive occupationally—politicians who sought their votes and journalists who required their patronage (Daniels, 1988: 51–52). Thus the economic factor played a major role in whites' response to early Chinese immigration.

Eventually Congress decided to take a decisive step to quell the violence and to protect jobs for white workers. The Chinese Exclusion Act of 1882 halted the immigration of laborers and helped to alleviate if not eliminate anti-Chinese violence, which continued through the 1880s (Knoll, 1982: 24–27).

The Japanese arrived on the West coast several decades after the Chinese, and they inherited much of the racist feeling. "Now the Jap is a wily an' a crafty individual—more so than the Chink," warned a writer in the *Sacramento Bee* (Okimoto, 1971: 15). To many white Americans, newly arrived Japanese workers willing to work at the most menial, lowest-paying jobs simply extended the "Yellow Peril," threatening employment, housing, and even American culture itself. As Japanese immigration reached a peak of about 50,000 in the first decade of the twentieth century, Congress passed the United States Immigration Act of 1907, which authorized the president to restrict entrance of foreign workers if he deemed that their arrival would jeopardize opportunities for American workers. The following year President Theodore Roosevelt negotiated a deal with the Japanese government, permitting only the families of Japanese men already owning land or professionals to immigrate. This arrangement precluded the embarrassment of legislation similar to the Chinese Exclusion Act of 1882 and foreshadowed a trend of "respectable" racism, which, as we will see, is now prominent (Ima, 1982: 263–264; Knoll, 1982, 53–58).

Unlike Asian-Americans, the earliest Mexican-Americans (Chicanos) did not immigrate to the United States. They were living in Texas when, after the Mexican War, the United States gained permanent possession of the land which currently constitutes the states of Texas, New Mexico, and Arizona. As late as 1910, however, only about 250,000 Mexican-Americans, people of mixed Spanish and Native-American heritage, were residents of the United States.

At that time several events in Mexico, including the release of workers from forced labor on large haciendas (ranches) and the violence produced by revolution, encouraged many Mexicans to flee their homeland. Along the U.S. border, work was available because legislation had compelled many large cattle and sheep ranchers to give way to crop farmers, who badly needed laborers. In the 1920s Mexicans also moved to such Northern manufacturing cities as Chicago, Detroit, and Milwaukee, where they became factory employees. By the early 1930s, there were nearly 1.5 million Mexican-Americans in the United States. During that decade, however, there was a great surplus of workers because of the high unemployment accompanying the Great Depression. About 400,000 Mexican-Americans who were out of work either returned to Mexico voluntarily or were forced to leave by government officials intent on reducing welfare roles.

With the outbreak of World War II, the employment picture once again changed dramatically. Mobilizing for war, the United States badly needed workers to fill farm-labor jobs left by departing soldiers. In 1942 the *bracero* program, which existed briefly during World War I, was reestablished. This program was a bilateral agreement between Mexico and the United States involving the supply of labor. The American government underwrote Mexicans' travel costs and promised both a minimum wage and just treatment for *braceros* (temporary laborers) working on privately owned farms in the United States. Essentially the program provided federal subsidy for agricultural interests, and while originally intended only to meet wartime labor shortages, it continued for two decades after the war because it proved useful on both sides of the border. For Mexico the *bracero* program served as a partial solution for high unemployment, and for U.S. farmers it produced a steady supply of cheap labor.

Frequently employers violated the program's conditions, and although the Mexican government protested the violations, few official efforts sought to prevent them; the U.S. government, in fact, permitted agricultural interests almost complete control of wages, housing conditions, and other factors affecting workers' welfare. Although the *bracero* program was officially discontinued in 1964, many American farmers still maintain it informally, illegally hiring Mexican farm workers.

At present the majority of Chicano citizens live in Southwestern urban areas. A substantial number, however, live elsewhere, especially in the Midwest (Feagin, 1989: 258–261; Heyman, 1990; Keefe and Padilla, 1987; Maldonado, 1982; Stoddard, 1973: 2–30).

Puerto Ricans, another major Hispanic group, began reaching the United States in the nineteenth century, but their relations with whites began much earlier. On November 19, 1493, on his second voyage to the New World, Columbus arrived in Puerto Rico. At that time the island inhabitants were members of the Tainos tribe, and when the Spanish conquered the island, most of the Tainos died because of exposure to European diseases. As a result of this annihilation of indigenous people, the Spanish had no source of cheap labor. In 1511 they started bringing in African slaves to remedy the situation, and the practice of slavery continued for over three-and-a-half centuries until it was abolished in 1873. In 1898 following Spain's defeat in the Spanish-American War, the island became a possession of the United States. American-owned sugar plantations dominated the economy until after World War II when the local government started a program of economic expansion that produced over 1000 factories by 1970. For American businesspeople it has been very profitable to establish factories in Puerto Rico since local workers could be hired for considerably less than mainland laborers (Fitzpatrick, 1987: 28–29, 33–34). Commenting on 500 years of white exploitation, Jesus Colon wrote:

> The first thing we must realize is that . . . strangers have been knocking at the door of the Puerto Rican nation for centuries always in search of something,

to get something or to take away something from Puerto Ricans. This has been done many times with the forceful and openly criminal way of the pirate. (Colon, 1961: 147)

Before the Spanish-American War, most of the Puerto Rican immigrants were political exiles who used New York as a base for seeking support for the island's independence. Obviously these people were disappointed when the United States took over the island instead of granting independent status.

In the 1950s large numbers of primarily poor Puerto Ricans started coming to the mainland. In 1945 there were about 34,000 departures from Puerto Rico, with people primarily bound to the mainland United States. In 1950 the figure rose to about 170,000, then to 315,000 in 1955, jumped to over 1.5 million in 1971, and remained at or above that number each year through the 1970s and 1980s. A rapidly growing population in an undeveloped economy where unemployment has remained high has spurred the migratory flow. Furthermore as American citizens, Puerto Ricans do not face legal restrictions entering the country, and since the island is close to the mainland, flights from and to the island are fairly cheap.

Race and racism have been complicated issues for Puerto Ricans. While firmly established segregation patterns never existed on the island, Puerto Ricans have been aware of racial differences. Traditionally upper-class individuals prided themselves on what they claimed to be their pure Spanish lineage, and among other social-class groups, there has often been a preoccupation with color. But while a concern with people's skin color and other racial characteristics has existed, Puerto Ricans claim that social-class location, not race, determines how one person will treat another. In Puerto Rico, they say, an upper-class white Puerto Rican will treat lower-class Puerto Ricans the same way, regardless of whether they appear to be white or racially mixed. In the United States, in contrast, people's color often determines how they are treated, regardless of their social class. For Puerto Ricans with African and Native-American heritage, such explicit racial discrimination is very painful to encounter (Fitzpatrick, 1987: 18–19, 105–106).

We move rapidly toward the present, introducing important factors setting the stage for race relations in the late-industrial era, which will be discussed in detail in later chapters.

THE LATE-INDUSTRIAL PERIOD

By the middle of the current century, all racial groups examined in this book had substantial membership in the United States. While significant changes have continued to occur, it appears that the racial stratification system was essentially in place. Thus at this juncture, it seems reasonable to suspend the use of Noel's theory on the development of racial stratification and employ the internal-colonialist theory. Table 3.1 summarizes the relationship of theory to events in the three historical sections examined in this chapter.

During World War II, an executive order banning discrimination in defense plants and government agencies, along with an acute labor shortage, permitted blacks and other racial minorities to move into semi-skilled manufacturing jobs and some white-collar positions. While some individuals belonging to racial minorities lost their positions to returning veterans after the war, the expanding economy provided improved opportunities for many of them.

At the time the economy was starting to shift from one focused on goods-producing industries (manufacturing, construction, mining, and agriculture) to one primarily concerned with service (government, transportation, public utilities, trade, and later information transmission). In this new economy, members of racial minorities with appropriate educational and training credentials, sometimes assisted by affirmative-action standards, could often locate well-paying jobs (Wilson, 1978: 88–93).

But in recent decades, racial discrimination has continued to be widespread, and protest against it has been extensive.

Table 3.1   HISTORICAL STAGES OF AMERICAN RACISM

1. Preindustrial Stage (analyzed by Noel's theory of the origin of racial stratification)
   Ethnocentrism stressing Native Americans' and blacks' cultural inferiority
   Competition, with whites experiencing an expanding, unregulated economy: Native Americans' loss of land and traditional subsistence patterns; blacks' slavery
   Whites' superior power permitting complete control of Native Americans and blacks

2. Early-Industrial Stage (analyzed by Noel's theory)
   Social Darwinism, ethnocentrically declaring racial minorities "less fit" racially and culturally
   Competition pursued by whites in an expanding, largely unregulated economy
   Whites' greater power allowing nearly complete control of policies and practices affecting racial minorities

3. Late-Industrial Stage (analyzed by internal colonialism)
   Whites controlling the political structure and determining the policies structuring racial minorities' lives
   Ghettos and segregation forcing racial minorities to live in certain areas and making them highly vulnerable to economic downturns; sporadic violence against minorities limiting freedom of movement
   Consistent with the colonial-labor principle, racial minorities highly overrepresented in low-paid, menial jobs
   Blaming-the-victim ideology ignoring institutional racism and emphasizing that poor members of racial minorities possess cultural inferiority

Racial Minorities' Protest in Modern Times

On February 1, 1960, four black students from the Negro Agricultural College in Greensboro, North Carolina, entered a variety store, bought several items, and then sat down at a lunch counter and ordered coffee. At the time their action was remarkable, because the lunch counter, like other public facilities in the South, was officially segregated. The students were refused service, but they continued to sit at the counter until the store closed. This was the opening attack of the sit-in movement, which was a peaceful effort to destroy segregation in stores, libraries, hotels, buses, and other Southern public facilities.

During the early 1960s, peaceful protests demanding full civil rights for blacks spread throughout the South. In May 1961 the Congress of Racial Equality, a prominent civil-rights organization, sent "freedom riders" into the South to challenge segregation laws in interstate transportation. In several Alabama cities, the interracial teams encountered violence when their buses were attacked. Eventually Attorney General Robert Kennedy sent 600 federal officers to the scene to restore order (Franklin and Moss, 1988: 439–444). While blacks' civil rights were not high on the agenda for either Robert Kennedy or his brother, the president, the Kennedys basically supported freedom riders' efforts. Martin Luther King, Jr., suggested that the attorney general seek a ruling from the Interstate Commerce Commission to establish the rights of all interstate travelers. At first Robert Kennedy branded the scheme naive, but then he changed his mind, ordering Justice Department lawyers to keep after ICC commissioners until they issued a ruling protecting the rights of interstate travelers. In September Kennedy received the ICC statement. Taylor Branch indicated that Kennedy and his assistants had "telescoped a process that normally took years—even if the commissioners like the proposal, which in this case they did not—into less than four months. Experts considered the lobbying feat a bureaucratic miracle" (Branch, 1988: 478).

The unstable partnership between protesters in the South and the federal government also involved school integration and voting rights. Although black and white protesters were sometimes attacked, beaten, and even killed, government forces offered some protection and support. Advances occurred, most notably the Civil Rights Act of 1964 and the Voting Rights Act of 1965, which we discuss in the next chapter.

But for many people, both black and white, Martin Luther King, Jr., and civil-rights activists were not sufficiently confrontational. Besides segregated facilities were not the problem outside the South. Elsewhere blacks and other racial minorities were victims of institutional racism in politics, work, education, and housing. In 1966 Stokely Carmichael, a prominent civil-rights leader, started speaking about "black power"—that only if blacks provided strong, militant leadership for their own people would they obtain a fair share of the society's political, economic, and social rewards. Black leaders' style changed, and many began to predict that unless blacks started receiving equal rights, massive violence would occur. Riots in Los Angeles, Detroit, Newark, Washington, D.C., Cleveland, and a host of other cities indicated that the black-power leaders were not making idle statements. But while some members of these organizations appeared in public carrying guns, no evidence indicated that they initiated violent activity. They simply emphasized that continuing racial injustice would make rioting inevitable.

During the late 1960s, other racial minorities also became involved in protests. Among Native Americans the best-known protest group was the American Indian Movement (AIM). Founded in 1968 in Minneapolis, it soon became national and played a major part in several protests, including the 71-day, armed occupation of reservation land on the Pine Ridge reservation in Wounded Knee, South Dakota (Farley, 1988: 143). In the late 1960s and early 1970s, a group of radical Chicanos, disgusted with the failure of established political organizations to oppose discriminatory policies against Mexican-Americans, formed *La Raza Unida*, which ran candidates for statewide and local offices, winning a number of contests, and initiating educational and social programs that helped their primarily low-income constituents. In the spring of 1969, some Puerto Rican men in Chicago started the Young Lords, a militant organization, which soon initiated chapters in other cities. The New York City branch, for instance, occupied the First Spanish Methodist Church for 11 days and started a day-care center, a breakfast program, and a clothing distribution program. In the 1960s an Asian-American movement, led by Japanese-American students, began to challenge older leaders and traditional ways. Programs in Asian-American studies were established, and in their own new journals, Asian-Americans started to encourage their people to develop group pride and collective consciousness (Feagin, 1989: 271–272, 299, 319).

The Double Whammy: Racism and Poverty

Since the 1970s a new complex of destructive economic and social conditions has affected many minority-group members, particularly poor African-Americans and black Puerto Ricans. These people, considered members of the so-called "underclass," now seem to have little opportunity to escape poverty. One contributing factor has been the loss of jobs for unskilled minorities produced by the decline of manufacturing, the growth of service jobs, and the suburbanization of blue-collar employment (Wilson, 1987). In an important article, however, Douglas Massey (1990) argued that the most significant cause has been racial segregation in housing.

Focusing on African-Americans, Massey analyzed the significance of racial segregation in housing. He indicated that in a largely integrated area, particularly if it has diverse income groups, an increase in poverty, such as the one occurring during the economic downturn of the early

1970s, will adversely affect the area but will not alter its basic functioning: The economic strengths of the district will offset increased poverty, which will be dispersed throughout it. In contrast, if African-Americans face segregated housing, they will be forced to live in a restricted number of locales, which, given blacks' history of job discrimination, are likely to be in no better than fair economic condition in the best of times. An economic downturn will affect black residents more readily than whites since blacks' greater poverty makes them more vulnerable to the downturn. In addition, given housing segregation, poor blacks from other locales forced to move by the downturn most likely will be funnelled into the area, contributing significantly to its economic decline. As a result most businesses will fail or be forced to close; local opportunities for work will diminish in number or virtually disappear; with the loss of local income, clinics and hospitals will leave the area; schooling, which is highly dependent on district funding, will sharply decline in quality; local residents will be less able to maintain their homes, landlords will be less motivated to provide housing, and with the deterioration of residential buildings, the number of deserted buildings will increase; because of the growth of poverty, crime and violence will accelerate. Over the past two decades, this process has contributed substantially to the rapid growth of a black underclass.

But for many people, structural conditions producing poverty and racism receive little attention. Focus is on an individual's inability to be successful, to avoid poverty. Social Darwinist references to in-born inferiority, racial or otherwise, of certain groups no longer prevail. The modern fixation has become a person's cultural inferiority—an ethnocentrism that has been attached to racial minorities since Columbus's day but in the past was invariably linked to a group's racial composition. Currently what Monte Piliawsky (1984) called "respectable racism" is prevalent. No longer need whites make blatantly racist comments about African-Americans' stupidity or laziness. Instead they can speak of insufficient economic advancement for many blacks and suggest, with a reference to a limited work ethic or some other cultural deficiency, that the fault is their own. Certainly this approach is reminiscent of the internal-colonialist tenet emphasizing racial minorities' cultural inferiority.

William Ryan (1976) has called such a strategy "blaming the victim." The failure to achieve success is described as an individual's personal deficiency, and the economic and political conditions severely limiting that person's full participation in society—in short, conditions promoting institutional racism analyzed by internal-colonialist theory—are downplayed or ignored. In modern times politicians, policy makers, and social scientists have often endorsed the blaming-the-victim approach by emphasizing racial minorities' cultural inferiority. Widespread support for such a perspective is hardly surprising in a culture that has placed a premium on the importance of individuals' strivings and success in competitive settings.

Certainly minority-group members who are not successful are aware of the victim-blaming labels attached to them. One of the greatest dangers posed by this situation is the potential violence it creates. In a society where individual success is so strongly emphasized, those who see little likelihood of such success readily feel diminished, angry, and frustrated, and, as a result, are often poised to strike out against others—either in their own communities or outside of them. Violence seems to be a growing reality in our society. In the upcoming chapters, we will see that racism and blocked opportunity are conditions contributing to violence.

REFERENCES

Bailyn, Bernard, et al. 1977. *The Great Republic.* Lexington, MA: D.C. Heath.

Baker, Ray Stannard. 1973. "What Is Lynching?" pp. 304–328 in Donald P. DeNevi and Doris A. Holmes (eds.), *Racism at the Turn of the Century: Documentary Perspectives 1870–1910.* San Rafael, CA: Leswing. Article originally published in 1905.

Baker, Ray Stannard. 1973a. "The Negro's Struggle for Survival in the North," pp. 278–289 in Donald P. DeNevi and Doris A. Holmes (eds.), *Racism at the Turn of the Century: Documentary Perspectives 1870–1910.* San Rafael, CA: Leswing. Article originally published in 1908.

Bennett, Lerone, Jr. 1982. *Before the Mayflower: A History of Black America.* Chicago: Johnson Publishing Company. Fifth edition.

Berthrong, Donald J. 1986. "Legacies of the Dawes Act: Bureaucrats and Land Thieves at the Cheyenne-Arapaho Agencies of Oklahoma," pp. 204–217 in Roger L. Nichols (ed.), *The American Indian: Past and Present.* New York: Alfred A. Knopf. Third edition.

Branch, Taylor. 1988. *Parting the Waters: America in the King Years 1954–63.* New York: Simon and Schuster.

Brown, Dee. 1972. *Bury My Heart at Wounded Knee.* New York: Bantam Books.

Colon, Jesus. 1961. *A Puerto Rican in New York.* New York: Mainstream Publishers.

Cox, Oliver C. 1976. *Race Relations: Elements and Social Dynamics.* Detroit: Wayne State University Press.

Daniels, Edward, and Harry Kitano. 1970. *American Racism.* Englewood Cliffs, NJ: Prentice-Hall.

Daniels, Roger. 1988. *Asian Americans: Chinese and Japanese in the United States Since 1850.* Seattle: University of Washington Press.

Deloria, Vine, Jr. 1972. *Of Utmost Good Faith.* New York: Bantam Books.

Douglass, Frederick. 1968. *Narrative of the Life of Frederick Douglass.* New York: Signet Books. Originally published in 1845.

Farley, John E. 1988. *Majority-Minority Relations.* Englewood Cliffs, NJ: Prentice-Hall. Second edition.

Feagin, Joe R. 1989. *Racial & Ethnic Relations.* Englewood Cliffs, NJ: Prentice-Hall. Third edition.

Fitzpatrick, Joseph P. 1987. *Puerto Rican Americans: The Meaning of Migration to the Mainland.* Englewood Cliffs, NJ: Prentice-Hall. Second edition.

Franklin, John Hope, and Alfred A. Moss, Jr. 1988. *From Slavery to Freedom: A History of Negro Americans.* New York: Alfred A. Knopf. Sixth edition.

Goffman, Erving. 1974. *Stigma: Notes on the Management of Spoiled Identity.* New York: Jason Aronson.

Heyman, Josiah McC. 1990. "The Emergence of the Waged Life Course on the United States-Mexico Border." *American Ethnologist* 17 (May): 348–359.

Hofstadter, Richard. 1955. *Social Darwinism in American Thought.* Boston: Beacon Press. Revised edition.

Ima, Kenji. 1982. "Japanese Americans: The Making of 'Good' People," pp. 262–302 in Anthony Gary Dworkin and Rosalind J. Dworkin (eds.), *The Minority Report.* New York: Holt, Rinehart and Winston. Second edition.

Jacobs, Wilbur R. 1985. *Dispossessing the American Indian: Indians and Whites on the Colonial Frontier.* Norman: University of Oklahoma Press. Revised edition.

Keefe, Susan E., and Amado M. Padilla. 1987. *Chicano Ethnicity.* Albuquerque: University of New Mexico Press.

Knoll, Tricia. 1982. *Becoming Americans.* Portland, OR: Coast to Coast Books.

Luther Standing Bear. 1978. *Land of the Spotted Eagle.* Lincoln: University of Nebraska Press.

Maldonado, Lionel A. 1982. "Mexican-Americans: The Emergence of a Minority," pp. 168–195 in Anthony Gary Dworkin and Rosalind J. Dworkin (eds.), *The Minority Report.* New York: Holt, Rinehart and Winston. Second edition.

Massey, Douglas S. 1990. "American Apartheid: Segregation and the Making of the Underclass." *American Journal of Sociology* 96 (September): 329–357.

Nichols, Roger L. 1986. "The Indian in Nineteenth-Century America: A Unique Minority," pp. 127–136 in Nichols (ed.), *The American Indian: Past and Present.* New York: Alfred A. Knopf. Third edition.

Noel, Donald L. 1968. "A Theory of the Origin of Ethnic Stratification." *Social Problems* 16 (Fall): 157–172.

Okimoto, Daniel I. 1971. *American in Disguise.* New York: John Weatherhill.

Piliawsky, Monte. 1984. "Racial Equality in the United States: From Institutionalized to 'Respectable' Racism." *Phylon* 45 (June): 135–143.

Ryan, William. 1976. *Blaming the Victim.* New York: Vintage Books. Revised edition.

Shapiro, Herbert. 1988. *White Violence and Black Response: From Reconstruction to Montgomery.* Amherst: University of Massachusetts Press.

Stoddard, Ellwyn R. 1973. *Mexican Americans.* New York: Random House.

Trennert, Robert A. 1986. "Educating Indian Girls at Nonreservation Boarding Schools, 1878–1920," pp. 218–231 in Roger L. Nichols (ed.), *The American Indian: Past and Present.* New York: Alfred A. Knopf. Third edition.

Twain, Mark. 1868. "Persecution of the Chinese in California and Passage of the Burlingame Treaty to Protect Their Rights," pp. 98–99 in Maxwell Geismar (ed.), *Mark Twain and the Three R's.* Indianapolis: Bobbs-Merrill, 1973.

Wilson, William Julius. 1978. *The Declining Significance of Race: Blacks and Changing American Institutions.* Chicago: University of Chicago Press.

Wilson, William Julius, 1987. *The Truly Disadvantaged: The Inner City, the Underclass, and Public Policy.* Chicago: University of Chicago Press.

Wright, Richard. 1938. *Uncle Tom's Children.* New York: Harper & Brothers.

Chapter
4

Under the Thumb: Politics, the Criminal-Justice System, and Violence

*I*n 1954, early in his civil-rights activities, Martin Luther King, Jr., was a leader of the Montgomery bus boycott, in which black citizens were refusing to ride city buses until seating was integrated. At one point African-Americans advocating integrated busing and whites opposing it agreed to meet and form a committee, which would seek to reach a mutually satisfying resolution.

During one meeting a member of the White Citizens Council, a white supremacist organization, joined the group on the opponents' side of the table. Immediately King jumped up and protested the addition of someone else when committee membership had already been established. Furthermore, King added angrily, "we will never solve this problem so long as there are persons on the committee whose public pronouncements are anti-Negro" (Branch, 1988: 148).

Henry Parker, a white minister, reacted strongly to King's comment, indicating that the new man had as much right to join the committee as anyone, including King. Then other whites entered the discussion, asserting that King's comment had introduced hostility and mistrust into the negotiations. Some African-Americans defended King, and the exchanges became angry, with each side accusing the other of initiating bitterness and negative feelings.

Eventually King made a motion for recess, saying that the whites had come to the meeting with "preconceived ideas." This observation infuriated Mrs. Logan A. Hipp, a white woman who had been serving as secretary for the meeting. "You are the one who has come here with preconceived ideas," she told King, trembling with fury. "I resent very deeply the statement that we have come here with preconceived ideas" (Branch, 1988: 148).

The meeting broke up, and King felt a "terrible sense of guilt"—that he had not maintained sufficient control, and, as a result, had handled himself badly. The problem was that the whites' reaction had caught him off guard. Most of King's adult years had been spent in integrated situations with whites who accepted moral claims of racial equality, and he had expected whites on the committee to fall into two categories. Either they would have been enlightened and accepted his call for racial equality, or they would have been so blatantly racist that they would have appeared wicked and ridiculous to both African-Americans and whites.

It was unexpected to learn that the majority of the whites regarded a declared white supremacist as no more extreme than King and his associates who advocated the "shocking" practice of integrated busing. Taylor Branch wrote, "The whites had spoken as the diplomats of a large country might defend their interests to diplomats from a small one. Their technical approach had deprived King of the moral ground he had occupied all his life" (Branch, 1988: 149).

As this episode illustrates, historically whites have controlled American society, and central to that control has been dominance of the political process. We will see that the shadow of internal colonialism remains. While in the past couple of decades, racial minorities have made progress in the political realm, they remain relatively powerless, with their governance primarily in whites' hands. In the areas of criminal justice and violence, some basis for optimism exists, but many whites' sense of perceived threat to their established control still encourages destructive, racist outcomes.

The common factor uniting political activity, the criminal-justice system, and violence is "power." **Power** is the ability of an individual or group to implement wishes or policies, with or without the cooperation of others. **Authority** is power that people generally recognize as rightfully maintained by those who use it. In race relations people's sense of which concept applies to a given situation varies with their outlook. In the opening illustration, whites felt that in dealing with African-Americans, they exercised authority. Blacks, in contrast, stressed that whites maintained control by power, not authority: Whites simply had the personnel and weaponry to enforce their dominance. The first major section of this chapter discusses the **political institution**, which is the system of norms and roles that concerns the use and distribution of authority within a given society.

RACIAL MINORITIES IN THE POLITICAL PROCESS

At the end of World War II, many African-Americans moved from the rural South to the urban South or North, where they received work in factories at improved wage levels over their previous jobs. At this time many white business leaders realized that in an expanding business economy, blacks would be more effective workers if they obtained better education; furthermore support for their education appeared to discourage social disharmony and provide a tranquil atmosphere for high-level production.

By the 1950s urbanization of the South had also started to affect whites. The backing of segregationist policies, which had been widespread during agricultural times, became less common as Southern whites were increasingly exposed to higher education and national mass media. Recognizing that political opportunities were increasing, African-American organizations initiated sit-ins and boycotts to protest the continuation of segregation. Meanwhile, during the 1950s and 1960s, an expanded, active black electorate was beginning to make an impact in Northern cities. The increased black-voter strength in the North combined with civil-rights protest in the South to give the assertion of African-American political rights much greater prominence.

In the late 1950s and early 1960s, black leaders hoped that the media coverage of white Southerners' violent reactions to their antisegregation protests would encourage the federal government to overcome its traditional reluctance to interfere with Southern local and state governmental practice. This, in fact, did occur. After racial violence in Birmingham, Alabama, President John Kennedy proposed the Civil Rights Act, which was passed in 1964 soon after his death, and in 1965 renewed violence against African-Americans in Selma, Alabama, and the international uproar produced by this violence helped to ensure passage of the 1965 Voting Rights Act.

The Civil Rights Act of 1964 has been the broadest American legislative effort to eliminate racial discrimination. The act covers employment practices of all businesses with more than 25 employees, access to all public accommodations such as hotels, motels, and restaurants, and the use of such federally supported organizations as colleges and hospitals. The Voting Rights Act of 1965 has suspended various qualifying tests for voter registration that many Southern states used selectively to discriminate against African-Americans, and this act also authorized federal examiners to enter these states and register black voters, greatly increasing their number.

Significantly these two pieces of legislation developed when Americans' support for civil-rights issues was very high. At the time Congress was faced with these two bills, adult Americans indicated that civil rights was the "most important problem facing the country." By 1966 civil rights had lost that priority position, and it has never regained it (Jaynes and Williams, 1989: 221–223).

The Voting Rights Act has helped advance political interests of African-Americans and other racial minorities. Results have been most striking in the South. In 1952, before the passage of the Voting Rights Act, 13 percent of black adults voted; in 1984 the figure rose to 65 percent (Jaynes and Williams, 1989: 234).

Since 1965 African-Americans have been elected to every major political office except for the presidency and vice presidency; in November 1989 L. Douglas Wilder became the first African-American elected to the other major executive position when he became governor of Virginia. The national total of black elected officials was 7335 in 1990, 496 percent of the 1479 elected in 1970 (U.S. Bureau of the Census, *Statistical Abstract of the United States: 1991*. No. 447). Table 4.1 provides more detailed statistics on this topic.

These figures must remain in perspective. The percentage of black elected officials is very small. As of 1985, 1.2 percent of elected officials were African-Americans, with the South's 4 percent the highest of all

Table 4.1 BLACK ELECTED OFFICIALS BY OFFICE, 1970 TO 1990

	Total	U.S. and state legislatures[1]	City and county offices[2]	Law enforcement[3]	Education[4]
1970	1479	179	719	213	368
1975	3522	299	1885	387	951
1980	4963	326	2871	534	1232
1985	6312	407	3689	685	1531
1990	7335	440	4481	769	1645

[1]Includes elected state administrators

[2]Composed of county commissioners and councilmen, mayors, vice mayors, aldermen, and regional officers

[3]Involves judges, magistrates, constables, marshals, sheriffs, and justices of the peace

[4]Includes members of state education agencies, college boards, and school boards

Note: While blacks are underrepresented in elected office, there has been a significant increase over time in the number of elected black officials.

Source: U.S. Bureau of the Census. *Statistical Abstract of the United States: 1991.* No. 447.

regions. In a country with about 12 percent of the population black, there is a distinct underrepresentation of elected black officials (Jaynes and Williams, 1989: 238).

The figures, in fact, probably overstate blacks' political impact. In a well-known study of policy-making in Cook County, Illinois (which includes the city of Chicago), Harold Baron (1968) concluded that the actual power held by elected and appointed African-American officials in government, business, labor, education, and other major policy-making bodies was probably about one-third as great as the percentage of posts they held. The problem was that these officials primarily worked in black areas or interacted only with blacks and had little or no opportunity to make policy decisions in such critical areas as housing, jobs, and education.

Other racial minorities are also underrepresented politically. Among Native Americans political activity primarily involves reservation elections. Not until 1924 did Native Americans have the right to vote in elections outside of reservations. Since 1900 about two dozen Native Americans have served in state legislatures, and there have been a half-dozen Native-American members of the House of Representatives and two senators (Feagin, 1989: 187–188).

Asian-Americans have been more successful politically, especially Japanese-Americans. In Hawaii they have dominated congressional positions, with both senators and both representatives usually Japanese-Americans. In 1987 three Japanese-Americans were also serving in the California House of Representatives (Daniels, 1988: 311). A two-generation study of Japanese-Americans suggested that one prominent factor contributing to their political success has been a high level of participation in their own ethnic organizations, where they have been able to develop both skills and contacts for involvement in outside political structures (Fugita and O'-Brien, 1985).

Mexican-Americans have had a comparable level of political success. By 1988 there were ten Mexican-American members of the House of Representatives, up from four in 1982, but no senators. The growth of the Chicano population, along with the elimination of discriminatory statutes, such as a California law requiring English literacy for voters, have encouraged steady expansion of Mexican-American voting turnout (Feagin, 1989: 270). A recent study conducted in Texas provided two reasons why the Chicano population is increasingly likely to vote. First, Mexican-Americans' level of education has been rising, and voting studies indicate that level of education is the factor best predicting people's inclination to vote. Second, with the growth of the Chicano population, the major parties have increased their efforts to mobilize support from this group, in particular offering Chicano candidates on statewide ballots (Longoria, Wrinkle, and Polinard, 1990).

In New York City, Puerto Ricans have had modest political success, with Herman Badillo the first Puerto Rican elected to the House of Representatives in 1971. Badillo's successor, Robert Garcia, attempted to establish closer political ties to African-Americans, claiming that their common location at the bottom of the income ladder makes them obvious allies. Outside of New York City, Puerto Ricans have had little success in politics. In Chicago, for instance, a study indicated that Puerto Ricans and other Hispanic-Americans have been unable to demonstrate sufficient political voting power to force the city's political leadership to incorporate them (Feagin, 1989: 297–298; Gann and Duignan, 1986: 224–231).

Conditions Affecting Racial Minorities' Political Success

To be elected to political office, minority candidates are usually dependent on heavy voting support from their own racial group. A study of mayoral and city-council elections between 1965 and 1986 in New Orleans indicated that in elections where less than 40 percent of registered voters were African-American, most candidates were white and those elected were overwhelmingly white, with few blacks supporting black candidates. With between 40 percent and 55 percent of registered voters black, there were candidates of both races, and generally voting broke along racial lines. In elections with over 55 percent of registered voters African-American, the majority of candidates were African-American, and, in fact, in districts with over 60 percent black registered voters, both candidates were invariably black (Vanderleeuw, 1990).

Sometimes members of racial minorities can be elected, even when their group is small. A study of the conditions permitting the election and reelection of Federico Pena, the Mexican-American mayor of Denver, suggested two factors that can help accomplish this goal. First, the candidate must obtain almost complete support from his or her own racial group. Even though he did not present himself as a "minority" candidate, Pena was able to perform this task by stressing such issues as "neighborhoods" and "openness"—abstract concerns that had great meaning to Mexican-Americans traditionally denied effective political participation but concerns that would not offend whites. Second, the minority candidate must make special efforts to appeal to nonminority voters or, at least, to lessen their opposition. One way Pena accomplished this goal was to emphasize prominent citywide concerns, such as more and better city planning and sounder government management (Hero and Beatty, 1989).

Besides seeking political-leadership positions, racial minorities face another important challenge in the political arena: Are they able to accomplish significant political goals? A study of black and Chicano urban leadership in 12 northern California cities produced a notable result: Researchers found that the extent of minority representation in city government was not a decisive indicator of whether or not local government was responsive to minority needs.

Much more significant was what researchers called **political incorporation**—inclusion of racial minority-group members as significant players in political coalitions which contain some whites and successfully challenge established white conservative groups for control over a city's political activity. When African-Americans and Mexican-Americans achieved substantial political incorporation, important improvements for their groups were likely to occur. These included:

1. A sharp increase in the city employment of minorities
2. The creation of police review boards, which investigated cases in which racial minority-group members claimed police abuse
3. A significant rise in the numbers of minority representatives appointed to city boards and commissions
4. The establishment of many minority-oriented programs
5. City governments' greater responsiveness to minority interests in the delivery of services and the formation of city policies in such key areas as economic development and education (Browning, Marshall, and Tabb, 1986)

The link between political incorporation and internal colonialism seems clear. The colonial mentality persists among whites, especially the governance principle emphasizing whites' control of racial minorities in political situations. Thus as political leaders, African-Americans and other minority-group members are only able to produce significant political change when allied with whites.

A cautionary note should be added. Minority politicians' political incorporation does not inevitably produce programs aiding members of their racial group. In the 1980s in Philadelphia, African-Americans constituted a major voting block within the city council and occupied many positions of governmental authority. However, most black politicians, including the black mayor, failed to support a local bill, widely backed by African-Americans and advocating a hiring preference for minority candidates, because their interracial coalition depended on cooperation from the white business community and construction unions, which opposed the bill (Beauregard, 1990).

Minority Politics Outside of Government

One racial minority—Native Americans—has conducted much of its political activity outside of the established governmental structure. Forced to confine most of their political involvement to reservations and supported by governmental emphasis on the revival of tribalism, many modern Native Americans have started to mobilize politically around issues of tribal identity and reservation roots (Hagan, 1986).

Since the United States government historically negotiated treaties with tribes, current members of those tribes are in a strong legal position to demand that the government maintain these official agreements. In 1984 Ojibway men renewed the practice of spearfishing, which had been a traditional spring practice of the tribe. The fishing is done in the Upper Great Lakes area on territory sold to the United States. Treaties signed in

1837 and 1842 permitted the Ojibway to fish the area, but for over a century, the state of Wisconsin refused to recognize those rights, imposing its fish and game laws and jailing Ojibway people who violated them. In recent years court orders have allowed the activity to continue while the issue is being litigated. Although the tribe's legal efforts have permitted the Ojibway to return to this traditional practice, at least temporarily, there has also been a negative development—extensive, sometimes violent outsider resistance to the Ojibway fishing practices (Harjo, 1989).

While the pursuit of political rights through the courts does not always produce the results desired, other benefits can emerge. Since 1920 there have been a string of court cases initiated by the tribes deprived of control of the Black Hills, a huge tract of western land comprising about 7 percent of the contiguous 48 states. While this series of lawsuits has been unsuccessful, it has helped maintain a vital sense of unity among members of participating tribes and has won a number of admissions from the Supreme Court, such as their 1975 statement that the treatment of Native Americans in this giant land deal represented "a national disgrace." Such admissions have produced much more national support for these tribes than they could have obtained if they had just made a one-sided presentation of their case (Churchill, 1990).

Chicanos have also sought to accomplish political goals by using organizations outside of the established political process. In 1929 the League of United Latin American Citizens (LULAC) was founded in southern Texas to use moderate political means to oppose discrimination against Mexican-Americans. Currently the organization has active councils in 28 states, a national headquarters in Washington, D.C., and a professional staff. White politicians have seldom criticized LULAC's efforts because its heavily middle-class membership has made strenuous efforts to strongly support most American political and economic practices and has never condemned the society as discriminatory. LULAC has approached political activism cautiously, avoiding demonstrations or disruptive practices but using such widely supported techniques as voter-registration drives, petitions, and legal pressure (Marquez, 1989).

In the 1960s and 1970s, poor Mexican-Americans, feeling that they had little or no representation in the political process, believed that La Raza Unida, a Chicano political party, more effectively served their interest. In 1972 the organization ran a third-party slate in Texas, and the candidate for governor received 6 percent of the vote. In Crystal City, Texas, a small city primarily composed of poor Mexican-Americans, La Raza Unida candidates won three of seven school-board positions and two of five city-council positions and were able to establish education, health, and urban renewal programs that benefited both Chicanos and whites. By the middle 1970s, however, La Raza Unida was in disarray. Disagreements within the organization and also the delay by state politicians of federal money for programs the party had started were contributing factors (Hirsch, 1982).

As the following situation illustrates, minority-group members often face the dire effects of limited political representation.

Florence Grier: African-American Political Activist

During the 1960s Florence Grier, who was interviewed by sociologist Bob Blauner, was an active community worker in a poor black district in Sacramento, California. Eventually she became an employee of the federally funded anti-poverty program. She was so successful that when a local housing office opened, many local citizens insisted that Grier be hired. As soon as she was working, people started coming to her office with an array of problems—grievances about the police, eviction notices, and requests for emergency funds to buy food for their children.

In summarizing her regular contacts and activities, Grier concluded that between the early 1960s and the early 1980s, some improvements had occurred but overall the political and economic picture had not significantly altered. With reduced protest, police were now freer to be repressive toward African-Americans than they were in the 1960s; schools for poor blacks were so bad that many children were not learning to read; many young black people were unable to find jobs and, in their desperate desire for drugs or sometimes merely for food, were increasingly likely to resort to robbery, with fellow African-Americans the most common victims. On page 68 we noted that only with political incorporation can a racial minority initiate programs that will measurably benefit members of their own racial group. In this case, where no appreciable African-American leadership had yet begun to emerge, blacks had not even established the political foundation for building toward that goal.

As a long-time political organizer, Grier realized that no guardian angels were going to lead her people: They had to take the initiative themselves. But one of the difficulties was that oppression had diminished their sense of identity. Grier stated that African-Americans "have not outgrown the slave mentality—that you have to depend on the white man to breathe and to think and to do what you need to do" (Blauner, 1989: 188).

Blauner asked Grier how she had changed over the past 10 or 15 years. She began to speak about the criminal-justice system, and he interrupted her, observing that she did not like to talk about herself. Grier conceded the point, saying that in a community where African-Americans "have not got a pot to pee in," individuals should not brag about personal accomplishments until local citizens' pressing needs were addressed effectively (Blauner, 1989: 194).

Warming to the discussion, Grier explained that to accomplish community political tasks, there needed to be 50 or 60 local people who would spearhead such activities as preventing a nearby law school from taking over the people's park or investigating and publicizing police misdeeds against black citizens. There were simply too many important things for the few politically active people in the community to do.

Earlier in the conversation, Grier had seen a policeman drive over the curb and into the nearby park, which she loved. Now, as the interview drew toward an end, she wondered what gave him the right to do that. She concluded, "I don't exactly understand it. Well, I guess I'm a grumble. If I was closer to him, I'd get his badge number and his car number and call down" (Blauner, 1989: 196).

Florence Grier clearly understood the political situation in which she was involved. She realized that she and other African-Americans were largely powerless victims of internal colonialism. Grier believed that the most effective course of action was to fight politically to remove the impact of that powerlessness and to recruit a host of black citizens for that fight.

One of Florence Grier's major concerns was police mistreatment of African-Americans. In the following section, we analyze the police's role in the criminal-justice process.

RACIAL MINORITIES AND THE CRIMINAL-JUSTICE SYSTEM

At the beginning of 1987, American federal and state prisons contained about 545,000 people, comprised of about 275,000 whites, 247,000 African-Americans, 20,600 Mexican-Americans, 10,500 Puerto Ricans, 5,300 Native Americans or Alaskans, 4,200 Puerto Ricans, and 1,850 Asian-Americans (U.S. Department of Justice, *Correctional Populations in the United States,* 1988. Table 5.6).

It is revealing to compare racial groups' representation in the prison population adjusted for their numbers in the overall American population: African-Americans stand out. Blacks are 17 times more highly represented as state and federal prisoners than Asian-Americans; six times more than whites; five times more than Mexican-Americans; nearly three times more than Native Americans; and two times more than Puerto Ricans (U.S. Department of Justice, *Correctional Populations in the United States.* Table 5.6; U.S. Bureau of the Census, *Statistical Abstract of the United States: 1989.* No. 44, No. 45). We need to consider why that situation has developed.

Alfred Blumstein (1982) and Patrick Langan (1985) sought to determine whether racial discrimination explains African-American overrepresentation in prisons. Their studies of state prisons produced similar results, with both researchers concluding that the disproportionate number of blacks arrested, particularly for major crimes carrying severe penalties, largely explained their overrepresentation in the prison population. Thus Langan indicated that his study demonstrated that "even if racism exists, it might explain only a small part of the gap between the 11 percent [currently 12 percent] black representation in the United States adult population and the now nearly 50 percent black representation among persons entering state prisons each year in the United States" (Langan, 1985: 682).

Two comments on these studies seem appropriate. First, since both compare the number of individuals arrested with those who eventually end up in prison, they are not examining the issue of whether racism enters the criminal-justice process during the arrest phase.

Second, these investigations might have underestimated the extent to which racism exists throughout the entire criminal-justice system. Marjorie Zatz (1987) suggested that such studies may concentrate on readily detectable measures of bias and overlook less obvious racist displays—for instance, a prosecutor's request for a long sentence for a black man not officially sought because of his race but because of his history of criminal activity. In addition, Zatz emphasized that participants in the criminal-justice system inevitably try to hide racist policies since such activities would cast doubt on the legitimacy and rationality of the entire system. Other researchers have indicated that most research on racial discrimination in the criminal-justice system has focused on specific points—arrest, arraignment, sentencing, and so forth. Such studies tend to ignore or deemphasize that accused people's involvement in this system is a process. Thus seemingly trivial bits of information or commentaries that are racially discriminatory can remain in an individual's file or be transmitted verbally, appearing to have no effect in the early stages of the criminal-justice process but then having an impact when individuals are sentenced or incarcerated (Bridges and Crutchfield, 1988; Swigert and Farrell, 1977).

In 1991 the 17-member New York State Judicial Commission on Minorities composed of judges, lawyers, law professors, and an official from the State Education Department concluded that the state court system is "infested with racism." The Commission concluded that minority-group members are less likely than whites to receive favorable actions from the courts; that judges and prosecuting attorneys are more hostile and racially biased toward minorities than are other court employees; that minority lawyers are often subjected to opposing attorneys' racial stereotyping and racist jokes (Gray, 1991).

In short, there is the distinct possibility that racism is more prevalent within the criminal-justice system than the Blumstein and Langan investigations indicated. Blacks and Puerto Ricans, whose incarceration rate is closest to blacks, are the most likely victims. We will now consider why racism permeates this system.

Sense of Threat: Key to Racism in the Criminal-Justice System

Several years ago sociologist Darnell F. Hawkins (1987) wrote about the relationship between race and the criminal-justice system. Hawkins made a specific point reminiscent of a more general issue discussed within the first chapter's introduction of internal colonialism—that conflict theorists have tended either to ignore the role played by race in relation to criminal justice or have subordinated its significance to social class. The result,

Hawkins indicated, is that conflict theorists have simply lumped all of the poor together, whether members of racial minorities or white, assuming that people's socioeconomic class is the major factor determining their treatment in the criminal-justice system. For this issue, however, race appears to play a critical role.

Hawkins concluded that a sense of threat is the key factor encouraging racial discrimination in the criminal-justice process. When whites see the criminal behavior of blacks as threatening, they are likely to deal with them harshly. On the other hand, when whites do not see African-Americans' crimes as threatening, they will not subject blacks to discriminatory treatment (Hawkins, 1987). This idea seems consistent with the internal-colonialist perspective, suggesting that whites fixate on controlling racial minorities' activities. A sense of threat emerges when whites believe that blacks' actions would loosen their controlling grip, and often criminal behavior can produce that sense.

Studies dealing with both arrest and sentencing support Hawkins's thesis. In an investigation of 77 American cities with populations of over 100,000 people, there was no relationship between cities' proportion of poor and their arrest rates. On the other hand, the proportion of racial minority-group members and the extent of racial segregation within cities correlated to minority individuals' arrest rates. In fact, the higher the proportion of minority-group members and the greater racial segregation, the higher the arrest rate, both for minority-group members and whites. Why did this precise result occur? The researchers reasoned that the combination of a high percentage of minority-group members and a low level of racial integration were optimal conditions promoting whites' perceived threat of crime. In essence, whites were frightened by what they considered a large alien force of minority-group members. These perceptions increased pressure on police to control crime, and the result was an accelerated rate of arrests for both racial minorities and whites (Liska, Chamlin, and Reed, 1985).

A study drawing its data from a representative sample of American 11- to 17-year-olds concluded that for serious offenses (in particular, felony theft, felony assault, robbery, hard drug use, and fraud) African-Americans were two to three times more likely to be arrested and charged than whites. But this finding does not mean that racial discrimination definitely occurred. Perhaps black and white youths differed in some other significant respect besides race. Investigators examined a couple of the most likely possibilities. Did the youthful blacks have a more extensive history of delinquencies? No! Perhaps the blacks were more likely to have committed crimes involving either greater physical injury or the use of guns? Once again, no! The researchers concluded that young African-Americans "appear to be at greater risk for being charged with more serious offenses than whites involved in comparable levels of delinquent behavior, a factor that may eventually result in higher incarceration levels" (Huizinga and Elliott, 1987: 221).

Another study found that black youths were not only more likely to be arrested than whites but also were more frequently held, charged, sentenced, and incarcerated. The researchers suggested that when black youths "discern differential and more lenient treatment for their Anglo counterparts, a bitter and ironic form of accountability is taught" (Fagan, Slaughter, and Hartstone, 1987: 253). A self-fulfilling prophecy develops. Motivated by their perception that young African-Americans represent a greater threat than white youth, police, judges, and other court officials treat them more harshly. The black youth perceive their biased treatment, and, indeed, are likely to become a more substantial threat than they would have been without exposure to racism in the criminal-justice system.

A number of studies demonstrate racial bias in sentencing, with the relationship between threat and race apparent once more. An investigation done in 39 states found that blacks typically served longer sentences than whites for robbery, rape, and murder (Hacker, 1988). A growing body of research indicates that in many cases the key factor is the race of the victim. Preliminary evidence suggests that when the victim of rape or robbery is white, the sentence is likely to be more severe (LaFree, 1980; Thomson and Zingraff, 1981).

A related conclusion appears in murder cases. Researchers have found that when the level of seriousness is controlled—that is, the four possible racial combinations of offender and victim are compared for similar degrees of severity, such as whether only one person was killed or whether multiple killings were involved—prosecutors and juries are more likely to demand the death penalty if the victim is white and the offender is black than in any of the other three possible racial combinations—white offender/black victim, black offender/black victim, or white offender/white victim (Ekland-Olson, 1988; Jaynes and Williams, 1989: 488–489; Keil and Vito, 1989). Once again the concept of threat seems relevant. When a black person kills a white person, he or she is not only offending the individual whom the state has an obligation to protect but also the state itself by challenging whites' control of the social order. African-Americans killing whites present the specter of insurrection. White murderers generally create a similar sense of threat only if they kill public officials or law-enforcement personnel (Hawkins, 1987: 726).

In a study of state prisons in 48 states, George S. Bridges and Robert D. Crutchfield (1988) found that African-Americans were disproportionately imprisoned in states where the black citizenry was relatively poor compared to whites, primarily urban, and a fairly small percentage of the overall population. North-central states had the disproportionately highest number of black prison inmates and Southern states the lowest. The researchers decided that while racial differences in arrest rates was a factor in the disproportionate imprisonment of blacks, it was a much less significant factor than indicated in the Blumstein and Langan studies.

Bridges and Crutchfield hypothesized that one factor that might have contributed to the high proportion of African-Americans in the prison population in states where blacks were poorer and concentrated in urban areas might have been longer criminal records among blacks. But blacks' records were not longer than whites'. As did Darnell Hawkins, these researchers eventually endorsed the idea of threat, suggesting that an effective analysis of their findings needed to consider that disproportionate punishment is the dominant white group's means of signaling its determination to maintain control over African-Americans and other racial minorities in a situation where they consider the stable social order threatened (Bridges and Crutchfield, 1988: 719).

But why, one might ask, do people in the North-central states—in particular Minnesota, Nebraska, Wisconsin, and Iowa according to the Bridges and Crutchfield data—appear to feel the strongest sense of threat from blacks? One contributing factor might be that in such states many rural whites find racial confrontation a horrifying abstraction. They have had little or no contact with blacks but are painfully aware that not far away—in Minneapolis, Omaha, Milwaukee, or DesMoines—there is a heavy concentration of poor blacks who, television news programs and newspapers daily inform them in gruesome detail, are heavily engaged in crime, much of it violent. As a result these people are frightened, and they react by pressuring their politicians, police, sheriffs, prosecutors, and judges to crack down on African-Americans and other minorities.

In the late 1960s, I recall watching a news program during which a reporter standing in a remote cornfield in one of the North-central states reported that where he was, 100 miles from the nearest city, people were far more terrified of being victims of rioting inner-city blacks than any urban residents he had ever encountered.

The sense of threat also seems to be a factor encouraging racial violence.

VIOLENCE AGAINST RACIAL MINORITIES AND THE CONDITIONS ENCOURAGING IT

In his well-known study of a Southern town in the 1930s, John Dollard (1937) summed up his perception of whites' motivation for aggression against African-Americans with the following statement. He wrote:

> In the end it seems . . . [most accurate] to say that white people fear Negroes. They fear them, of course, in a special context, that is, when the Negro attempts to claim any of the white prerogatives or gains. . . . By a series of hostile acts and social limitations the white caste maintains a continuous threatening atmosphere against the possibility of . . . demands by Negroes; when successful, . . . the effect is to keep the social order intact. (Dollard, 1937: 316–317)

Sometimes whites' violence against racial minorities has served to keep the social order intact, and sometimes violence provided a means of winning control over minorities.

From the seventeenth through the nineteenth centuries, white invaders battled Native Americans in the continuous effort to take over their land and their lives. Broken treaties and the slaughter of defenseless women, children, and elderly people were common practice. Richard Maxwell Brown indicated that the effect of whites' dealings with Native Americans "has not been a healthy one; it has done much to further our proclivity to violence" (Brown, 1979: 50).

One could make the same point about whites' violent treatment of blacks. With the end of slavery, Southern whites developed a special organization for dealing with African-Americans—the Ku Klux Klan. In three waves—during the 1860s and 1870s, the 1920s, and from the 1950s to the present—Klan members have used intimidation and violence to terrorize blacks and to discourage them from making political and economic advances.

Even before the development of the Klan, racial riots served to intimidate blacks. Antiblack riots, which occurred in the North in the 1820s and 1830s and continued in both the South and North for about four decades after the Civil War, were one-sided attacks on blacks by whites. From about 1915 through the 1940s, whites still initiated riots, but blacks began to develop their own counterrioting gangs. From 1964 through 1967, certain circumstances encouraged some inner-city residents to initiate riots. Generally the rioters were infused with black pride, frustrated by the limit on economic opportunities available to them, and mobilized by local incidents, such as a beating by a white policeman or a killing of a black resident.

Other racial minorities have also encountered extensive violence. For instance, in the 1870s and 1880s, Chinese workers competing with whites for jobs were often run out of town, beaten, or even killed. In Los Angeles in 1871, between 18 and 21 Chinese men were hanged or burned to death, and in 1887 in desolate Hell's Canyon on the Idaho-Oregon border, 31 Chinese gold miners were robbed and murdered (Kitano and Daniels, 1988: 22).

In the 1990s, to be sure, those who want to contain racial minorities' advancement are no longer "successful" in Dollard's 1930s sense. The relationship between threat and violence, however, is probably similar— with whites who want African-Americans or other racial minorities "kept in their place" using violence as a means of intimidation.

One issue that has received considerable attention has been the number of blacks killed by the police. In any given year, a disproportionate number of blacks will be killed by police—about a fourfold greater number than one would expect by their overall proportion of the population. However, some researchers suggested that violence is more likely to develop when police arrest or attempt to arrest individuals for serious offenses. They pointed out that when analysts consider not only offenders' race but the seriousness of the crimes with which they are charged, the number of African-Americans killed is not disproportionate (Jaynes and Williams, 1989: 477–478).

The same statistical murkiness discussed in the previous section develops once more: Since researchers do not systematically observe law-enforcement officials on the job, they cannot determine to what extent racial bias enters at the arrest stage—either in the decision to arrest or to use deadly force.

But while those data are not available, sociologist William B. Waegel did a study that gets at least some relevant, behind-the-scenes information. Waegel spent about ten months as a participant-observer in a police department in a Northeastern city. He concluded that politicians' calls for the harsh treatment of criminals along with victims', friends', or family members' demands for revenge create a moral climate encouraging violence against offenders. Widespread racism, Waegel believed, plays into the process. In urban areas, where minorities are overrepresented in serious crimes, police are likely to feel that race itself is a major cause of crime. Frequently Waegel heard comments supporting such a position. For instance, during the investigation of a homicide involving a member of a racial minority (Waegel did not specify which group), the researcher heard one detective tell another, "Maybe Hitler was right, he just had the wrong group." And during another investigation in which all the parties involved were black, a veteran officer told Waegel, "You've got to understand, these people are animals, and we're here to keep peace among animals." In the aftermath of a police shooting, a colleague approached the officer responsible and asked what happened. The officer described the circumstances, which included shooting the suspect while he was lying unarmed on the ground, and then concluded, "What was I supposed to do?" Without hesitation the other policeman replied, "What's another dead nigger anyway?" (Waegel, 1984: 148)

Sometimes incidents of police violence against minority-group members are highly publicized. In September 1990 John Andrews, a black man, was standing in an otherwise all-white crowd whose members were asking two white police officers to stop a tow truck from hauling off a woman's car, which had been parked illegally. According to witnesses, even though Andrews was acting just like everyone else in the crowd, the officers pulled him out, slammed him against the car, and arrested him. One of the witnesses explained that "the younger cop . . . totally lost control. He punched the kid in the stomach and at one point unsnapped his holster. And the kid never laid a hand on the officer" (Prial, 1990: 26).

In March 1991 in Los Angeles, the most celebrated recent incident of police violence against a minority-group member occurred. Four police officers kicked and beat Rodney G. King, a local African-American, for two minutes while 11 other officers and 20 local residents watched. What was unique about the incident was that one of the local residents filmed the beating, and it was widely shown on national television. The large number of police present during the beating and transcripts of squad-car communications, which indicated that such incidents occurred frequently, supported the widespread belief in the Los Angeles area that police violence against black and Chicano citizens is commonplace. Jerome Skolnick, a sociologist specializing in police behavior, indicated, "This is going to be the defining incident in police brutality; it's going to be the historical event for police in our time" (Mydans, 1991: B7).

Besides racist violence by police, ordinary citizens sometimes engage in it. In the past decade, analysts of racism have emphasized the apparent rise in white citizens' initiation of violence, particularly on college campuses. For instance, the Justice Department indicated that the number of campuses in which race-related incidents occurred rose from 48 in 1986 to 77 the following year.

Commenting on a racial killing that occurred in New York City and will presently be discussed, sociologist Bob Blauner noted, "We're not used to seeing incidents of racial violence spearheaded by the young—this is something new and it cuts across class lines" (Johnson, 1989: section 1, p. 32).

Janet Caldwell, a member of the Center for Democratic Renewal, an Atlanta-based research group that monitors the Ku Klux Klan and other white-supremacist groups, suggested that in the modern world, a white skin no longer translates to automatic privilege. Caldwell said "Young whites are facing things they never had to face before" (Johnson, 1989: section 1, p. 32). No longer do whites monopolize high-paying, prestigious jobs. Many resent the situation, and they can find support from various media sources, notably white-power rock and roll groups such as Guns N' Roses, whose debut album sold nine million copies and included vicious put-downs of African-Americans and other racial minorities (Pareles, 1989).

In a study of the Ku Klux Klan, researchers found extensive evidence of youthful racism, learning to their surprise that even though Klan membership had been greater in the past, support was unrelated to age—that "favorable attitudes toward the Klan are not dying out in the younger generation" (Seltzer and Lopes, 1986: 96). The investigators discovered that the social variable that most predicted support for the Klan was education or, actually, the lack of it: the less education received, the greater the expressed support. The researchers did not know whether this relationship resulted because better educated people have learned to tone down their racist expression or actually are less inclined to be racist (Seltzer and Lopes, 1986: 98).

Another study conducted in Wilkes-Barre, Pennsylvania, illustrated how Ku Klux Klan members have learned to gain support by exploiting whites' fears. When new owners of the local newspaper anticipated a workers' strike, they hired a security company, which deployed guards throughout the building—in rest rooms, on the shop floor, in most work areas, and in the places where workers gathered to talk or eat lunch. The workers deeply resented the guards' presence, feeling that the company was trying to intimidate them into not striking. The fact that the guards were primarily black while the newspaper workers were mainly white compounded the tension, and in the weeks that preceded the strike, the workers' frustration centered on the guards, whom they constantly threatened and insulted with racial slurs.

Eventually the strike occurred, and workers began mass picketing in front of the newspaper headquarters. At this point built-up frustrations were released on the guards, who were spat upon, hit by objects, and punched.

After the outbreak of violence, Klan organizers approached the strikers, suggesting that their fury toward the black guards should extend to the entire black community of Wilkes-Barre. What was particularly disturbing to local African-American leaders was that few whites expressed alarm or even concern about the Klan actions. Eventually the security company was replaced with one using exclusively white guards. Tensions lessened, and finally the strike was settled. It appeared, however, that the events described placed a long-term strain on race relations in Wilkes-Barre (Keil, 1985).

When jobs are on the line in interracial situations, there is likely to be racially targeted resentment, which can turn violent. Visitors to Detroit-area auto plants have found racist anti-Japanese posters and graffiti very prevalent. Some United Auto Worker locals have ordered and distributed bumper stickers reading "Toyota-Datsun-Honda = Pearl Harbor" and "Unemployment—Made in Japan." A number of auto executives have been equally unrestrained. In particular, Bennett E. Bidwell, Chrysler's executive vice president for sales and marketing, suggested that the most effective means of limiting car imports would be to charter the *Enola Gay* (the airplane that dropped the first atomic bomb on Japan) (Daniels, 1988: 342–343).

The most celebrated violent incident emerging from this situation occurred on June 19, 1982. Vincent Chin, a Chinese-American, went with three friends to a topless bar, where a white automobile-industry foreman mistook him for Japanese and started making racial slurs, suggesting that Chin was responsible for his unemployment. A scuffle developed, and all participants were thrown out of the bar. Later that evening the white foreman and his stepson saw Chin at a restaurant, waited for him to leave, and then, while the stepson held Chin, the older man beat him with a baseball bat. Chin died four days later. Originally charged with second-degree murder, the whites were allowed to plead guilty to manslaughter; they were fined $3780 each and put on three years probation. The local Asian-American community was outraged, charging that a racist deevaluation of Asian-Americans led to the light sentences. Eventually their protests produced a federal investigation and a federal indictment of the older man, who was found guilty of depriving Chin of his civil rights. In September 1984 he received 25 years in prison, but upon appeal, witnesses' conflicting and vague testimony produced an acquittal (Kitano and Daniels, 1988: 189).

Modern Native Americans sometimes are victims of violence when they use the court system to obtain illegally removed tribal rights. After the Ojibway of northern Wisconsin sued for return of traditional fishing rights, hundreds of whites gathered on different occasions to protest. During the 1987 fishing season, 12 Ojibway spearers were trapped on a small point of land by about 500 whites, who hurled rocks and racial insults and blocked escape until a tactical squad arrived and dispersed the mob. In the spring of 1989, several anti-tribal organizations, with such names as Protect Americans' Rights and Resources, and Stop Treaty Abuses organized against Ojibway fishermen, throwing rocks, shooting ball bearings from high-powered slingshots, shouting racist vulgarities, and taking to the water to swamp the Ojibway's boats. Over 200 of the members of these organizations were arrested during a 12-day span. It is not readily apparent why the return of Ojibway fishing rights so angered whites. Did they feel threatened? One Native-American writer stated:

> It seems to enrage white people whenever Indians manage to hold onto any vestige of their land, their heritage, their rights. The racist resentment unleashed in northern Wisconsin is never far from the surface in areas with an Indian presence. The thin veneer of civilization is easily stripped away. (Harjo, 1989: 25)

For racial minorities negative living conditions can encourage violence. In a study conducted in Baltimore, Taylor and Covington (1990) found that murder and assault rates rose rapidly in largely black neighborhoods in which a rapid increase in poverty indicated that the residents' quality of life was declining.

James W. Balkwell provided consistent findings. In research done in 150 urban areas each containing 50,000 or more inhabitants, Balkwell (1990) found that what he called "ethnic inequality" was the social factor best predicting the homicide rate. Balkwell obtained income data from five ethnic categories—non-Hispanic whites; African-Americans; Native Americans, Eskimos or Aleuts; Asian-Americans; and Hispanic-Americans. He found that the greater the proportion of poor racial minority-group members, the higher the homicide rate. Balkwell suspected that a version of the frustration-aggression theory applied here: Frustrated and angered by restrictions for achieving economic success and unable to confront the true sources of their frustration, poor members of racial minorities sometimes lashed out at the people at hand, who served as scapegoats. This situation brings to mind the internal-colonialist theme of powerful whites and white-dominated structures imposing oppressive limits on racial minorities. Indeed, after considering a host of theoretical explanations for African-Americans' high homicide rate, Darnell Hawkins (1990) concluded that internal colonialism, with its emphasis on the legacy of racial oppression imposed on blacks since the days of slavery, appears to provide the most accurate analysis.

Evidence indicates that minority-group aggression most often is against members of the individual's own group. Low-income blacks have higher rates of violent-crime victimization than any other race-and-income subgroup, with a very high proportion of these crimes performed by blacks (Oliver, 1989). Because of their limited physical strength, children are especially vulnerable to violence. A study reported that between 1976 and 1983 in Illinois, the homicide rate for black children was nearly nine times the rate for white children; about 98 percent of the time, suspects in black childrens' killings were black, with parents, other family members, or other individuals known to the child accounting for over 90 percent of the homicides (Silverman, Riedel, and Kennedy, 1990). A pattern of violence against members of one's own minority group has also been apparent with another type of crime. In spite of widespread belief to the contrary, recent evidence indicated that during robberies involving strangers, black men were slightly more likely to rape black women than white women (South and Felson, 1990).

The following situation involves a highly publicized incident of racial violence.

A Killing in Bensonhurst

On the evening of August 23, 1989, four young black men came to an all-white neighborhood in Bensonhurst, a section of Brooklyn, to sell a used car. Unknown to these four men, they were watched by a group of young white men carrying baseball bats and, in one case, a .32-caliber handgun. A witness said that the whites approached the African-Americans, and one suggested that they club them. No, they should kill one of them, another said. A moment later one of the young white men shot Yusuf K. Hawkins twice in the chest, and he died.

Within a few days, the public learned the circumstances behind the killing. Bensonhurst is a closed, protected world primarily inhabited by Italian immigrants. As one resident said, "This neighborhood, it's like a family." Like a family, neighbors knew one another's problems and often became involved in one another's disputes and feuds.

An 18-year-old woman named Gina Feliciano was the former girlfriend of 19-year-old Keith Mondello. She was no longer interested in him and emphasized her disinterest by telling him that she was going to bring a bunch of her African-American and Puerto Rican friends to the neighborhood for a party. Feelings against Feliciano were already negative because she violated neighborhood norms by dating blacks and dark-skinned Puerto Ricans. Her statement served as a threat, and when Hawkins and his friends showed up, they were mistaken for Feliciano's friends.

The issue of threat, that has been so prominent in this section and in the discussion of the criminal-justice system, seems relevant here. Residents of Bensonhurst felt a strong sense of threat from black outsiders, and they endorsed norms consistent with that sense of threat, norms invoking a sense of caste: One should date and associate only with "one's own kind." Gina Feliciano violated this norm by dating members of racial minorities.

She further betrayed her own people by threatening to bring in minority-group members to her own neighborhood. Sociologist Gerry Krase, who has studied Bensonhurst, indicated that residents' sense of threat from blacks produced the feeling "that they have to defend the family, the neighborhood against incursion" (Kifner, 1989: B4).

Comments from Bensonhurst residents were consistent with this theme. Many residents expressed the idea that the killing "was being blown out of proportion"—that African-Americans simply entering their neighborhood represented a physical threat, even though Gina had never suggested that her friends would be coming in to engage in violence. Carolyn Scalici, a young woman who was interviewed while leaning against the candy store where the youths charged in the killing regularly gathered, indicated that Mondello's friends were just helping him when he was in trouble. She added, "The same thing would have happened if it was white guys came in. He was defending himself." An interesting view of local racism was provided by one young woman. In a contradictory statement, she declared, "This wasn't racial and I've never been racial in my life. But white people should stick together for ourselves" (Kifner, 1989: B4).

The Bensonhurst killing shows how savage racial confrontations can become when people perceive a sense of threat. In this case an isolated, racist white group felt threatened by blacks and killed an innocent black man, who was viewed as a threatening outsider.

While most white Americans are less isolated than Bensonhurst residents, it appears that the sense of racial threat found in that community thrives.

REFERENCES

Balkwell, James W. 1990. "Ethnic Inequality and the Rate of Homicide." *Social Forces* 69 (September): 53–70.

Baron, Harold M. 1968. "Black Powerlessness in Chicago." *Trans-Action* 6 (November): 27–35.

Beauregard, Robert A. 1990. "Tenacious Inequalities: Politics and Race in Philadelphia." *Urban Affairs Quarterly* 25 (March): 420–434.

Blauner, Bob. 1989. *Black Lives, Whites Lives.* Berkeley: University of California Press.

Blumstein, Alfred. 1982. "On the Racial Disproportionality of United States' Prison Populations." *Journal of Criminal Law and Criminology* 73 (Fall): 1259–1281.

Branch, Taylor. 1988. *Parting the Waters: America in the King Years, 1954–1963.* New York: Simon and Schuster.

Bridges, George S., and Robert D. Crutchfield. 1988. "Law, Social Standing and Racial Disparities in Imprisonment." *Social Forces* 66 (March): 699–724.

Brown, Richard Maxwell. 1979. "Historical Patterns of American Violence," pp. 49–76 in Hugh Davis Graham and Ted Robert Gurr (eds.), *Violence in America: Historical & Comparative Perspectives.* Beverly Hills, CA: Sage Publications. Revised edition.

Browning, Rufus P., Dale Rogers Marshall, and David H. Tabb. 1986. "Protest Is Not Enough: A Theory of Political Incorporation." *PS* 19 (Summer): 576–581.

Churchill, Ward. 1990. "The Black Hills Are Not for Sale: A Summary of the Lakota Struggle for the 1868 Treaty Territory." *Journal of Ethnic Studies* (Spring): 127–142.

Daniels, Roger. 1988. *Asian Americans: Chinese and Japanese in the United States since 1850.* Seattle: University of Washington Press.

Dollard, John. 1937. *Caste & Class in a Southern Town.* New Haven: Yale University Press.

Ekland-Olson, Sheldon. 1988. "Structured Discretion, Racial Bias, and the Death Penalty: The First Decade after *Furman* in Texas." *Social Science Quarterly* 69 (December): 853–873.

Fagan, Jeffrey, Ellen Slaughter, and Eliot Hartstone. 1987. "Blind Justice? The Impact of Race on the Juvenile Process." *Crime & Delinquency* 33 (April): 224–258.

Feagin, Joe R. 1989. *Racial & Ethnic Relations.* Englewood Cliffs, NJ: Prentice-Hall. Third edition.

Fugita, Stephen S., and David J. O'Brien. 1985. "Structural Assimilation, Ethnic Group Membership, and Political Participation among Japanese Americans: A Research Note." *Social Forces* 63 (June): 986–995.

Gann, L. H., and Peter J. Duignan. 1986. *The Hispanics in the United States: A History.* Boulder: Westview Press.

Gray, Jerry. 1991. "Panel Says Courts Are 'Infested with Racism.'" *New York Times* (June 5): B1.

Hacker, Andrew. 1988. "Black Crime, White Racism." *New York Review of Books* 35 (March 3): 36–41.

Hagan, William T. 1986. "Tribalism Rejuvenated: The Native American Since the Era of Termination," pp. 295–304 in Roger L. Nichols (ed.), *The American Indian: Past and Present.* New York: Alfred A. Knopf. Third edition.

Harjo, Suzanne Shown. 1989. "Rights of Spring: Racism in Wisconsin." *Daybreak* 3 (Spring): 24–25.

Hawkins, Darnell F. 1987. "Beyond Anomalies: Rethinking the Conflict Perspective on Race and Criminal Punishment." *Social Forces* 65 (March): 719–745.

Hawkins, Darnell F. 1990. "Explaining the Black Homicide Rate." *Journal of Interpersonal Violence* 5 (June): 151–163.

Hero, Rodney E., and Kathleen M. Beatty. 1989. "The Elections of Federico Pena as Mayor of Denver: Analysis and Implications." *Social Science Quarterly* 70 (June): 300–310.

Hirsch, Herbert. 1982. "Political Activation and the Socialization of Support for a Third Party: Mexican-American Children and the Future of *La Raza Unida* Party," pp. 249–265 in Z. Anthony Kruszewski et al. (eds.), *Politics and Society in the Southwest.* Boulder: Westview Press.

Huizinga, David, and Delbert S. Elliott. 1987. "Juvenile Offenders: Prevalence, Offender Incidence, and Arrest Rates by Race." *Crime & Delinquency* 33 (April): 206–223.

Jaynes, Gerald David, and Robin M. Williams, Jr. (eds.). 1989. *A Common Destiny: Blacks and American Society.* Washington, DC: National Academy Press.

Johnson, Kirk. 1989. "Racism and the Young: Some See a Rising Tide." *New York Times* (August 27): 32.

Keil, Thomas J. 1985. "Capital, Labor, and the Klan: A Case Study in the Deterioration of Local Racial Relationships." *Phylon* 46 (Winter): 341–352.

Keil, Thomas J., and Gennaro F. Vito. 1989. "Race, Homicide Severity, and Application of the Death Penalty: A Consideration of the Barnett Scale." *Criminology* 27 (August): 511–531.

Kifner, John. 1989. "Bensonhurst: A Tough Code in Defense of a Closed World." *New York Times* (September 1): A1.

Kitano, Harry H. L., and Roger Daniels. 1988. *Asian Americans: Emerging Minorities.* Englewood-Cliffs, NJ: Prentice-Hall.

LaFree, Gary. 1980. "The Effect of Sexual Stratification by Race on Official Reactions to Rape." *American Sociological Review* 45 (October): 842–854.

Langan, Patrick A. 1985. "Racism on Trial: New Evidence to Explain the Racial Composition of Prisons in the United States." *Criminology* 76 (Fall): 666–683.

Liska, Allen E., Mitchell B. Chamlin, and Mark D. Reed. 1985. "Testing the Economic Production and Conflict Models of Crime Control." *Social Forces* 64 (September): 119–138.

Longoria, Thomas, Jr., Robert D. Wrinkle, and J. L. Polinard. 1990. "Mexican American Voter Registration." *Social Science Quarterly* (June): 356–361.

Marquez, Benjamin. 1989. "The Politics of Race and Assimilation: The League of United Latin American Citizens, 1929–40." *Western Political Quarterly* 42 (June): 355–375.

Mydans, Seth. 1991. "Videotape of Beating by Officers Puts Full Glare on Brutality Issue." *New York Times* (March 18): A1.

Oliver, William. 1989. "Sexual Conquest and Patterns of Black-on-Black Violence: A Structural-Cultural Perspective." *Violence and Victims* 4 (Winter): 257–273.

Pareles, Jon. 1989. "There's a New Sound in Pop Music: Bigotry." *New York Times* (September 10): Sec. 2, 1.

Prial, Frank J. 1990. "Man Is Still in Jail After Dispute over Towing." *New York Times* (September 15): 26.

Seltzer, Rick, and Grace M. Lopes. 1986. "The Ku Klux Klan: Reasons for Support or Opposition among White Respondents." *Journal of Black Studies* 17 (September): 91–109.

Silverman, Robert A., Marc Riedel, and Leslie W. Kennedy. 1990. "Murdered Children: A Comparison of Racial Differences Across Two Jurisdictions." *Journal of Criminal Justice* 18: 401–416.

South, Scott J., and Richard B. Felson. 1990. "The Racial Patterning of Rape." *Social Forces* 69 (September): 71–93.

Swigert, Victoria, and Ronald A. Farrell. 1977. "Normal Homicides and the Law." *American Sociological Review* 42 (February): 16–32.

Taylor, Ralph B., and Jeanette Covington. 1990. "Ecological Change, Changes in Violence, and Risk Prediction." *Journal of Interpersonal Violence* 5 (June): 164–175.

Thomson, Randall J., and Matthew T. Zingraff. 1981. "Detecting Sentence Disparity: Some Problems and Evidence." *American Journal of Sociology* 86 (January): 869–880.

U.S. Bureau of the Census. 1989. *Statistical Abstract of the United States: 1989.* Washington, DC: U.S. Government Printing Office. 109th edition.

U.S. Bureau of the Census. 1991. *Statistical Abstract of the United States: 1991.* Washington, DC: U.S. Government Printing Office. 111th edition.

U.S. Department of Justice. 1988. *Correctional Populations in the United States.* Washington, DC: U.S. Government Printing Office.

Vanderleeuw, James M. 1990. "A City in Transition: The Impact of Changing Racial Composition on Voting Behavior." *Social Science Quarterly* 71 (June): 326–338.

Waegel, William B. 1984. "How the Police Justify the Use of Deadly Force." *Social Problems* 32 (December): 144–155.

Zatz, Marjorie S. 1987. "The Changing Forms of Racial/Ethnic Differences in Sentencing." *Journal of Research in Crime and Delinquency* 24: 69–72.

Chapter
5

Knowing Your Place: Work and Housing

*F*or twenty years—from 1917 to 1937—the best third baseman in the country might have been William Julius "Judy" Johnson. He was a line-drive hitter, who consistently batted well above .330 and also fielded his position superbly. As both a batter and fielder, Johnson was frequently compared to the legendary "Pie" Traynor of the Pittsburgh Pirates.

Who was better, Johnson or Traynor? It was impossible to make an accurate comparison, because Judy Johnson could never play in the major leagues. He was black, and until 1947 black players were barred from Major League Baseball.

Watching Johnson play in his prime, Connie Mack, a well-known judge of baseball talent, stated, "If Judy were only white, he could name his price." About being barred from playing Major League Baseball, Johnson said, "You have to take life in stride. Sometimes your heart may ache, but you can't let it get you down. There's always a better day coming" (Harvin, 1989: 29).

One might argue that Johnson's "better day" came in 1975 when he was the sixth player from the segregated Negro baseball league elected by a special committee to the baseball Hall of Fame, an honor restricted to top ball players regardless of color. Still this belated recognition did not remove the injustice Johnson encountered in his playing days.

But, someone might ask, hasn't such blatant racism in sports been banished? It has. As we see later in the chapter, however, evidence of racial discrimination still occurs in baseball and in other sports. In fact, evidence of racism occurs widely in both work and housing, the topics featured in this chapter.

The internal-colonialist perspective fits comfortably here—with emphasis upon racial minorities accepting whites' control and knowing their place. As we saw in the first chapter, one of the theory's basic ideas is the colonial-labor principle, which indicates that racial minorities must serve white controllers' interests and needs. We consider its relevance in the upcoming discussion of work.

Another fundamental tenet of internal colonialism involves restricted freedom of movement, and one illustration concerns residential location. To what extent do racial minorities face discrimination in housing? The second major section of the chapter answers this question.

RACIAL MINORITIES' WORK WORLD

At the end of the nineteenth century, Horatio Alger wrote a series of best-selling novels about hard-working, clean-living boys whose perseverance paid off. Their virtuous efforts produced a rise from poverty and obscurity to wealth and fame. Horatio Alger never bothered to emphasize that all his young heroes were white. For racial minorities of that era, the road to economic and social success was virtually nonexistent.

Before World War II, African-Americans still largely lived in the rural South. With the outbreak of war, they started moving to both Southern and Northern cities, where wartime industrial jobs paid much higher wages than they had previously received. The labor force transformation continued after the war, as we see upon examining job categories in which African-American men and women made their statistically largest shifts.

In 1939, 41 percent of black men were farmers or farm workers; by 1984 the figure had dropped sharply to 5 percent. Meanwhile the proportion in clerical and sales, machine operation, and crafts rose from 19 percent to nearly 52 percent. During that period the proportion of women providing domestic service shifted from 60 to 6 percent while clerical and sales, machine operation, and crafts went from less than 8 to nearly 48 percent.

The shift from rural to urban living also gave African-Americans increasing access to American consumer technology—plumbing, electricity, automobiles, refrigerators, telephones, radios, and eventually television. They also benefitted from improved medical care, especially in the late 1960s after the establishment of government-subsidized health care for the poor (Medicaid) and for the elderly (Medicare).

Overall, however, African-Americans' economic advancement in the past half-century has been at best mixed. Through the 1970s and the 1980s, blacks' wages rose relative to whites, but African-Americans experienced higher unemployment rates than whites, with the least-educated workers most adversely affected. Poverty among African-Americans has become increasingly evident. For instance, keeping the dollar's buying power at the 1984 level, one finds that in 1984 about 40 percent of black men earned less than $10,000, up from 25 percent in 1969. For white men the respective percentages were 20 and 10 (Jaynes and Williams, 1989: 272–275).

Why have African-Americans historically had lower incomes than whites? Differences of opinion exist. Wacquant and Wilson concluded that the dominant factors are the flight of manufacturing jobs out of Northern and Midwestern cities and the general economic shift toward service industries and occupations. When these conditions occur, they suggested, "even mild forms of racial discrimination—mild by historical standards— have a bigger impact on those at the bottom of the American class order" (Wacquant and Wilson, 1989: 11). For these observers poor blacks' poverty is largely the result of impersonal, color-blind factors, primarily affecting low-income people.

Many scholars more strongly emphasize racism, offering recent evidence that racial discrimination has been a significant factor affecting African-Americans at all income levels, limiting them in management (Morrison and Von Glinow, 1990; Larwood, Szwajkowski, and Rose, 1988) and male-dominated professions (Sokoloff, 1988); pushing them into low-skill as opposed to high-skill work (Kaufman, 1986); holding down wage levels (Cotton, 1988; Geschwender and Carroll-Seguin, 1990; Killian, 1990) and advancement from low-paying jobs (Beauregard, 1990; Pomer, 1986); and increasing the likelihood of unemployment or underemployment (Burstein and Pitchford, 1990; Farley, 1987; Johnson, 1990; Killian, 1990; Lichter, 1988; Shulman, 1987).

Furthermore as we noted in Chapter 3, racial segregation has played a major role in the creation of a black underclass. Forced to live in restricted urban areas, poor African-Americans find their residential areas particularly hard hit by such economic downturns as the one occurring in the early 1970s, especially when segregation policies make it likely or inevitable that large numbers of poor blacks from other districts are funnelled into them. Businesses leave; vital services, including medical care and schooling deteriorate, and crime and violence sharply increase (Massey, 1990). These are prime conditions fostering the **vicious cycle of pov-**

erty—a pattern in which parents' minimal income significantly limits children's educational and occupational pursuits, thereby keeping them locked into the same low economic status. It is being argued here that in modern times, a poor minority member's residential area contributes significantly to the perpetuation of poverty. Given these conditions it is not surprising that in 1988 the proportion of African-Americans living below the poverty level was more than three times greater than the white proportion—31.6 percent compared to 10.1 percent (U.S. Bureau of the Census, *Statistical Abstract of the United States: 1991.* No. 751). Table 5.1 provides more information on racial minorities' poverty.

Research has also indicated that housing segregation affects middle-class blacks' job prospects. Often prevented from living in primarily white suburbs, which have become prominent sites for retail and service trade industries in the last couple of decades (Darden, 1990), or restricted to living in racially segregated suburbs that provide few such job opportunities (Schneider and Phelan, 1990), middle-class African-Americans often have much less immediate physical access to good-paying jobs than whites.

Like African-Americans other racial minorities have historically suffered job discrimination. For instance, during the 1950s and 1960s, increasing numbers of Japanese- and Chinese-Americans graduated from college and obtained jobs outside their ethnic locales, but they tended to be denied supervisory and higher administrative positions. The most formidable barrier to their advancement seemed to be white employers' reluctance to put Asian-Americans into positions where they could hire and fire whites (Daniels, 1988: 315–316).

To many white Americans, Asian-Americans' occupational success is impressive, and, in fact, the success image has often become the dominant element in modern whites' stereotype of Asian-Americans. Like any stereotype, however, this one provides a disservice for the group in point. Asian-Americans' success image often overshadows significant amounts of underemployment, poverty among the elderly, mental illness, divorce and family disorganization, and juvenile delinquency. As a result government agencies, educational institutions, and private corporations are less likely to attend to such problems among Asian-Americans than among other racial minorities (Crystal, 1989; Hurh and Kim, 1989).

Historically Mexican-Americans have also suffered job discrimination, with workers in farming, oil, mining, and manufacturing jobs often classified as "nonwhites" and systematically paid less than their white counterparts. Many current employers have selectively hired illegal Chicano immigrants, who could be forced to accept sub-minimum wages and oppressive working conditions because they have no papers for legal jobs. Studies conducted primarily on Mexican-Americans living in the Southwestern states indicated that they are more likely to be successful occupationally if they speak English, live in areas where they represent a substantial proportion of the population, and have elected representatives in local government (Mladenka, 1989; Stolzenberg, 1990).

Table 5.1   MINORITY FAMILIES' POVERTY[1]

Percentage of various racial groups' families below the poverty level[2]

Puerto Ricans	42.7
Vietnamese-Americans	35.1
African-Americans	32.5
Native Americans	23.7
Mexican-Americans	23.5
Korean-Americans	13.1
Chinese-Americans	10.5
Whites	10.2
Japanese-Americans	4.2

Percentage of Blacks' and Whites' poverty: 1959 to 1988

	African-Americans	Whites
1959	55.1	18.1
1966	41.8	12.2
1970	33.5	9.9
1975	31.3	9.7
1980	32.5	10.2
1985	31.3	11.4
1988	31.6	10.1

[1]The poverty index, which is updated each year, is an estimate of the money necessary to purchase basic consumer products and services. Families falling below the poverty line simply possess insufficient funds to make these purchases.

[2]The figures in this table come from the 1980 Census of Population.

Note: While poverty has been an unrelenting American problem, data in this table make it clear that it has been a consistently greater threat to most racial minorities than to whites.

Sources: U.S. Bureau of the Census. *Current Population Reports,* "Characteristics of the Population Below the Poverty Level: 1980." Table 38; U.S. Bureau of the Census. *Statistical Abstract of the United States: 1991.* No. 44 and No. 750.

Research has indicated that besides blacks, Puerto Ricans are the only major racial group suffering racial segregation so severe that they are locked into residential areas that have been steadily deteriorating since the advent of the 1970s economic downturn (Massey and Eggers, 1990). Partly as a result of this segregation, Puerto Ricans have been the only major racial group besides blacks in which an underclass has been rapidly expanding. About one-third of the Puerto Rican population in the United States—33.7 percent in 1988—falls below the poverty line (Feagin, 1989:

293; U.S. Bureau of the Census, *Statistical Abstract of the United States: 1991*. No. 45).

For Puerto Ricans institutional racism has also been a common barrier. In New York City, for example, applicants for many low-level service jobs such as trash collection have been required to take tests written in English that are not job-related and that, besides, could be translated easily into Spanish. Another illustration of institutional racism is that Puerto Ricans, who tend to be smaller than average American citizens, find that height and weight requirements for police and fire-department jobs can rule them ineligible (Feagin, 1989: 293).

A recent study of Puerto Rican women in the New York City area indicated that respondents with 11 or more years of formal education, a good ability to speak English, no children under five, and previous work experience were considerably more likely to be employed than women without all or most of these characteristics. About 30 percent of the women studied lacked the traits making employment likely, and as education and English-language skills become increasingly required for employment, such women's chances of getting a job will grow even more remote (Falcon, Gurak, and Powers, 1990).

A number of state and national studies indicated that Native Americans frequently suffer discrimination in employment in towns located near reservations. Their work difficulties have been compounded by limited amounts of formal education and on reservations by the fact that a surplus of potential workers has tended to keep wages for such positions as laborer, truck driver, and typist scarcely half what they would be off the reservation (Olson and Wilson, 1984: 186–187).

Do most Americans appreciate these conditions? When a national sample was asked in July 1989 if lack of effort or circumstances is more often to blame if a person is poor, 38 percent indicated lack of effort, 42 percent opted for circumstances, 17 percent selected both, and 3 percent had no opinion. Of whites 39 percent chose lack of effort compared to 32 percent for members of racial minorities; among whites 41 percent selected circumstances while 48 percent of racial minority members chose that option (Gallup, 1989). Clearly whites were more inclined than minority members to focus on individuals' failure and hold them responsible—"blame the victim" in the phrase introduced in Chapter 3—while members of racial minorities were more likely to take a sociological perspective, focusing on conditions promoting poverty in people's lives. Why the difference? While the survey did not examine this issue, it seems probable that racial minorities' more intimate contact with poverty, and, perhaps in particular, their knowledge of the role racism plays, encourage them to be aware of social conditions producing poverty.

Abundant evidence suggests that racism affects racial minorities in the economy. One way to examine the situation systematically is to analyze employment as a process involving three phases.

RACIAL MINORITIES AND THE EMPLOYMENT PROCESS

When a national survey team asked Americans whether or not blacks in their community have as good a chance as whites to receive any job for which they are qualified, seven out of ten (70 percent) agreed that they did. Respondents' race was a significant factor. Compared to 73 percent of whites, only 43 percent of blacks replied affirmatively (Gallup and Hugick, 1990).

At each stage of racial minorities' work experience, evidence of racism is prevalent. We examine the job-candidate stage, the job-screening stage, and the job-promotion stage. Then we consider black managers' experiences.

Job-Candidate Stage

Research has indicated that African-Americans are excluded from entire job areas, especially well-paid positions requiring minimal education and experience. For instance, African-Americans who seek jobs in large restaurants are usually kept out of such positions as waiter and cook, that lead to promotion and supervisory roles. Instead they are pushed into low-paying, dead-end jobs—dishwasher and busboy. A 1985 study done in New York City found blacks were virtually unrepresented in 130 of 193 private-sector industries, and the few working in these industries were primarily in clerical positions (Steinberg, 1989: 49). Individual racism helps produce this outcome, but the lack of social networks also contributes significantly.

In a society where racial segregation permeates all major structures, members of different races are primarily involved in social networks—composed of friends, neighbors, colleagues, and other work-related associates—containing members of their own race. This situation has a significant impact on job applicants. At the job-candidate stage, there are fertile possibilities for institutional racism: Members of racial minorities are indirectly discriminated against because frequently they lack access to whites' social networks, which generally provide better leads and informal recommendations for jobs than their own.

When social networks are a chief means of job recruitment, minority members confronting white networks are more likely than whites to be denied employment or to receive low-paying jobs. For poor, young members of racial minorities who live in residentially segregated areas, have limited schooling, and modest or no work histories, social networks to obtain employment are deficient (Jaynes and Williams, 1989: 320–321). For this reason alone, they are at a distinct disadvantage to other groups competing for jobs.

As the prestige and pay of jobs increase, use of social networks for locating candidates declines. For positions requiring college degrees, employers are much more likely to place advertisements in the local mass media than they do when hiring people for lower-level slots.

Nonetheless social networks are also used for higher-level jobs. In a study of 4078 employers, when respondents indicated that they relied on social networks as a chief means of recruitment for college-degree jobs, their openings were more likely to be filled by whites than when they indicated limited reliance on these networks.

Besides determining whether individuals will be hired, access to social networks appears to affect job candidates' income. In the same investigation, black high-school graduates who used segregated networks averaged $5.69 per hour, those who did not use networks averaged $5.74 per hour, and, in contrast, those who had access to desegregated networks averaged $6.45 per hour (Braddock and McPartland, 1987).

To counteract institutional racism in employment, lawsuits have been initiated based on affirmative-action standards established by the federal government and requiring that racial minorities' representation in a given workforce roughly reflect their proportion of the local population. For instance, one major court case focused on the fact that the Akron police department was only 3 percent African-American in a city with an 18 percent black population (Feagin, 1986: 122).

Job-Screening Stage

When employers confront a pool of job candidates, they usually have certain desirable traits in mind. First, they are likely to set a minimum educational standard, and this practice represents institutional racism when it is irrelevant to on-the-job performance and yet disproportionately eliminates racial minorities whose members are on the whole less educated than whites. A study of equal-employment-opportunity cases brought to federal appellate court showed that employers were usually unable to demonstrate that educational credentials and test scores related to productivity (Burstein and Pitchford, 1990).

Screening candidates also involves an evaluation of individuals, and individual racism can appear at this time. One study found that many companies frequently eliminated 30 to 40 percent of applicants by a screening interview. In such situations employers did not need to make direct reference to race, even among themselves. They could discuss impressions of candidates' "intelligence," "appearance," "vigor," and "self-confidence," with such references intentionally or perhaps unintentionally playing into interviewers' racial stereotypes (Lopez, 1976). Without explicit references to it, racism can be the crucial consideration.

In the previously cited study of 4078 employers, investigators found that whites were more likely to be chosen for jobs when employers valued such traits as quick learning, advanced reading skill, math excellence, and good judgment. This trend was most apparent for jobs requiring high-school certificates and less though still evident for jobs needing some college or a college degree (Braddock and McPartland, 1987). With such stereotyping occurring, blacks seeking jobs which possess a distinct intellectual component have little hope of getting them unless they are fully qualified or overqualified educationally while for whites educational criteria might be applied less stringently.

It is sobering to learn that when researchers asked members of the college class of 1957 from three Ivy-League colleges, which have traditionally supplied about two-fifths of America's business elite, whether they agreed with the conclusion that blacks are as intelligent as whites, just 36 percent of the Princeton class, 47 percent at Yale, and 55 percent at Harvard agreed (Jones, 1986: 88). If a similar mind-set exists throughout the business world, it is hardly surprising that blacks face widespread job discrimination.

Job-Promotion Stage

The national study of 4078 employers indicated that for promotion African-Americans' chances were closer to whites' if candidates came from within instead of outside an organization. Nonetheless blacks also were not as likely to be promoted as whites when only internal candidates were involved; the researchers learned that within organizations when workers' qualifications were held constant, blacks' salaries tended to be distinctly lower than whites' (Braddock and McPartland, 1987: 23).

On the job African-Americans and members of other racial minorities tend to face "a triple jeopardy"—racial stereotyping, the role of being the solo member of a racial minority on the job, and the token role, where whites consider them inferior if they obtained their positions through affirmative action. The impact of these three factors is likely to affect blacks negatively when they apply for promotions (Pettigrew and Martin, 1987).

Individuals who are the only or nearly the only representatives of racial minorities in an organization frequently encounter stereotypes. If an African-American employee does something that an observer can interpret negatively, such as speaking somewhat harshly to a colleague, then that behavior is more likely attributed to a basic deficiency in the person's character than in the case of a white person who acted similarly. In the latter instance, the white colleague would probably attribute the harsh statement to a situational factor, saying, "Oh, she's just having a bad day."

On the other hand, when minority workers perform effectively, co-workers who stereotype will rationalize the situation. Of an employee belonging to a racial minority, white colleagues might say, "He works so hard because he has to compensate for his lack of intelligence." Or they might claim that this person's success was the result of favoritism from a boss sensitive to pressures to incorporate minority individuals in high positions.

The second element in the triple jeopardy is the solo role. As the only or almost only member of their own group, African-Americans or mem-

bers of other racial minorities are likely to experience unrealistic evaluation from whites who have had little or no previous contact with racial
minorities. White workers often expect poor performances from African-
Americans. One solo black worker reported, "They were astonished to
find that I could write a basic memo. Even the completion of an easy task
brought surprised compliments" (Pettigrew and Martin, 1987: 55). Sometimes minority solo employees find the opposite—that expectations are
unrealistically high. In either case the situation is not useful to them.
Considered different from whites, they are not evaluated equitably and
thus do not receive realistic feedback that provides a helpful evaluation
of their progress on the job.

The third factor is the token role. If fellow workers or supervisors feel
that a member of a racial minority received a position because of affirmative action, then these people are likely to assume the individual is incom-
petent, only able to obtain the job when given unfair advantage because
of race.

Perhaps no situation portrays racial minorities' special job pressures
better than black managers' experiences.

Black Managers: The Dream in Jeopardy

As black managers move into the white corporate world, they must make
major adjustments. Often they have come from very different backgrounds than their white colleagues. To be able to survive, they must learn
norms governing behavior in what often feels like an alien world and
make the necessary adjustments. Whites' stereotypes or discriminatory
practices can complicate such adjustments.

Few, if any people enter business management with the feeling that
the job will prove easy and tension-free. All executives must work hard
and produce tangible results that lead to increased company profits. If
unsuccessful, they will not advance and might lose their jobs. This issue
alone is a source of considerable stress to many executives, both black and
white. We see, however, that blacks face additional stresses.

Because African-Americans entering executive positions often have
very different backgrounds from whites', they are frequently unsure about
standards of conduct and feel nervous and confused about interracial
relations. As the solo African-American management trainee in a department with over 8000 employees, Edward Jones faced such problems. In
a detailed account of his opening months on the job, Jones indicated that
he worked very hard and did everything he could imagine to receive good
evaluations, and yet he was nearly fired, being told to his astonishment
that he lacked tact and was constantly rocking the boat.

In his evaluation of this experience, Jones concluded that his style of
relating to coworkers and bosses was sometimes inappropriate—that the
world of white business required a low-key behavioral style with which he
was unfamiliar.

But, according to Jones, there was another issue. He was convinced that his fellow employees felt he "was out of the 'place' normally filled by black people in the company, and since no black person had preceded me successfully, it was easy for my antagonists to believe I was inadequate" (Jones, 1973: 114). As the colonial-labor principle emphasizes, blacks have traditionally been assigned menial jobs, and Jones's placement in a management position opposed whites' expectations. Hostile white colleagues responded to the confusing situation by unleashing their racial stereotypes, placing Jones in the triple jeopardy we previously discussed.

Entering corporations, black managers often find that the unrelenting emphasis on making profits permits little attention to be paid to race relations. As a result prevailing standards about racial issues are abundantly unclear. To survive and do well, African-American executives usually try to conform, but to what standards, in fact, are they supposed to conform? Sometimes top leaders within a corporation try to pretend that race is not an issue, and so all employees, regardless of race, are expected to support such a position. Moreover some white managers become defensive if racism is ever mentioned. Jones indicated that since "it's un-American to be prejudiced, . . . white and black managers, fearful of confronting the issue, take part in a charade" (Jones, 1986: 90). The result is that communications between African-Americans and whites are adversely affected.

The isolated, confusing circumstances in which black managers often find themselves are special problems when they seek promotion, which is highly dependent on effective relations with coworkers and superiors. A black middle manager described a situation in which a black manager working for her demanded an overdue merit raise. Convinced that he deserved it, the middle manager gathered relevant documentation and went to the appraisal meeting. That meeting involved several white male colleagues who spoke without documentation of their respective candidates, voted down her nominee, and awarded merit raises to several of their own people. According to the black middle manager, there was a "buddy system" in which these important men took turns providing promotions for each other's followers (Jones, 1986: 89). Within this system African-Americans, who are new arrivals and widely considered "different" or inferior, are often victims of severe discrimination.

In business, high-level executives often become sponsors of younger subordinates, but a prominent white consultant told Edward Jones that white managers are usually uncomfortable sponsoring African-Americans, fearing negative reactions from other whites (Jones, 1986: 89). As a result black executives often find themselves shunted into slots out of the corporate mainstream—into community relations, personnel, or anything to do with minorities. Furthermore many black executives claim that their superiors withhold more strategic information from them than from their white colleagues. As a result African-Americans claim that they can be much less effective than white colleagues (Campbell, 1982).

Most black executives believe that to obtain promotion they must demonstrate competence and loyalty in ways not required of whites. What happens, a black executive wonders, if he hires a black secretary? He is likely to decide against it, realizing, as one black manager noted, that peers and superiors might say "that's a black operation over there, so it can't be too effective" (Jones, 1986: 90). Or consider the case of Charlie, a junior executive, who was straightforward and honest, if not militant about racial issues. One day several lower-level black managers approached him, expressing concern about what they saw as a pattern of discrimination limiting their careers. Charlie felt that the top officers ought to hear their account and arranged a meeting with them. Two days before that meeting, the president took Charlie aside and said, "Charlie, I'm disappointed that you met with those people. I thought we could trust you" (Jones 1986: 90). Certainly this statement made it clear that Charlie's superiors were giving him little maneuvering room: If he were going to keep rising in the company, he would need to reject racial loyalties, making loyalty to his white superiors and the company his only concern.

With the preceding information as background, it should not be surprising to learn that surveys of the Fortune 1000 (the largest American corporations) indicated that there has been no significant movement of racial minorities and women into top management. A 1979 survey of 1708 senior executives indicated that three were African-American, two Asian, two Hispanic, and eight women while a 1985 survey of 1362 senior executives found four African-Americans, six Asians, three Hispanics, and 29 women (Jones, 1986: 84). The barrier faced by minorities and women seeking to move into top management has sometimes been called a "glass ceiling"—so subtle that it is nearly invisible but also strong enough to block candidates from moving to the top rungs of the corporate ladder (Morrison and Von Glinow, 1990).

For African-Americans the move into the alien corporate world offers the same rewards of wealth, power, and prestige whites receive. It is a journey, however, that promises special difficulties and tensions: Often blacks need to learn new rules and to adjust to special, race-related demands made on them. Even when they adjust successfully, their rewards are likely to be less extensive than whites'.

Besides seeking work in the mainstream economy, members of racial minorities have pursued some distinctive approaches.

TWO SPECIAL STRATEGIES

One plan is to establish businesses that offer select products or services not provided by the mainstream economy—Japanese-Americans in farming, for example—and the other is to seek employment in areas where minorities' participation has traditionally been encouraged—blacks in professional sports, for instance.

Japanese-Americans in Farming

How can a racial minority survive in a repressive, racist society? While there is no foolproof answer to this question, many Asian immigrants developed a response: Find a business that provides a potentially profitable product or service that is minimally competitive with those supplied by established whites. Chinese opened restaurants, laundries, and garment factories (Sanders and Nee, 1987; Wong, 1987). The Japanese produced a variety of agricultural products, and their experience in California serves to illustrate this strategy for seeking economic success (Jiobu, 1988).

In the 1890s Japanese immigrants, many of them with a background in farming, began to work as farm laborers. In the next two decades, government officials became concerned that the hard-working Japanese would dominate agriculture, and so their immigration was restricted, their political rights were removed, and, if not citizens, they were prevented from owning land.

Still Japanese farmers prospered. Often the laws prohibiting land ownership were poorly enforced, and white land owners and bankers were generally eager to do business with the Japanese, selling them marginal land at high prices. The Japanese approach to farming was to concentrate on crops that required intensive labor and specialized care and that could be grown in profitable amounts on fairly small plots of marginal land. Besides their farming expertise, Japanese efforts benefitted from an ancient cultural tradition emphasizing hard work, sacrifice for the future, and patience in the face of adversity. Their efforts paid off. In the early 1920s, in the Sacramento area, for instance, Japanese farmers grew 80 percent of the tomatoes, 61 percent of the asparagus, and 78 percent of the spinach. By the outbreak of World War II, estimates indicated that throughout the state Japanese-Americans, who were about 2 percent of the population, were producing over 90 percent of snap beans, strawberries, and celery, and about 50 percent of artichokes, cauliflower, cucumbers, and tomatoes.

Forced relocation of all Japanese-Americans living on the West Coast during World War II produced significant economic losses for farmers, but their overall capital investment was fairly modest, and thus the majority managed to reestablish themselves in the farming business after the war.

In the past 20 or 30 years, there has been a steady decline in the proportion of Japanese-Americans entering agriculture. But early success in farming seems to have served several important purposes: It provided funding that subsidized the education and training of many members of the next generation of Japanese-Americans; it also established Japanese-Americans as a hard-working, reputable people in the eyes of the majority group, thus making it easier for youthful Japanese-Americans to enter the broader economy.

Blacks in Sport

For African-Americans two avenues to possible financial success have traditionally been open: Entertainment was one and sports was the other. The openness of entertainment and sports suggests the internal-colonialist issue mentioned in the chapter title—knowing one's place. In the realm of the physical, whites experienced little sense of threat from blacks, as long as blacks were merely strong or physically capable. The key issue for whites was maintaining control. In the well-known book *Soul on Ice,* Eldridge Cleaver analyzed racism in American society, classifying white men as "Omnipotent Administrators—all mind and no body—and labeling black men "Supermasculine Menials"—all body and no mind (Cleaver, 1970: 166). According to Cleaver, the reality of modern sport in which large numbers of black professional athletes perform impressive physical feats for primarily white audiences simply confirms in the racist's mind the natural order of things.

But while blacks have found the world of professional sport open to them, the question remains whether they have experienced racial discrimination within it. We consider this question, examining research involving professional baseball, football, and basketball.

Writing about big-league baseball, Robert M. Jiobu (1988a) suggested that for a number of reasons related to the game itself, one would expect baseball to be relatively free of racial discrimination. First, Major League Baseball, which has been voluntarily integrated since 1947, has a longer history of integration than most American activities. Second, with constant exposure to the mass media, baseball officials are fully aware that incidents of racism will be exposed. Third, widespread agreement exists on the basis for evaluating good performance, and major statistics on batting, pitching, and fielding are well publicized. Fourth, the goal of winning dominates professional baseball, and there is general acceptance that regardless of race, the best players are the ones that most effectively help a team to win. So these four reasons would discourage racial discrimination in baseball.

To find out whether racism occurred in the game, Jiobu looked at the records of Major League Baseball players involved in at least 50 games between 1971 and 1985. He learned that African-Americans' performance levels were higher than those for either Hispanics or whites. Blacks' lifetime slugging average (total bases per thousand times at bat) was .381 contrasted to .337 for Hispanics and .348 for whites, and blacks' lifetime batting average (hits per thousand times at bat) was .258 compared to .245 for Hispanics and .241 for whites.

Because of their superior performances, African-Americans last longer in the major leagues than the other two groups. For blacks the median survival time is 11.8 years while for whites and Hispanics it is 10.0 years.

So far there has been no evidence of racism. According to the data, African-Americans perform better and as a result maintain longer careers in Major League Baseball. But Jiobu realized that another issue required analysis. What happens if performance levels among the three groups are controlled (kept constant)? When this occurs, it turns out that African-Americans' careers are shorter than either Hispanics' or whites'. Jiobu concluded that blacks are "simultaneously rewarded for their performance and penalized for their race" (Jiobu, 1988a: 532).

Why are African-Americans penalized for their race? Jiobu speculated that a major factor might be owners' and management's concern that the predominantly white fans will not support a largely black team. To prevent such a result and yet to produce a winning team, owners and managers appear to place a distinct limit on the number of black players, eliminating African-Americans as soon as their skills start to decline while keeping a certain number of white players of comparably marginal ability. Many prominent writers and academics have suggested that there is no activity more typically American than baseball. In contrast to those positive commentaries, Jiobu's findings suggest a strictly negative side to the observation.

Research on football players in the National Football League, the second major U.S. professional sport, has examined another racism issue—whether or not a player's race affects his position. Investigators' basic assumption is that the more central positions in a football formation—on offense centers, quarterbacks, and guards—are not only central physically but also socially and politically: These positions are central to communication and leadership, and players at the seven other positions simply must follow orders. If professional football reflects the racial stratification system prevailing in American society, then one would expect that whites would dominate the central positions and African-Americans the less central ones. Let's consider.

Between 1975 and 1985, the percentage of black players in the National Football League increased from 41.6 to 51.3. Nonetheless during that time period, the proportion of whites in central positions remained disproportionately high on both offense and defense, with some impressive statistical increases in the offensive pattern. Most notably among quarterbacks, whose position is the most cerebral and most involved in decision making, the increase was from 95.5 to 97.1 percent. While the researchers unfortunately did not distinguish centers and guards, the most central of offensive linemen, from the other offensive linemen, they did indicate that during the same ten-year span, the percentage of white offensive linemen increased from 76 to 89 percent. (Since on a given team, the guards and center represent about 43 percent of the offensive line—it varies with the formation—one can guess that between 1975 and 1985, the proportion of central linemen who were white increased.) In contrast, African-Americans' participation rose in noncentral positions. The proportion of black running backs increased dramatically from 65 to 86 percent, and the proportion of black receivers rose from 55 to 62 percent. The authors concluded, "The positions requiring leadership and thinking ability have become even more 'white' and the positions necessitating speed, quickness, and 'instinct' have become even more 'black' " (Schneider and Eitzen, 1986: 260).

In basketball, the third major professional sport, a study found that as a group African-American players outperformed white players and as a result were better paid. Discrimination was revealed when performance statistics were held constant for the 1984–85 professional season: Researchers learned that blacks as a group averaged about $26,000 less per year than whites (Koch and Vander Hill, 1988). The authors suggested that while it "is difficult to avoid the conclusion that race discrimination . . . is the cause" (Koch and Vander Hill, 1988: 92), other factors, such as the possibility that upon entering professional basketball blacks are less knowledgeable or aggressive bargainers than whites, might also be relevant.

Besides athletes, management personnel are significant players in the world of professional sport. Although black management personnel in professional basketball, baseball, and football remain considerably below the proportion of black athletes in their respective sports, their numbers have been slowly increasing. Since the 1970s there have been a few black managers in Major League Baseball and head coaches in the National Basketball Association. In 1989—finally—the Oakland Raiders became the first team in the National Football League to hire a black head coach.

Commenting on Major League Baseball, Hank Aaron, a senior vice president for the Atlanta Braves and baseball's all-time home-run champion, indicated that blacks' involvement in baseball management has been minimal. Aaron cited the impact of social networks discussed earlier. He concluded, "Baseball was and continues to be a good-old-boy network." Aaron added that the commissioner of baseball and the president of the United States should push for significant change (Araton, 1991).

Recently Drew Pearson, a former All-Pro wide receiver for the Dallas Cowboys and now the president of a successful sportswear manufacturing company, has raised another issue involving blacks' participation in professional sport. Black athletes, Pearson argued, have been restricted in their range of roles. For example, while top black athletes have made large sums of money doing endorsements for athletic products, they could make more money and even provide jobs for poor, inner-city African-Americans if they started their own companies. Black athletes have not pursued this course of action because they have been brought up to see themselves narrowly—as just athletes. Pearson added:

> You don't really see yourself as a coach or as someone running these concession stands that generate money. Power people see us as being participants,

not the ones that set up these leagues, not the ones making any decision concerning the welfare of the league. (Rhoden, 1990: B7)

According to Pearson, black athletes need to recognize both for their own good and for the benefit of young, struggling African-Americans, that they should consider trying to become major players in the commercial and administrative areas of professional sport.

As we shift from jobs to housing, we once again find ample evidence of racism.

RACIAL MINORITIES AND HOUSING

One of the basic points in the internal-colonialist perspective involves freedom of movement. To what extent are members of racial minorities restricted in where they go and, in particular, where they live?

Since the 1920s sociologists have been interested in residential segregation. As they watched various European groups settling in this country, they predicted that as groups' socioeconomic status rose, residential restrictions would disappear. For white groups this proved true, and it has been generally accurate for Native Americans, Asian-Americans, and Mexican-Americans (Darden, 1990; Massey and Eggers, 1990). By 1988, however, a secondary pattern was absolutely clear. Nancy Denton and Douglas Massey, a pair of sociologists specializing in housing discrimination, wrote, "Blacks represent a major exception to the pattern of declining segregation with rising socioeconomic status" (Denton and Massey, 1988: 798).

Denton and Massey found that this conclusion about residential segregation for blacks held across different socioeconomic levels. For metropolitan areas with the largest black populations, they calculated the **index of dissimilarity**, which indicates the proportion of a particular racial group that would need to change residential area in order to achieve racial balance, a condition in which that group's percentage in a given census district would be similar to their percentage in that city.

In the metropolitan areas with the 60 largest black populations, the index of dissimilarity for African-Americans with none to four years of schooling completed was 83 percent, for those with 12 years of schooling 71 percent, and for those with 17 or more years of schooling (schooling beyond college) 68 percent. There was, in short, only a slight decline in the index of dissimilarity as African-Americans' education increased. When the researchers calculated the index of dissimilarity for income in those same 60 metropolitan areas, a similar pattern emerged. For blacks making under $2500 per year, the dissimilarity index was 80 percent; it dropped to 73 percent for those with income of $15,000 or $20,000 per year; but then it rose to 80 percent for those with income of $50,000 per year or more (Denton and Massey, 1988: 803). Table 5.2 presents blacks'

Table 5.2   BLACKS' RESIDENTIAL SEGREGATION

	Index of racial dissimilarity for years of school completed				
	0–4	8	12	16	17+
Mean, metropolitan areas with 10 largest black populations	84%[1]	84%	78%	72%	73%
Mean, metropolitan areas with 20 largest black populations	80%	80%	75%	70%	70%
Mean, metropolitan areas with 60 largest black populations	83%	81%	70%	68%	68%

	Index of racial dissimilarity for yearly income				
	$2,500	$5,000	$10,000	$20,000	$50,000+
Mean, metropolitan areas with 10 largest black populations	84%	82%	79%	76%	79%
Mean, metropolitan areas with 20 largest black populations	81%	79%	76%	74%	77%
Mean, metropolitan areas with 60 largest black populations	80%	78%	74%	73%	80%

[1]Figures are rounded off to the nearest percentage.

Note: This table concerns two measures of blacks' indexes of dissimilarity—the percentage of blacks that would need to change residential areas to achieve a racially balanced outcome in a given city. Two distinct trends are apparent. First, as blacks' years of schooling and income increase, there is little change in the index of dissimilarity; in fact, in all three classifications of metropolitan areas, the highest income group scored a higher index of dissimilarity than the second highest income group. Second, the larger the black populations of metropolitan areas, the higher the indexes of dissimilarity across educational and income levels.

Source: Adapted from Nancy A. Denton and Douglas S. Massey. "Residential Segregation of Blacks, Hispanics, and Asians by Socioeconomic Status and Generation." *Social Science Quarterly.* V. 69. December 1988, pp. 797–817.

indexes of dissimilarity for education and income in three sets of metropolitan areas.*

Another factor affecting blacks' residential segregation is the population density of the area in which they live. African-Americans living in the suburbs do experience more segregation than other groups but less than blacks in large metropolitan areas (Massey and Denton, 1988). The most profound residential segregation experienced by African-Americans occurs in the following large cities—Baltimore, Chicago, Cleveland, Detroit, Milwaukee, and Philadelphia. They are closely followed by Gary, Los Angeles, and New York. In these cities massive physical areas are exclusively black. As a result residents are likely to be largely or completely isolated from whites, most decisively affecting black citizens' opportunities for effective education and employment (Massey and Denton, 1989).

There is only one other major group that suffers a high level of residential segregation across all socioeconomic levels—black Puerto Ricans and other black Caribbean Hispanics who do not identify themselves as white. While white Puerto Ricans become increasingly integrated as their socioeconomic status rises, this is decisively not the case with black Puerto Ricans, whose most frequent non-Puerto Rican neighbors are African-Americans. It seems clear that for many white Americans a powerful desire is not to live near black people (Denton and Massey, 1988; 1989; Massey and Fong, 1990).

In the opening chapter, we encountered William J. Wilson's thesis about the declining significance of race. Lower-class status is the dominant source of oppression for blacks, Wilson argued. But researchers with data on residential location question this conclusion: For African-Americans a high-education or high-income level does little to overcome residential segregation.

For Asian-Americans and Mexican-Americans, the situation contrasts sharply. In metropolitan areas containing the heaviest concentrations of these two racial groups, their indexes of dissimilarity declined more sharply with rising socioeconomic status than blacks'. Well-educated Asian-Americans and Mexican-Americans are accepted as neighbors by most whites, even in metropolitan areas where they live in large numbers (Denton and Massey, 1988: 810–812). The least segregated Asian-American group is Japanese, with the Chinese, Filipino, Korean, Indian, and Vietnamese following in that order. It appears that the proportion of immigrants in an Asian-American group affects its residential integration: The smaller the proportion of immigrants, the higher the group's residential integration (Langberg and Farley, 1985). Studies on Mexican-Americans indicated that they are slightly less likely than Asian-Americans but

---

*It should be emphasized that indexes of dissimilarity do not reveal residents' feelings about segregated housing. While many African-Americans want to escape segregated housing areas, some undoubtedly have various reasons for wanting to remain in them.

much more likely than blacks to share a neighborhood with whites (Darden, 1990; Massey and Fong, 1990).

Thus the dominant research finding is that African-Americans' index of dissimilarity is much higher than other racial groups'. In the 10, 20, and 60 cities with the largest black populations, blacks with postgraduate schooling lived in more highly segregated areas than Asians with between no and four years of schooling. Furthermore in those same three sets of cities, African-Americans earning $50,000 or more per year resided in more highly segregated neighborhoods than Hispanic-Americans earning between $2500 and $5000 a year (Denton and Massey, 1988).

Racial segregation serves as a vivid, destructive illustration of internal colonialism's conclusion about minority groups' restricted movement. Forced to live in a deteriorating area, members of the African-American and Puerto Rican underclass suffer low-quality housing, a physically unhealthy environment, dangers and tensions produced by high-crime rates, and substandard schooling for their children (Massey, 1990; Massey, Condran, and Denton, 1987; Massey and Eggers, 1990).

In addition, as problems mount, victims of these areas are increasingly likely to be subjected to racial stereotypes that emphasize "crime, family disruption, and dependency" (Massey, 1990: 353). Citizens, their elected representatives, and government bureaucrats will become increasingly committed to controlling underclass members' "deviant ways." The result will be a hardening of discriminatory practice, with racial segregation for minorities consistently reinforced.

We have considered the significance of housing discrimination. We should also examine how the process develops.

Racist Tactics in Housing

We are now examining racism delivered with a smile, often with a distinct show of courtesy and even deference. Investigations have found that realtors selling homes to blacks have often invested less time and energy with them or steered them to restricted locales.

Research on this topic has used what are called "fair housing audits," in which a black couple and a white couple with comparable incomes and credit ratings, and seeking similar residence requirements contact the same set of realtors and are shown houses or apartments. With this technique, investigators are able to determine whether or not differences occur in white and black couples' treatment. Robert Weink and associates (1979) pioneered this use of testers, studying real-estate activity in 40 large cities throughout the country and finding that discrimination against African-Americans appeared in both rental housing and home sales. The investigation concluded that black clients had a 50 percent chance with houses and a 70 percent likelihood with apartments of encountering discrimination.

Realtors have discriminated against black clients in various ways. The body of research using testers seeking to rent has indicated that racial discrimination against African-Americans occurred with respect to the number of available units, number of units offered for inspection, and length of waiting list. For home buying black testers received less time, more limited information about houses in higher price ranges or more select neighborhoods, less discussion about financing, fewer house showings, and more discourteous or rude treatment, such as canceling appointments or showing up late for them (Leigh, 1989: 74–75).

A major factor in housing discrimination has been the issue of steering clients toward particular residential areas (Galster, 1990). Research in Boston indicated that the most significant consideration seemed to be the prospective residential section—in particular, whether or not it was currently an all-white area or one undergoing racial transition. In the latter case, African-Americans were much more likely to be shown housing. This research suggested that the primary cause of housing discrimination against blacks was agents' catering to their white clients' racism (Yinger, 1986).

Not surprisingly blacks are more attuned than whites to racial discrimination in housing. When in 1990 a national survey team asked Americans whether blacks have as good a chance as whites in their community to get any housing they could afford, 75 percent of whites answered affirmatively. Among blacks the figure was a much lower 47 percent (Gallup and Hugick, 1990).

Besides steering, realtors sometimes use a less subtle technique—"blockbusting." Once a few black families have moved into a residential area, a realtor can exploit home owners' racial and financial fears, suggesting by telephone, mail, or visits that the neighborhood is starting to deteriorate rapidly, becoming a distasteful and dangerous place to live, and that they had better get out before their property becomes nearly worthless. Successful blockbusting campaigns can transform an all-white to an all-black neighborhood in just a few years (Galster, 1990a).

The success of such tactics suggests that in order to avoid living near African-Americans, many whites readily leave an area when blacks move into their neighborhood. One study conducted in the greater Cleveland area with data from the years 1970 to 1980 concluded that two factors determined whites' departure—their desire to live in racial segregation and the percentage of African-American residents in the district. In locales that were 2 percent black, racially motivated departure occurred only among whites strongly wanting to live apart from blacks. In contrast, for whites with a mild desire for residential segregation, no such departures occurred until blacks represented 47 percent of the neighborhood. Any district with half its population black rapidly lost at least 25 percent of its white residents (Galster, 1990a).

Recent data have also addressed this issue. When in 1990 a national survey team asked nonblack Americans whether they would leave if "large numbers" of black people entered their neighborhood, 8 percent of the sample indicated that they definitely would move and an additional

18 percent concluded that they might. While the 26 percent demonstrating at least some likelihood of moving was down from the 1978 total of 51 percent (Gallup and Hugick, 1990), the recent figure suggests that a substantial proportion of whites remains vulnerable to the blockbusting tactic.

Along with many citizens and realtors, bank officials often support racist policies. A study by the Federal Reserve System indicated that banks and savings institutions in the Boston area were discriminating racially in the awarding of mortgages. After income, property values, and other nonracial factors were taken into account, a sharp difference remained between the percentage of mortgages granted in white and in African-American neighborhoods. Other studies had found a similar pattern in Detroit and Atlanta (Gold, 1989). Earlier research conducted in eight large metropolitan areas throughout the country produced a comparable result (Shear and Yezer, 1985).

The disposition of housing complaints is an important issue. If a local fair housing agency does not vigorously perform its task, then those engaging in housing discrimination are likely to continue the practice. In the period 1979 to 1982 in Houston, for example, there was a lukewarm effort to enforce fair housing standards. The local agency readily dismissed two-thirds of the complaints, often for such trivial reasons as an incorrect signature, and the most frequent resolution was "voluntary" compliance, with the concerned parties informally working out the situation. Of 175 complaints, officials considered only six to be sufficiently serious to refer them to the city's legal department (Bullard, 1990).

Minority-group members sometimes suffer negative experiences affecting their willingness to live in a certain area. For instance, one day in September 1990, Dee Brown, a rookie guard for the Boston Celtics, had parked his car in Wellesley, a wealthy Boston suburb, and was reading mail with his fiancée. Suddenly several policemen approached the car with guns drawn, ordered Brown out, and forced him to lie on the ground. Apparently Brown was mistaken for another black man, who had recently robbed a bank in the area. Brown and his fiancée had considered buying a house in the area, but the incident changed their minds (*New York Times,* 1990). We might wonder how frequently minority-group members have similar experiences convincing them not to live in affluent, largely white residential areas.

Having seen that housing discrimination is a widespread pattern, we can examine a more intimate situation in which it occurred.

What Happened When a Puerto Rican Tried to Sell His House in an All-White Neighborhood

In *Stigma* Erving Goffman suggested that oppressed individuals often experience a "phantom acceptance," which means that the nonoppressed members of the society treat them as normal during superficial contacts as long as the latter support the charade by pretending that they are treated like everyone else. In order to establish the fantasy, oppressed people generally must keep their distance (Goffman, 1974: 122) or, as the phrase goes in this chapter, know their place.

When African-Americans or black Puerto Ricans, the two groups most likely to suffer housing discrimination, attempt to move into a white neighborhood, they are rejecting the phantom-acceptance game. If members of these minorities pursue this course of action, they are likely to encounter discriminatory tactics.

Piri Thomas, a black Puerto Rican, bought two houses on Long Island, New York, from Don Baldwin, his white brother-in-law, and moved into one of them. At first both he and his wife were very happy and proud to have moved from an inner-city neighborhood to the suburbs, and Thomas worked hard getting both houses into shape. Soon, however, he noticed that the neighbors would walk by and stare, often insolently, apparently suggesting that he shouldn't have dared to move into their neighborhood.

Once Thomas overheard a couple discussing the situation. The wife wondered "who could have sold that nigger a house in her community" (Thomas, 1973: 199). The husband replied that it had been Don Baldwin and that the family was Puerto Rican, not black. Thomas was infuriated, noting that in their bigoted minds being Puerto Rican was a notch above being black. Thomas wrote:

> Who makes the damned rules of who's better than who? I looked back at the two so-called Christians walking with their child and just to get their attention, I let out a mighty yell. They looked back and I made a most exaggerated bow and the gesture let them know I'd heard the bullshit that they, white Christian God-loving God-fearing [people], had put down. (Thomas, 1973: 199)

Eventually the Thomases decided to move back to New York City. While local racism played some role, the primary reason was that Thomas was working in the city, and the commute on top of a long day's work was backbreaking. So deciding to sell the houses, Thomas went to see Paul Hendricks, a realtor.

As soon as Hendricks saw Thomas, he tried to steer him toward an area where he indicated some of the best African-American families lived. No, Thomas indicated, he didn't want to buy a house but wanted to sell two of them. Hendricks was puzzled, not recalling what he believed was a black family in that locale. When Thomas mentioned that he had bought the houses from Don Baldwin, Hendricks's face lit up with recognition. "Oh . . . ha ha, of course, you're the Spanish family I've heard about" (Thomas, 1973: 208). Puerto Rican, replied Thomas. They talked some more, and in spite of distinct reservations about Hendricks, Thomas decided to use him as a realtor.

Hendricks brought a few people to see the houses, but none of them were interested in buying. Eventually Thomas himself found a buyer. At first Hendricks was enthusiastic that a buyer had been found. But as soon as Thomas handed him a piece of paper on which the name and address were written, the enthusiasm faded. What was the matter?, Thomas wanted to know. Was the family black? Mr. Hendricks asked.

> "That's right. Why?" I asked knowing the why all the way.
>
> "Really, Mr. Thomas, I don't know quite how to say this, but you certainly must know that Silver View is a, er . . . white community and they wouldn't be happy there . . . and you bought your house from Mr. Baldwin, who's lived here many years and his parents before him, and, well, you being, er . . . Spanish is not like . . ."
>
> My blood was tearing itself up into my eyeball.
>
> "Why don't you just come out with it, fella?" My eyes just stared into his.
>
> "Well, it's not that I mind, but the people, I mean their homes, they've worked hard and they do mind, ah . . . mixing, and well, dammit, I have lived here all my life. Real estate is my livelihood and if I sold to a colored family property in Silver View, well . . . Can you understand? I mean, put yourself in my place?" (Thomas, 1973: 210)

No, he wouldn't do that, Thomas replied. He got rid of the agent and prepared to sell the house directly to the black family, but threatened by members of the all-white Better Civic Improvement Committee, the prospective purchaser withdrew.

The Thomases moved back to New York City, still hoping to sell to whomever they wished. Returning during the winter, they found that the house in which they had been living had been broken into, many windows were smashed, water had been turned on in the unheated house, thereby bursting the pipes, and dog dung had been smeared throughout the house.

Piri Thomas had challenged the phantom-acceptance game by attempting to sell his house to a black couple. Eventually he was defeated by the racist system he attempted to overcome. The couple to whom he had planned to sell his house was intimidated and decided not to buy it, and Thomas was punished when his house was broken into and damaged.

REFERENCES

Araton, Harvey. 1991. "Aaron Speaks with Vincent on Remarks about Hiring." *New York Times* (May 15): B5.

Beauregard, Robert A. 1990. "Tenacious Inequalities: Politics and Race in Philadelphia." *Urban Affairs Quarterly* 25 (March): 420–434.

Braddock, Jomills Henry, II, and James N. McPartland. 1987. "How Minorities Continue To Be Excluded from Equal Employment Opportunities: Research on Labor Market and Institutional Barriers." *Journal of Social Issues* 43: 5–39.

Bullard, Robert D. 1990. "Housing Barriers: Trends in the Nation's Fourth-Largest City." *Journal of Black Studies* (September): 4–14.

Burstein, Paul, and Susan Pitchford. 1990. "Social-Scientific and Legal Challenges to Education and Test Requirements in Employment." *Social Problems* 37 (May): 243–257.

Campbell, Bebe Moore. 1982. "Black Executives and Corporate Stress." *New York Times Magazine* (December 12): 36–39.

Cleaver, Eldridge. 1970. *Soul on Ice.* New York: Dell Publishing.

Cotton, Jeremiah. 1988. "Discrimination and Favoritism in the U.S. Labor Market: The Cost to a Wage Earner of Being Female and Black and the Benefit of Being Male and White." *American Journal of Economics and Sociology* 47 (January): 15–28.

Crystal, David. 1989. "Asian Americans and the Myth of the Model Minority." *Social Casework* 70 (September): 405–413.

Daniels, Roger. 1988. *Asian Americans: Chinese and Japanese in the United States since 1850.* Seattle: University of Washington Press.

Darden, Joe T. 1990. "Differential Access to Housing in the Suburbs." *Journal of Black Studies* 21 (September): 15–22.

Denton, Nancy A., and Douglas S. Massey. 1988. "Residential Segregation of Blacks, Hispanics, and Asians by Socioeconomic Status and Generation." *Social Science Quarterly* 69 (December): 797–817.

Denton, Nancy A., and Douglas S. Massey. 1989. "Racial Identity among Caribbean Hispanics." *American Sociological Review* 54 (October): 790–808.

Falcon, Luis M., Douglas T. Gurak, and Mary G. Powers. 1990. "Labor Force Participation of Puerto Rican Women in Greater New York City." *Sociology and Social Research* 74 (January): 110–114.

Farley, John E. 1987. "Disproportionate Black and Hispanic Unemployment in U.S. Metropolitan Areas: The Role of Racial Inequality, Segregation and Discrimination in Male Joblessness." *American Journal of Economics and Sociology* 46 (April): 129–150.

Feagin, Joe R. 1986. *Social Problems.* Englewood Cliffs, NJ: Prentice-Hall. Second edition.

Feagin, Joe R. 1989. *Racial & Ethnic Relations.* Englewood Cliffs, NJ: Prentice-Hall. Third edition.

Gallup, George, Jr. 1989. *Gallup Report* (August).

Gallup, George, Jr., and Larry Hugick. 1990. "Racial Tolerance Grows, Progress on Racial Equality Less Evident." *Gallup Poll Monthly* (June): 23–32.

Galster, George C. 1990. "Racial Steering in Urban Housing Markets: A Review of the Audit Evidence." *Review of Black Political Economy* 18 (Winter): 105–129.

Galster, George C. 1990a. "White Flight from Racially Integrated Neighborhoods in the 1970s." *Urban Studies* 27 (June): 385–399.

Geschwender, James A., and Rita Carroll-Seguin. 1990. "Exploding the Myth of African-American Progress." *Signs* 15 (Winter): 285–299.

Goffman, Erving. 1974. *Stigma: Notes on the Management of Spoiled Identity.* New York: Jason Aronson.

Gold, Allan R. 1989. "Racial Pattern Is Found in Boston Mortgages." *New York Times* (September 1): A1.

Harvin, Al. 1989. "Judy Johnson, a Star 3rd Baseman in the Negro Leagues, Dies at 89." *New York Times* (June 17): 29.

Hurh, Won Moo, and Kwang Chung Kim. 1989. "The 'Success' Image of Asian Americans: Its Validity, and Its Practical and Theoretical Implications." *Ethnic and Racial Studies* 12 (October): 512–538.

Jaynes, Gerald David, and Robin M. Williams, Jr. (eds.). 1989. *A Common Destiny: Blacks and American Society.* Washington, DC: National Academy Press.

Jiobu, Robert M. 1988. "Ethnic Hegemony and the Japanese of California." *American Sociological Review* 53 (June): 353–367.

Jiobu, Robert M. 1988a. "Racial Inequality in a Public Arena: The Case of Professional Baseball." *Social Forces* 67 (December): 524–533.

Johnson, Gloria Jones. 1990. "Underemployment, Underpayment, Attributions, and Self-Esteem Among Working Black Men." *Journal of Black Psychology* 16 (Spring): 23–43.

Jones, Edward W., Jr. 1973. "What It's like to Be a Black Manager." *Harvard Business Review* 51 (July/August): 108–116.

Jones, Edward W., Jr. 1986. "Black Managers: The Dream Deferred." *Harvard Business Review* 64 (May/June): 84–93.

Kaufman, Robert L. 1986. "The Impact of Industrial and Occupational Structure on Black-White Employment Allocation." *American Sociological Review* 51 (June): 310–323.

Killian, Lewis M. 1990. "Race Relations and the Nineties: Where Are the Dreams of the Sixties?" *Social Forces* 69 (September): 1–13.

Koch, James V., and C. Warren Vander Hill. 1988. "Is There Discrimination in the 'Black Man's Game'?" *Social Science Quarterly* 69 (March): 83–94.

Langberg, Mark, and Reynolds Farley. 1985. "Residential Segregation of Asian Americans in 1980." *Sociology and Social Research* 70 (October): 71–75.

Larwood, Laurie, Eugene Szwajkowski, and Suzanna Rose. 1988. "Sex and Race Discrimination Resulting from Manager-Client Relationships: Applying the Rational Bias Theory of Managerial Discrimination." *Sex Roles* 18 (January): 9–29.

Leigh, Wilhelmina A. 1989. "Barriers to Fair Housing for Black Women." *Sex Roles* 21 (July): 71–84.

Lichter, Daniel T. 1988. "Racial Differences in Underemployment in American Cities." *American Journal of Sociology* 93 (January): 771–792.

Lopez, Felix. 1976. "The Bell System's Non-Management Personnel Selection Strategy," pp. 226–227 in Phyllis A. Wallace (ed.), *Equal Opportunity and the AT&T Case.* Cambridge, MA: M.I.T. Press.

Massey, Douglas S. 1990. "American Apartheid: Segregation and the Making of the Underclass." *American Journal of Sociology* 96 (September): 329–357.

Massey, Douglas S., Gretchen A. Condran, and Nancy A. Denton. 1987. "The Effect of Residential Segregation on Black Social and Economic Well-Being." *Social Forces* 66 (September): 29–56.

Massey, Douglas S., and Nancy A. Denton. 1988. "Suburbanization and Segregation in U.S. Metropolitan Areas." *American Journal of Sociology* 94 (November): 592–626.

Massey, Douglas S., and Nancy A. Denton. 1989. "Segregation along Five Dimensions." *Demography* 26 (August): 373–391.

Massey, Douglas S., and Mitchell L. Eggers. 1990. "The Ecology of Inequality: Minorities and the Concentration of Poverty, 1970–1980." *American Journal of Sociology* 95 (March): 1153–1188.

Massey, Douglas S., and Eric Fong. 1990. "Segregation and Neighborhood Quality: Blacks, Hispanics, and Asians in the San Francisco Metropolitan Area." *Social Forces* 69 (September): 15–32.

Mladenka, Kenneth R. 1989. "Barriers to Hispanic Employment Success in 1,200 Cities." *Social Science Quarterly* 70 (June): 391–407.

Morrison, Ann M., and Mary Ann Von Glinow. 1990. "Women and Minorities in Management." *American Psychologist* 45 (February): 200–208.

New York Times. 1990. "Change of Heart." (September 23): Sec. 8, 10.

Olson, James S., and Raymond Wilson. 1984. *Native Americans in the Twentieth Century.* Provo, UT: Brigham Young University Press.

Pettigrew, Thomas F., and Joanne Martin. 1987. "Shaping the Organizational Context for Black American Inclusion." *Journal of Social Issues* 43: 41–78.

Pomer, Marshall I. 1986. "Labor Market Structure, Intragenerational Mobility, and Discrimination: Black Male Advancement Out of Low-Paying Occupations, 1962–1973." *American Sociological Review* 51 (October): 650–659.

Rhoden, William C. 1990. "The Man Who Has His Own." *New York Times* (May 25): B5.

Sanders, Jimy M., and Victor Nee. 1987. "Limits of Ethnic Solidarity in the Enclave Economy." *American Sociological Review* 52 (December): 745–773.

Schneider, John J., and D. Stanley Eitzen. 1986. "Racial Segregation by Professional Football Positions, 1960–1985." *Sociology and Social Research* 70 (July): 259–261.

Schneider, Mark, and Thomas Phelan. 1990. "Blacks and Jobs: Never the Twain Shall Meet?" *Urban Affairs Quarterly* 26 (December): 299–312.

Shear, William B., and Anthony M. J. Yezer. 1985. "Discrimination in Urban Housing Finance: An Empirical Study across Cities." *Land Economics* 61 (August): 292–302.

Shulman, Steven. 1987. "Discrimination, Human Capital, and Black-White Unemployment: Evidence from Cities." *Journal of Human Resources* 22 (Summer): 361–376.

Sokoloff, Natalie J. 1988. "Evaluating Gains and Losses by Black and White Women and Men in the Professions, 1960–1980." *Social Problems* 35 (February): 36–53.

Steinberg, Stephen. 1989. "The Underclass: A Case of Color Blindness." *New Politics* 2 (Summer): 42–60.

Stolzenberg, Ross M. 1990. "Ethnicity, Geography, and Occupational Achievement in Hispanic Men in the United States." *American Sociological Review* 55 (February): 143–154.

Thomas, Piri. 1973. *Savior, Savior, Hold My Hand.* New York: Bantam Books.

U.S. Bureau of the Census. 1991. *Statistical Abstract of the United States: 1991.* Washington, DC: U.S. Government Printing Office. 111th edition.

Wacquant, Loic J. D., and William Julius Wilson. 1989. "The Cost of Racial and Class Exclusion in the Inner City." *Annals of the American Academy of Political and Social Science* 501 (January): 8–25.

Weink, Ronald E., et al. 1979. *Measuring Racial Discrimination in American Housing Markets.* Washington, DC: U.S. Government Printing Office.

Wong, Bernard. 1987. "The Role of Ethnicity in Enclave Enterprises: A Study of the Chinese Garment Factories in New York City." *Human Organization* 46 (Summer): 120–130.

Yinger, John. 1986. "Measuring Racial Discrimination with Fair Housing Audits: Caught in the Act." *American Economic Review* 76 (December): 881–893.

Chapter
6

Blocking the Gateway: Education

A Brief History of Racial Minorities' Schooling *117*

Controversial Issues in Minorities' Education: Racism or What? *122*

References *136*

*F*ifteen-year-old Mark Jenkins lives with his mother and two of his three siblings in the all-black Cabrini-Green housing project in Chicago in a building that many feel looks like a prison. In 1987 he was caught in a cross fire between two gangs fighting outside his apartment building, and a bullet lodged in his left arm just below the shoulder, shattering the bone. Mark explained, "They sniped me. I couldn't get out of the way in time." It was an automatic rifle, Mark explained. He hears them every day.

Like thousands of young African-Americans enclosed in the inner city, Mark finds himself surrounded by violence and frustration, and he is a member of a statistical category—poor black male teenagers—that is more likely to commit crimes and sell and use drugs than any other population group.

Mark, however, is determined to avoid such an outcome. He has not joined a gang; he goes to school regularly; he sells newspapers on weekends; and he often surprises his mother by cleaning the apartment and then complaining when his siblings mess it up. The violence around Mark, however, has affected him. In 1987 he spent two weeks in a juvenile detention center on assault charges. Later the charges were dropped, with the probation officer reporting that Mark was wrongly accused.

So here is a young person struggling to survive and do well in an environment that makes his efforts difficult or perhaps futile. What role has schooling played? Early on in elementary school, Mark earned good grades but then had to repeat the sixth grade when standardized tests revealed that he was reading at only a second-grade level. In the fall of 1987, he had to transfer to Lincoln Park High School in spite of poor grades because he had become too old for elementary school.

Mark labors at schoolwork but does not do well. It would be miraculous if he did. All his life he has attended poorly financed, overcrowded inner-city schools. Seldom have teachers paid much attention to him; never have they systematically tried to overcome his life-long educational disadvantage. The high school is little help in this regard. While it brings together students from various areas, Mark and other poor African-American students with weak academic backgrounds tend to be separated in classes from students with stronger academic preparation. In the hallways Mark passes middle-class white and black students wearing T-shirts and sweatshirts representing top universities; he imagines that they live in nice homes where they don't need to dodge bullets and explained that they deserve a better life than he because "they're smarter than me." This, according to experts, is not an unusual analysis; while poor delinquents tend to blame society for their plight, poor nondelinquents are likely to blame themselves. Having grown up in an all-black housing project, Mark has had almost no contact with whites and is wary of them. He said that he has no white friends and added, "We don't have nothing in common."

Mark's goals in life are modest by many Americans' standards. He would like to graduate from high school and either go on to college or the navy. He would enjoy visiting New York. But he is failing several of his courses; the circulation manager is cutting back the number of paperboys and so Mark is probably going to lose his job; and several of the local gangs are trying to recruit him (Wilkerson, 1988).

This is not a pleasant, inspiring account. It doesn't coincide with the American dream, emphasizing that hard-working, ambitious young men, in the Horatio-Alger mold, are sure bets for success and glory. What that dream fails to recognize is that for people who are poor and belong to racial minorities, circumstances dictate that the dream either never exists or starts to fade rapidly at an early age. And schools, we find, play a significant role in the absence or death of that dream.

At this point let us consider the role of education in American society and then assess how racism links to educational policy. To begin, in preindustrial life, education had relatively little career significance for most individuals. They pursued a line of work, often that of their parents—

farming, a trade, some activity where expertise developed strictly out of experience and credentials were seldom an issue.

But as society industrialized, literacy and other educational skills became increasingly necessary, or—what was equally important—policy makers and employers perceived them as necessary. For a large proportion of modern jobs, American citizens must have formal educational credentials—high-school certificates, college degrees, and frequently graduate degrees.

Supposedly American society endorses equal opportunity for all citizens. However, given the link between education and job success, equal opportunity is nothing but an abstract principle unless all children, regardless of race and family income, have access to sufficiently high-quality schooling to make them eligible for respectable, good-paying positions. Absence of such schooling produces the opposite condition—a society in which the economic and social status quo is maintained.

In Chapter 5 we noted that the rapid buildup of the urban underclass has been produced by funneling large numbers of black and Puerto Rican citizens into segregated, already poor inner-city areas, causing them to deteriorate much more rapidly. Education is one of the important areas seriously affected by this deterioration. In the American public-education system, local property tax is a prominent contributor to public education, and in poverty-stricken areas, such funding will be minimal, perhaps nearly nonexistent. With local funding for education in such areas very low, the quality will suffer seriously. One can readily argue that institutional racism is embedded in the public-education system: The economic condition of a residential area affects the quality of education its children receive, and racial minorities are disproportionately located in low-income districts, which receive inferior schooling. Figure 6.1 represents the relationship of factors described here.

A close relationship between racism and inferior schooling seems to exist. These are negative conditions that will be discussed frequently in this chapter. But as a foundation for this discussion, it seems necessary to convey some sense of the goals maintained in effective schooling. Consider, for instance, the following statement issued by Cold Spring School, a widely acclaimed elementary school in New Haven, Connecticut.

> The cornerstone of Cold Spring School's program for elementary age children is active, personally fulfilling learning with an emphasis on inquiry and problem solving. The program encourages self-awareness and creativity. This approach to learning challenges children to think as well as act, finding alternative ways to reach solutions. At Cold Spring, children experience school as a stimulating, nurturing extension of family life. Children learn not only cognitive skills but also independence, responsibility, and sensitivity. . . . The sense of community enables them to take the intellectual risks necessary to stretch academically. (Fiss, 1989)

The statement suggests that an effective school provides a supportive environment that develops for children both a highly positive image and

Racial ————————→ Rundown ————————→ Provision ————————————→ Inferior
segregation   inner-city   of limited   inner-city
                                    areas   property tax for   schools
                                                                  school funding

Figure 6.1 Factors Contributing to Inferior Inner-City Schools for Minority Children

understanding of themselves, and also the intellectual and emotional tools to do well in the modern world.

Let's recall internal-colonialist theory, with its emphasis in modern times on dominant whites continuing a colonial system of control. One tenet of the internal-colonialist perspective is the colonial-labor principle, which asserts that racial minorities' work is menial and low-status, simply serving the dominant group's interest. If members of racial minorities are deprived of effective education, their opportunity for achieving good-paying, satisfying work is minimal. Then there is the internal-colonialist principle asserting that racial minorities' culture is invariably inferior. As we see at several places in this chapter, this tendency has appeared in the American education system as efforts to Americanize students, ignoring other cultural traditions.

In the next section, we survey the historical development of racial minorities' education in the United States. The second major part of the chapter assesses some of the complicated, contemporary issues involving the relationship between education and race—issues that address the relevance of internal colonialism to modern education.

A BRIEF HISTORY OF RACIAL MINORITIES' SCHOOLING

Most of the slave states passed laws prohibiting people from teaching slaves to read and write. Masters felt that if they became literate, they might read antislavery newspapers and become discontent or forge passes and escape (Rothenberg, 1988: 191). Still some, like Frederick Douglass, learned how to read. In his autobiography Douglass indicated that while working in Baltimore, he traded bread to poor white boys for "that more valuable bread of knowledge" (Douglass, 1968: 54).

In the mid-nineteenth century, Northern public schools excluded African-Americans. Many towns and cities made no provisions for blacks' education while others, including Boston and New York, supplied modest funding for segregated, highly inferior schools (Bailyn et al., 1977: 503).

Educational discrimination carried into the twentieth century, with inequality greater in the South than in the North. In 1940, for example, data compiled by the U.S. Department of Education from a dozen Southern states indicated that per-pupil expenditures for whites averaged over three times those for blacks, with white students in Mississippi receiving seven times the amount provided to blacks (Jaynes and Williams, 1989: 58). Clearly the Southern states operating under a legally mandated "separate but equal" doctrine were providing educational facilities for African-Americans that were far short of equal.

Through the 1940s and early 1950s, there was an accumulation of legal precedents challenging the "separate but equal" doctrine, but the decisions used cautious wording. Then in 1954 in *Brown* v. *Topeka Board of Education,* the Supreme Court took a bolder step, declaring separate educational facilities for different racial groups to be unequal and inhumane. The following year the Supreme Court stated that school desegregation should proceed "with all deliberate speed" (Bailyn et al., 1977: 1219–1220).

But there was strong opposition from many Southern whites. In 1957, in the first effort to desegregate Southern public schools, Governor Orval Faubus of Arkansas ordered the National Guard to prevent nine African-American students from enrolling in previously all-white Central High School. Each morning the students vainly tried to enter the school and were turned away by the Guard troops. An increasingly large mob of angry whites gathered each day to make certain that the black students were forced to leave. Several times violence broke out, and one day two black reporters were beaten and school windows and doors were broken. President Eisenhower, a former general, saw the situation strictly in military terms—as an insurrection against the federal government. The solution, he decided, was to deploy a thousand riot-trained troops of the 101st Airborne Division. Through the school year, the troops occupied the school, and while violence declined, black students encountered countless incidents where they were mocked and ridiculed (Branch, 1988: 223–224).

School desegregation proceeded very slowly in the South. White groups like the White Citizens Councils threatened and intimidated African-American students integrating schools, and many administrators resisted the law or simply closed their schools. In 1954 in 11 Southern states, the proportion of African-Americans attending classes with whites was less than one-tenth of 1 percent. Ten years later the proportion had only risen to about 2 percent. The factor producing a major increase in desegregated schooling was the 1964 Civil Rights Act, which stated that until compliance with desegregation laws occurred, there would be no federal aid to local school districts. As a result the proportion of black students in formerly segregated Southern schools rose to 18 percent in 1968 and then 46 percent in 1973. Since that time, however, there has been little or no increase in Southern school desegregation (Jaynes and Williams, 1989: 75–76).

An explanation of this pattern seems useful. Many Southern school districts have been organized on a countywide basis, combining cities and suburbs, and thus a mandate to desegregate quickly produced a sharply increased racial mix of students even though whites are more inclined than African-Americans to live in suburban areas. In some Southern school districts, however, separation of cities and suburbs occurs, and as a result blacks, who are disproportionately located in cities, find themselves in largely segregated schools. In the North the latter pattern of school districting has dominated.

In the middle 1960s, the segregated nature of Northern public schools became a publicized issue. As mandated by the Civil Rights Act of 1964, Congress ordered the federal Commissioner of Education to conduct a study of the availability of educational opportunities for Americans of different races, religions, and national origins, and sociologist James S. Coleman was put in charge. What became known as the Coleman Report was a massive study conducted throughout the country involving 600,000 children, 60,000 teachers, several thousand principals, and several hundred school superintendents. One major conclusion was that minority-group students from poor areas could frequently improve their academic performance when they attended schools with students living in affluent districts (Coleman et al., 1966). This conclusion led directly to the practice of busing.

The plan was that busing minority students from inner-city to suburban schools and white students from suburban to inner-city facilities would produce an educational atmosphere that would prove beneficial to racial minorities. Busing has provoked considerable controversy and even violence. Most white parents have not cited integrated classrooms as their reason for opposition. Instead they have claimed to be concerned about the inferiority of inner-city schools, their unfamiliarity with these facilities, lengthy schools days that result from long-distance busing, the danger their children face by entering high-crime areas, and the destruction to community spirit produced by the loss of neighborhood schools (Armor, 1989: 26). One study concluded that nonracial factors like those just cited were at least as important as the racial composition of inner-city schools in predicting white students' refusal to be bused to inner-city schools (Rossell, 1988). Sixteen years after the Coleman Report appeared, James Coleman wrote about busing, acknowledging "the general unpopularity of this policy, greatest among whites, but also true for Hispanics and blacks" (Coleman et al., 1982: 197).

Like African-Americans early Asian immigrants to the United States faced educational discrimination. In nineteenth-century California, the children of Chinese immigrants, the first Asians in the United States, were not permitted to enter public schools even though their parents, forced to pay extra taxes, contributed to them at a higher rate than most residents. To rectify the situation, Chinese immigrants sued to gain access to schools. In 1885 a judge in San Francisco ruled in favor of the Chinese, declaring that there was no legal basis for excluding Chinese children from the public-school system and requiring the city to establish a special school for Chinese children.

Two decades later Japanese immigrants to the San Francisco area were more difficult to satisfy. Compelled to send their children to the Asian school originally established for Chinese children, Japanese parents rebelled, rallying support against school segregation from the Japanese government, which at the time had a strong relationship with top American leaders. In 1907 President Theodore Roosevelt temporarily resolved the situation by negotiating with the Japanese government a "gentleman's agreement" whereby the segregation policy would be removed if the Japanese government agreed to block the flow of immigrants competing with Californians for jobs (Hsia, 1988: 11–12).

Since the second decade of the twentieth century, Asian-Americans have been very successful educationally, surpassing whites in the number of years of schooling completed. Curiously racism contributed to this success. Beginning with the Chinese Exclusion Act of 1882 and continuing with the Immigration Act of 1924, restrictive legislation relieved pressure on local Asian-American communities previously forced to absorb new immigrants, permitting funds that would have been used to help new arrivals to be invested in children's education. In addition, those Asian immigrants allowed to come to the United States were highly selected, with educational qualifications well above the national average.

Prevented from entering most professions and excluded from the relatively well-paid craft industries, Asian immigrants devoted themselves to an ethnic economy centered in agriculture, trade, and services. They strongly encouraged their children to obtain a good education either as a means of entering a profession or of preparing themselves to run the family business more effectively.

With declining discrimination Asian-Americans' level of educational attainment has increased markedly, with a college degree becoming the standard. Continuing emphasis on education, particularly higher education, seems to be the rational response of people who are less involved in ethnic industries than in the past, who cherish professional careers, and recognize that in modern times these positions are unobtainable without appropriate degrees (Hirschman and Wong, 1986).

Mexican-Americans have been much less successful educationally. Early in this century, education officials classified Mexican immigrants as farm laborers and decided that for them and their children schooling was a low priority. Language also played an important role in impeding their educational advancement. With Spanish as their first language, young Mexican-American children often found themselves falling rapidly behind children whose native language was English. Evaluated by IQ tests given in English, Chicano children were often classified EMR ("educable/mentally retarded") and were placed in lower tracks that prepared them for low-level jobs requiring minimal formal education. Mexican-American children whose parents had a fairly high level of education and used English in the home were more likely to do well in school. Until at least the early 1970s, the principal response to this language problem made by many school officials was a blaming-the-victim action—establishing a "no-Spanish" rule for Mexican-American students. Caught speaking Spanish at school, they were punished. As internal-colonialist theory indicates, such a move was a clear assertion of the inferiority of the Spanish language and created considerable resentment among Chicano students. Not surprisingly in 1974, the U.S. Commission on Civil Rights concluded that the curriculum in Southwestern schools did not meet Chicano students' needs; it effectively served just one group—white, middle-class, English-speaking children (Simpson and Yinger, 1985: 342–345).

For over three decades, Puerto Rican children have been having serious difficulties in the American public-school system. A 1958 study indicated that two major sources of children's difficulties were language handicaps and ineffective relationships between teachers and parents. The report concluded with 23 recommendations, many stressing closer personal attention to the individual child and much greater contact with children's parents. A decade later a nationwide conference on Puerto Rican education indicated that instead of improving, problems were worsening. The trend continues. In New York City, for example, the performance of Puerto Rican children is currently poor on standarized tests and the high-school dropout rate is alarmingly high, about 60 percent (Fitzpatrick, 1987: 141–142).

From the early colonial era until well into the twentieth century, Native Americans have faced a criticism highlighted by internal colonialism—that they have suffered from an inferior cultural tradition. As we noted in Chapter 3, many officials believed that the most efficient means of Americanizing Native-American children was to send them to boarding schools where they could be systematically "civilized." This sometimes brutal, often humiliating practice was never particularly successful, and it ended during the 1920s.

Native-American children generally fall below national averages on standardized tests. At the third-grade level, they are about one year below the national average, and that margin increases to two years for high-school students. What factors produce this result? Researchers have indicated that the environment in which children develop plays a major role. Frequently their families offer limited effective preparation for school performance; many Native-American parents are illiterate or minimally educated and speak little or no English. In addition, communities in which the children live provide mixed messages about doing well in school and seeking success in "the white world" (Fuchs and Havighurst, 1972: 118–135; Simpson and Yinger, 1985: 348–351).

Recent figures show that among people over age 25, Asian–Indians obtain more schooling than any other major ethnic or racial group, including whites. While 51.9 percent of Asian–Indians completed four years of college or more, the figure for whites was 20.5 percent. Four Asian-Ameri-

Table 6.1   WHITES' AND RACIAL MINORITIES' AMOUNT OF SCHOOLING

Group	Number of years in school for people aged 25 or more[1]		
	Less than four years of high school	Four years of high school but no college degree	College degree or more
Asian-Indians	19.9%	28.2%	51.9%
Chinese-Americans	28.7%	34.7%	36.6%
Korean-Americans	21.9%	44.4%	33.7%
Japanese-Americans	18.4%	55.2%	26.4%
Whites	23.0%	56.4%	20.5%
Vietnamese-Americans	37.8%	49.3%	12.9%
African-Americans	36.6%	52.8%	10.7%
Native Americans	44.2%	48.1%	7.7%
Mexican-Americans	59.3%	34.1%	6.6%
Puerto Ricans	59.7%	33.8%	6.5%

[1]Figures in this table come from the 1980 Census of Population.

Note: The higher a group appears in this table, the greater the proportion of the group with a college degree or additional education. Thus it is apparent that four Asian-American groups have been more successful in obtaining higher education than whites, who, in turn, have graduated a higher proportion from college than Vietnamese-Americans, African-Americans, Native Americans, Mexican-Americans, and Puerto Ricans.

Source: U.S. Bureau of the Census. *Statistical Abstract of the United States: 1981*. Table 44; U.S. Bureau of the Census. *Statistical Abstract of the United States: 1991*. No. 44.

can groups had a higher college-completion percentage than whites while the other racial minorities examined in this text fell below the average for whites (U.S. Bureau of the Census, *Statistical Abstract of the United States: 1981*. No. 44; U.S. Bureau of the Census, *Statistical Abstract of the United States: 1991*. No. 44). Table 6.1 provides more detailed information about different racial groups' amount of schooling.

In the following section, we examine a number of topics involving race and education.

CONTROVERSIAL ISSUES IN MINORITIES' EDUCATION: RACISM OR WHAT?

Recall the two points about the relationship between education and the internal-colonialist perspective raised at the beginning of the chapter. Racial minorities traditionally have been forced to perform menial, low-status work and also have been labeled culturally inferior. In this section both issues frequently arise as we examine racial minorities' access to education and organizational policies affecting schooling.

Opening the Gate: Racial Minorities' Access to Education

We analyze two policy topics here—affirmative action and school desegregation. In both areas people feel strongly and raise arguments to support their respective positions.

Affirmative Action in Education   Affirmative action is a government-supported directive requiring employers and schools to develop timetables and goals for increasing employment and educational opportunities for women and minority-group members. Roots of affirmative action appear in the Civil Rights Act of 1964, an executive order issued by President Lyndon Johnson in 1965, and a Labor-Department statement produced in 1970.

Supporters of affirmative action stress that this policy is traditionally American, representing our culture's emphasis on equal opportunity by helping to remedy historical disadvantages suffered by racial minorities in access to education. One team of writers noted that until the Civil Rights Act of 1964, there was "a legally sanctioned and pervasive system of discrimination" against blacks and other racial minorities (Wigdor and Hartigan, 1990: 12). African-Americans and other racial minorities are especially disadvantaged because unlike many of the white immigrant groups arriving in the nineteenth and early twentieth centuries, they seek educational advancement in a highly competitive time period against majority-group members whose educational preparation has often been better than theirs.

Affirmative action can offset some subtle racist practice, the advocates emphasize. For example, interviewers for college or graduate programs might claim that certain personality factors are the basis for dismissing some minority candidates, but in many cases such observations are nothing but coded references to the candidates' race.

A final point stressed by advocates is that goals and timetables for affirmative action are not rigid. Goals need not become quotas specifying that an exact number of a certain minority must enter an upcoming college class; affirmative-action procedures are flexible guidelines but nonetheless guidelines to be taken seriously.

Like proponents of affirmative action, opponents might begin by stressing that theirs is the traditionally American position because it emphasizes that individuals must succeed in a competitive situation on their own, without governmental intervention.

One issue opponents raise is that goals might not start out as quotas but that over time they inevitably harden into them, and a quota system favoring minority educational candidates represents reverse discrimination. The claim about reverse discrimination, in fact, is the central concern expressed by opponents of affirmative action. They feel that this policy establishes two classes—those who benefit from affirmative action and those who do not. According to opponents this arrangement presents two major problems. First, its two-part division is impractical. Why, for instance, should Chinese-Americans and Japanese-Americans who, in spite of discrimination, have done very well educationally benefit from affirmative-action programs? On the other hand, what about poor white males? They are judged solely on the basis of their ethnicity and sex, and no consideration exists for the fact that they are just as clearly victims of poverty as members of racial minorities. Second, the system undermines the time-honored American tradition of judging people by their individual level of success. Affirmative action reestablishes the infamous "separate but equal" doctrine of the *Plessy* v. *Ferguson* case (Blits and Gottfredson, 1990: 9–10). When people are judged as members of separate categories, opponents argue, inequality—in this case reverse discrimination—is inevitable.

Finally opponents of affirmative action indicate that not even the supposed beneficiaries gain from it. Since members of racial minorities receive an unfair advantage, their qualifications will always be suspect, and they might even have some doubts about themselves.

The majority of Americans appear to oppose affirmative action. For example, in 1988, when a survey team asked adult Americans whether minorities should have preferences in college admission, 76 percent opposed such a policy (Media General-Associated Press Poll, August 1988).

Conflict theory, the body of theory to which internal colonialism belongs, emphasizes that there will invariably be a struggle for scarce resources, and certainly affirmative-action policies are a clear case in point. While one might feel compassion for white students whose test scores and grades must be better than minority-group members to be accepted in select colleges or universities, one should appreciate historical conditions that produced the current underrepresentation of many racial minorities and recognize that justice demands compensation for those conditions.

Actually one major racial minority—Asian-Americans—bears a unique relationship to affirmative action. Because of special historical conditions, some of which we have discussed, they have been unusually successful educationally, sometimes too successful from education officials' point of view. In some high-level education programs, a substantial portion of eligible Asian-American students are rejected. In spite of scores very similar to whites on the Standardized Aptitude Tests and comparable levels of participation in such nonacademic areas as sports and artistic activities, Asian-Americans' acceptance rate at Brown, Harvard, Princeton, and Stanford have been only about 70 percent of whites' rate (Bunzel and Au, 1987: 53–56). At such colleges Asian-Americans gain acceptance in greater proportion than their numbers in the population but, in spite of comparable levels of achievement, receive proportionately fewer places than whites.

Desegregation and Racial Equality   In 1988, when survey specialists asked a national sample of Americans whether school integration had improved the quality of education received by African-American students, 55 percent said yes, 29 percent said no, and 16 percent didn't know (Gallup and Elam, 1988: 39). Yet a recent study conducted in Montgomery County, Maryland, concluded that when permitted to choose their children's elementary school, whites generally preferred schools with a low proportion of minority students (African-American, Hispanic-American, and Asian-American) while minority parents usually chose minority-dominated schools. Both sets of parents seemed to want schools where their children would have classmates of similar racial and socioeconomic background (Henig, 1990).

Whether or not people support school integration, it is hardly a cure-all for racial minorities' educational problems. Derrick Bell, Jr., indicated that racism has been widespread in desegregated schools, reflected most significantly in the continuing wide gap in academic performance between African-Americans and whites (Bell, 1984). A review of the hundreds of studies on school desegregation suggested that modest gains in African-Americans' performances on standardized tests and in school grades result from one to two years in interracial schools (Jaynes and Williams, 1989: 373–374).

Braddock, Crain, and McPartland (1984) contended that the narrow relationship between school desegregation and blacks' academic performance has received too much attention. They examined ten major studies on the connection between segregation in schooling and segregation in other basic activities and concluded that besides short-term academic performance, segregated schooling affected students' lives in other important ways. Black students who attended desegregated elementary or secondary schools were more likely to enter integrated colleges, to complete those programs, to have white social contacts and friends, to work in desegregated businesses, and to live in integrated housing areas. The researchers concluded that "desegregation puts majorities and minorities together so that they can learn to coexist with one another, not so that they can learn to read" (Braddock, Crain, and McPartland, 1984: 260).

While African-American students recognize possible advantages of attending largely white colleges and universities, they often want to immerse themselves in black culture and study with black students and teachers. This outlook is particularly strong among some middle-class black students who attended largely white high schools. A senior at Howard University, an elite black school, stated, "My white friends from high school tried to talk me out of going to Howard. But I'd never had a black man teach me before, and when it happened, it made me feel kind of proud" (Alterman, 1989: 63).

Currently some black students are turning to black colleges because of racial tension at integrated schools and universities. According to the National Institute against Prejudice and Violence, between 1985 and 1990, 300 incidents of racial harassment or violence occurred at American colleges and universities. Kharis McLaughlin, a Boston guidance counselor who works with African-American students, explained that such incidents can have a significant effect. Following a trip with a group of black students to the University of Massachusetts at Amherst, where an outbreak of violence by whites against African-Americans had occurred several years earlier, she explained, "Some students were a bit fearful. Whether it's right or wrong, these things will sway people if they perceive a danger" (Wilkerson, 1990: A1). While racist incidents have deterred some African-American students from attending integrated colleges, about 80 percent of them enter such schools. Reginald Wilson, a senior scholar at the American Council on Education, indicated that "the chilly climate" in integrated colleges has kept some African-Americans away but that "it's not the parting of the Red Sea. There is not a flood of people leaving white schools" (Wilkerson, 1990: B10).

In many integrated colleges, minority-group members now engage in voluntary segregation. Rapid growth of racial and ethnic studies departments, separate dormitories, and racial and ethnic consciousness organizations has encouraged this trend. At the University of California at Berkeley, where minorities compose 55 percent of the enrollment, racial and ethnic organizations are highly specialized. For instance, if students have the appropriate combination of racial or ethnic status and career interest, they can join the Asian Business Association, the Black Sociology Student Association, or the Hispanic Engineering Society. Strong differences of opinion exist about whether separation is desirable (DePalma, 1991). On campuses people debate whether a largely separate existence strengthens minority students' self-image and performance, or fosters suspicion and antagonism among different racial and ethnic groups. Can members of college and university communities establish a middle ground, nurturing both the solidarity of individual racial and ethnic groups, and relations across racial and ethnic lines?

Besides the problems in access to schooling, educators feel that racism in schools is apparent when there is a careful examination of the actual programs.

The Terrible Twins: Racism and Alienation in School Policy

Florence Grier, the Sacramento community organizer who was discussed in Chapter 4, expressed frustration about school desegregation, noting that her all-black neighborhood had lost its junior-high school. She observed, "I'm so frustrated and disillusioned with the whole integration bit. A lot of mothers are beginning to complain. Because what are the kids getting? They can't read. I have people coming to me saying, 'Let's organize and bring our kids back here and demand quality education. Quality teachers' " (Blauner, 1989: 192).

As we have already noted, different opinions exist about the desirability of school desegregation, but everyone concerned about education recognizes the importance of high-quality schooling. Conditions that systematically prevent quality education for minority children are racist, or, at least, institutionally racist.

We examine two topics that involve race and racism and that significantly affect educational policy.

Minority Subcultures and Education The internal-colonialist perspective emphasizes that dominant whites declare racial minorities' cultures inferior. As a specialist in curriculum and instruction and a frequent observer of urban teachers, Carl A. Grant became convinced that white, middle-class students entering the teaching profession often have an unconscious belief in the superiority of white, middle-class cultural standards. For example, Grant observed a sixth-grade teacher, who was providing a lesson on topic sentences, telling his class of primarily African-American students that having heard rap music, he was convinced that it wouldn't help them learn the English needed to get and keep good jobs. Grant wrote, "The students silently tuned out this teacher and whatever instruction he might have offered on topic sentences. Had he introduced the lesson by using the words from rap songs to write a paragraph, the students would have remained interested" (Grant, 1989: 766).

Bilingual schools exist, and some of them have been very successful. For instance, in New York City, Public School 84 has provided alternate-day immersion in Spanish and English for both Hispanic and non-Hispanic children. Language itself is not taught but learned through informal classroom activities encouraging social interaction (Morison, 1990). In the Rock Point school, located on a Navaho reservation, students encounter both languages in all grades, with children gradually exposed to increasing amounts of English to help prepare them for participation in the outside world. The amount of class time conducted in Navaho declines from about two-thirds in kindergarten to 10 to 15 percent in junior high and high school (Holm and Holm, 1990).

Whether they are educators or not, Americans sharply disagree about racial minorities' rights to seek cultural diversity in schools. Proponents suggest that keeping African-American music or the Spanish language out of the curriculum represents a racist display—the assertion that these cultural traits are inferior. Opponents of cultural diversity disagree, saying that they are not being racist but simply focusing on elements of the mainstream culture.

Asian-Americans' educational progress has hardly helped those arguing for cultural diversity. People of Asian-Indian, Chinese, and Japanese heritage currently obtain higher percentages of high-school and college graduation, test scores, and prestigious prizes (such as winners in the Westinghouse Science Talent Search to identify the top 40 science students in American high schools) than whites. These accomplishments have occurred with Asian-American students "playing by the rules"—not insisting that educators consider their linguistic or cultural background. People who compare Asian-Americans' and African-Americans' academic accomplishments often conveniently overlook the fact that Asian-Americans have distinct background advantages over African-Americans, other racial minorities, and even many whites. Asian-American students have been more likely than whites to have fathers that graduated from college, attained postgraduate degrees, and have been employed in professional or managerial positions. Compared to whites, Asian-American students have had higher educational expectations and have been more likely to aspire to professional careers (Divoky, 1988; Wong, 1990).

Some researchers have argued that there are serious problems with an educational approach that makes no allowance for participants' varied cultural backgrounds. Janice Hale-Benson (1986) surveyed research on child development in Africa and black America, and concluded that behavioral similarities suggest that African-American children grow up in a culture rooted in African tradition and that when attending school, they must adjust to very different, often contradictory sets of demands.

Like Africans, Hale-Benson suggested, African-Americans are born into an expressive cultural setting, which emphasizes close, emotional contact. Use of language seems different in black culture. At home and in their communities, black children encounter a strong emphasis on black slang and extensive nonverbal communication, and their entire language experience builds around the idea of relationship—children interacting with adults and other children in a vibrant, emotionally and physically active environment. They master this body of skills and then, suddenly, they enter schools which primarily require analytic more than relational skills, written more than verbal expression, and much more constricted physical movement than previously experienced. What's the result? They are likely to receive such labels as "learning disadvantaged" or "hyperactive" and are destined to fail in the school system. Other researchers have reached similar conclusions (Abarry, 1990; Willis, 1989).

Hale-Benson's theory has been extensively criticized, with some scholars suggesting that her description of African-American children implies intellectual inferiority to whites (Hacker, 1989: 68) and fails to grasp the intellectual and personality diversity among African-Americans or, in fact, within any racial group. Dorothy S. Strickland, a professor of education at Teachers College, Columbia University, declared, "We may be pushing an Asian child too hard simply because we expect him to excel in science and he may be drawn to poetry and music while the black child may be the budding scientist" (Berger, 1988: B4). Controversy reigns on this topic. There is disagreement about the effects of special school programs on different racial minorities and also diverse opinions about the rights of racial minorities to make such a demand.

On the last point, African-Americans and members of other racial minorities who want quality schools to prepare their children for effective participation in the mainstream economy, and simultaneously want some of their own cultural elements—for instance, their literature, poetry, and music—featured in the education system are simply seeking full cultural equality with whites. After all, many whites are able to experience a combination of both integration is some spheres of life and self-segregation in others—choosing where to work, live, and play. As the dominant group, whites have had more personal options and have also possessed the power to control racial minorities' range of choices, including the content of school programs (Hacker, 1989: 68).

Hopefully an increasing number of Americans now realize that a nation that incorporates cultural contributions of various racial and ethnic groups into its educational programs not only acknowledges its diverse membership but in the process enriches all students.

Leaks in the Pipeline   At critical points in the educational pipeline, African-American, Mexican-American, Puerto Rican, and Native-American students drop out. Smaller proportions of these groups than either whites or Asian-Americans complete high school, enter college, complete college, enter graduate school, attain graduate degrees, and enter the teaching profession at all levels (Blackwell, 1989; Haberman, 1989; Lang, 1988). Marvel Lang, a specialist on minority participation in higher education, pointed out that while equal educational opportunity has been a national policy since the late 1960s, most primarily white colleges and universities did little until the 1980s to ensure equitable access and retention of black students. Lang noted, "Thus, the burden of historic exclusory and discriminatory racial practices are still being felt by black students attending predominantly white institutions. In practice, too few black students are being enrolled and too few graduating from these institutions" (Lang, 1988: 8). This position asserts that the failure of administrators at white-dominated colleges and universities to take necessary steps to recruit and graduate a substantial number of African-American students represents a clear illustration of institutional racism.

Institutional racism in higher education is a major issue. In the past two decades, changing governmental policies toward educational aid have disproportionately affected racial minorities, notably African-Americans. Between 1975 and 1986, outright grants as a percentage of total financial aid declined from 80 percent to 46 percent of financial aid while loans increased from 17 percent to 50 percent of the financial-aid package. For two reasons the change has probably reduced African-Americans' college-going chances more than whites'. First, the reduction in outright grants seems to have had a greater impact on African-Americans, because at an equal level of family income, black families are more vulnerable to unemployment and have fewer sources of wealth (economic assets such as stocks, bonds, and real estate). Second, African-Americans are less likely than whites of comparable family income to seek government loans for education. It is probable that a major factor contributing to this greater reticence is that African-Americans perceive more economic vulnerability than whites—because of the history of discrimination against them,

their more limited chances of obtaining good jobs, and the smaller proba-
bility for promotion—and so they are less inclined than whites to take a
chance and seek a government loan (Jaynes and Williams, 1989: 343). On
the surface federal government cuts in grants and an increased emphasis
on giving loans to college students would appear to be color-blind developments, but with a little investigation it becomes apparent that these funding cuts disproportionately discriminate against blacks—thus another case
of institutional racism.

Consider an additional condition encouraging leaks in the pipeline.
When colleges and universities have a small proportion of minority faculty, two factors promote an arid climate for minority attendance. First,
since minority faculty members are among the major recruiters of minority students, their absence deprives a school of this important recruiting
resource. In addition, minority students are less inclined to apply to a
college with few minority faculty members, because students recognize
that a small number of minority faculty suggests that the particular school
is no more than modestly committed to equal opportunity for minority
groups (Epps, 1989: 24). Thus the following statistics are instructive. In
American higher education, whites represent about 90 percent of the
teaching force. Asian-Americans comprise about 3.9 percent, African-
Americans about 1.7 percent, Hispanic-Americans 1.7 percent, and Native
Americans about 0.3 percent (Blackwell, 1989: 8). Once minority students
enter a particular school, various factors affect their success. One of these
factors is mentoring.

James Blackwell (1989), a leading authority on the subject, indicated
that **mentoring** is a process by which people of higher rank and achievement instruct and guide the intellectual or career development of less-
experienced individuals outside of classrooms. Through mentoring, students obtain extensive knowledge of the mentor's field and also receive
emotional support and stimulation to consider entering the field. Blackwell's impression is that faculty members seeking to become mentors
often want to reproduce themselves, thus subconsciously or even consciously choosing individuals whose social characteristics, including race,
ethnicity, and sex, are similar to their own (Blackwell, 1989: 11). With
small or even tiny percentages of minority faculty at most colleges, minority students have little or no opportunity to benefit from the unique
opportunity provided by mentoring.

Does the absence of mentoring represent racism? The answer, it
seems, depends on one's perspective. Certainly it would be unrealistic to
accuse a white person of racism because he or she chooses to serve as
mentor to an individual who happens to be white. On the other hand, one
can argue that the entire higher-education structure is institutionally racist, continuously failing in various ways, including mentoring, to offer
equal opportunity to racial minorities.

How can faculty members of a college or university respond to their
school's underrepresentation of minority-group members? In the spring

of 1990, Derrick Bell, Jr., an African-American professor at Harvard Law School, took a decisive position on this issue. Bell noted that at the time he was one of 61 tenured faculty at the Law School, including three African-American men and five women: There were, however, no African-American women. Until Harvard Law School offered a tenured position to a black woman, Bell declared, he would take a leave without pay. He couldn't afford a year without salary, Bell said, but added, "I cannot continue to urge students to take risks for what they believe if I do not practice my precepts" (Butterfield, 1990: A1).

From discussing upper-levels of education, we shift to the opposite end of the age continuum and finish the chapter with a crucial issue—alienation and race in children's education.

Ghosts in the Classroom

In this section we take a detailed look at how minority children suffer institutional racism in the schools and often become victims of a self-fulfilling prophecy designating them as inferior. We also examine some more optimistic material, which discusses successful schools or programs that educators, parents, and children have sometimes produced.

For minority children going to schools where the learning process is ineffective, the point about the self-fulfilling prophecy is particularly relevant: It is hammered home to the majority of them that they are "disadvantaged"—that it is unlikely that they will do well in school and that, even if they do graduate from high school, there is little likelihood that they will be able to obtain good jobs. So many of them begin to withdraw emotionally from life at school. They participate minimally in classroom activity, are barely known by their teachers, start skipping school, and eventually drop out entirely—in Nat Hentoff's haunting term become "ghosts" (Hentoff, 1989: 138).

Ineffective public education is a problem throughout the country, in the primarily white suburbs as well as the heavily minority inner-city areas, and inner cities contain white as well as minority students. However, the most overcrowded, poorly funded schools tend to have a high proportion of minority students. With these children the process of stereotyping most readily comes into play. Cultural inferiority and perhaps even limited intellectual capacity are reasons given for early failures in school. These children often become trapped in a self-fulfilling prophecy.

We consider some of the major components affecting the production of ghosts—the physical structure of the school, parents' role, teaching policy, and, finally, the children themselves.

The Physical Structure of Schools It might be possible to produce effective schooling in almost any environment, but pleasant, spacious surroundings certainly help. Often poor, inner-city schools are old, deteriorated buildings that look like fortresses, with chunks of missing ceiling, broken windows, nonfunctioning toilets, collapsing desks, outdated texts, chronic shortages of pencils, chalk, and erasers, and, inevitably, serious overcrowding (Hentoff, 1989: 141; Lukas, 1985: 100–102). One writer observed, "Students in those schools hardly get the sense that education is valued or that *they* are valued. And the same message, of course, is delivered to the parents" (Hentoff, 1989: 141). The physical structure, in short, can help convey a negative sense of self to students.

While destroying many current buildings and replacing them with smaller, brighter, less intimidating structures might be ideal, sometimes carefully planned program-oriented changes can compensate for physical disadvantages. If school administrators in old buildings can put the structures in running order and provide teachers with up-to-date books and other basic supplies, schools can be effective environments for learning. Rafael Hernandez School uses an early twentieth-century building in an inner-city neighborhood. It is a so-called "school of choice," to which parents from different parts of the greater Boston community can send their children. Given the age of the building and the neighborhood, one might suspect that it would be unpopular. Quite the opposite: Its highly successful program, where African-American, Puerto Rican, and white children are thoroughly integrated in all programs and expected to learn both languages, has produced a waiting list of children from all three groups (Glenn, 1989).

Parents   When minority parents examine their children's schools, they are likely to be deeply concerned but feel powerless to do anything to improve the situation. For instance, a black man who had been a school dropout in the South had come to New York City, where he had worked various menial jobs and was earning $90 a week. He had a daughter, and he was disturbed to see that each year her test scores were falling further and further behind the average for her age. He could visualize his daughter's future being as bleak as his own, and so in frustration he stood up at a board of education meeting to speak.

> The father stared at the variously attentive members of the school board. "You people," he said, "operate a goddamn monopoly, like the telephone company. I got no choice where I send my child to school. I can only send her where it's free. And she's not learning. Damn it, that's *your* responsibility, it's the principal's responsibility, it's the teacher's responsibility, that she's not learning."
>
> There was no answer from the board.
>
> "When you fail, when everybody fails my child," the father's voice had become hoarse with grief and frustration, "what happens? Nothing. Nobody gets fired. Nothing happens to nobody except my child." (Hentoff, 1989: 142)

Since parents are not the ones most responsible for education, they seldom are the prime movers. However, they can make a positive contribution when a school is effective. One elementary school in Brooklyn now stays open into the early evenings. As a result working parents who normally are unable to pick up their children come into the school and chat with the teachers. Because of the extra effort produced by school administrators and teachers, parents are also willing to make a greater commitment. Visiting the Brooklyn school, the state commissioner of education was very impressed, and partly as a result of this experience, he decided to launch a pilot project in which ten elementary schools in poor areas would become year-round centers of education open from early in the morning into the evening seven days a week (Hentoff, 1989: 145).

Psychiatrist James P. Comer's program provides a similar approach. After 22 years of research with black and Puerto Rican children in inner-city New Haven schools, Comer became convinced that such children "are in foreign territory" and that teachers and administrators are seldom aware precisely how students' cultural backgrounds make their adjustment to school life difficult. In New Haven Comer established an inner-city educational program in which parents can provide significant assistance to their children, becoming classroom aides or tutors or joining school governance committees. With parental participation students' needs can be more effectively identified and addressed, and as a result children are more likely to feel a welcome part of the school and confident about their activities in school. In recent years Comer's program has become nationally recognized and has been adopted by over 100 schools in eight states (Marriott, 1990).

The key to Comer's program has been effective parental involvement. Sometimes the means to elicit it is quite simple. At Rock Point, the Navaho school mentioned earlier, the fact that the Navaho language played a prominent part in the school demystified the education process for parents who could speak little or no English and made them much more likely to participate in school-board activities or join parents' committees (Holm and Holm, 1990: 183).

For many minority parents, however, efforts to influence their children's approach to schooling fail to yield positive results. According to John O. Ogbu (1990), poor black parents stressing the importance of education to their children often find themselves confronted by the harsh realities of an oppressive world, making it difficult to convey this message. These parents emphasize that success in school is a prerequisite to success in modern society, but children often see little evidence of such success. They observe parents struggling with low-level jobs, underemployment, and unemployment, and in their children's presence, parents are likely to complain to friends and relatives about "the system" they are encouraging their children to enter. Meanwhile in their neighborhoods, these young people learn about such survival strategies as stealing, drug dealing, and pimping: Norms supporting these strategies emphasize that success is possible without schooling, which is considered part of "the white man's thing" (Ogbu, 1990: 158–159).

Teaching Policy   A key—one might argue *the* key—to effective education is teaching policy. A positive, student-supporting policy makes a good teacher more effective. For both the policy and the individual teacher, the goal is to provide children with an opportunity to develop a positive self-image and the emotional and intellectual tools that permit them to be successful in the modern world. Educational policies frequently discriminate against minority children's pursuit of these goals.

In American public education, the "graded school" remains prominent. Students are expected to master a certain amount of material in a given year. Those who succeed are passed on to the next grade; those who don't will be held back. Since the widespread use of standardized tests began in the 1920s, the system of classification has become more precise: Testers can obtain numerical scores representing intelligence and achievement levels, and as a result students can be classified as gifted, superior, average, below-average, defective, dull, or whatever. Because of general cultural or language backgrounds that have left them relatively unprepared to do well in the American education system, many minority-group members tend to score lower on these tests than whites and thus receive the less exalted, more stigmatized labels. As one educator wrote, "Their labels . . . [become] badges—filed away in cumulative folders to follow them every step of the way through public school" (Cuban, 1989: 783). A self-fulfilling prophecy has been set in motion, and the impact for minority students is often negative.

But as Robert Rosenthal and Lenore Jacobson (1968) demonstrated, self-fulfilling prophecies also can produce positive results. The researchers conducted an experiment at Oak School, a public elementary school in a low-income section of a medium-sized city. The first step was to give all of the 650 children a standard nonverbal test of intelligence. Rosenthal and Jacobson told the teachers that the test would predict intellectual "blooming" or "spurting"—students' rapid intellectual growth. Then at the beginning of the following year, each of the 18 teachers of grades one through six received names of students who would supposedly be bloomers in the year ahead. While the researchers claimed that the list of names reflected test results, names actually had been chosen at random. Thus at first differences between designated bloomers and the remaining children existed only in teachers' minds.

Eventually, however, the teachers produced a self-fulfilling prophecy: They believed the bloomers were superior, treated them as such, and thereby encouraged superior performances from them. After a year these children scored higher on an IQ test than the other children. The difference was especially pronounced among first and second graders. While 19 percent of the regular children gained 20 or more IQ points, 47 percent of the "special" children produced such a gain. For the follow-up year, during which the supposed bloomers no longer had teachers who believed that they were superior, "special" first and second graders lost any advantage shown over their peers. The expected bloomers in grades three through six, however, showed higher scores compared to other children. Thus the impact of the self-fulfilling prophecy took effect more slowly on the older children but lasted longer.

This process unfolds in effective schools. Nat Hentoff, a well-known writer, visited Clara Barton High School in Brooklyn, where the school body is predominantly African-American, Puerto Rican, and Asian-American. He was immediately struck with the way the students carried themselves and spoke, especially to their teachers. Hentoff indicated that at Clara Barton "students looked directly at the teachers when they talked, and whether they were joking or in serious negotiation about an assignment, they were fully involved in the conversation. Their bearing showed considerable self-respect, not arrogance. They were comfortable with themselves, and so they were with others, including adults" (Hentoff, 1989: 137).

A consistent educational policy occurs in the Rafael Hernandez School, which was mentioned earlier. Throughout this school, children of diverse racial, ethnic, and linguistic backgrounds are put together and expected to develop verbal and written proficiency in both Spanish and English. By state law the school can exempt from state testing those students who require bilingual education or special-education services, but because of its policy emphasizing that students share all activities, school officials have not done it. As a result the average test scores are fairly low, but the children are thriving emotionally and intellectually, building an understanding of each others' cultural backgrounds. With all three major groups—African-Americans, Puerto Ricans, and whites—finding their own cultural experiences objects of positive, thorough inquiry, no students feel stigmatized or isolated (Glenn, 1989).

Students: Ghostlike or Alive?   In sociology a prominent concept related to socialization is Charles Horton Cooley's **looking-glass self**—individuals' understanding of what sort of person they are is based on how they think they appear to others. Members of racial minorities in inner-city schools have often received limited positive response from teachers, and thus their sense of self as students is diminished.

In ineffective schools most of class time involves teachers' telling students what to do. For many inner-city students, like Alicia in an all-black Harlem school, classroom knowledge becomes something to which they do not relate. Alicia said, "I'm wise, not smart. I knows what people are thinkin' and what's goin' down, but not what he be talkin' about in history" (Fine, 1985: 47).

Once Hentoff read and discussed poetry with the primarily minority-group children in an inner-city high school, acting against the advice of the regular teacher who had explained that the children weren't interested in reading. At the end he was approached by an extremely shy young woman who asked if he could tell her something more about this Emily Dickinson. Later she told Hentoff that while it was weird, she felt some of the same things that Emily Dickinson had felt so long ago. Then very hesitantly she handed Hentoff some of her poems, indicating that she had never shown them to anyone because she had suspected that nobody would believe she could write poetry. It was the first time that anyone in the classroom had communicated with this young woman in a way that suggested the possibility of interest in her work and, as a result, drew her out of the ghost world.

John Simon is a teacher who regularly accomplishes such tasks. He has taken tough, often delinquent, inner-city, primarily minority-group children and turned them into effective readers, writers, and sometimes college students. Simon indicated that there is nothing special about his approach. It is neither revolutionary, nor does it require a charismatic personality, but it does take time. Simon told Hentoff.

> First of all, . . . you have to listen. When I start working with a child I don't know too well, I spend a lot of time listening to him before I try to suggest a course of study. I have never fallen in with that dumb notion that you have to start teaching from the very first day of class—as if teaching is something that happens in a vacuum without having to take account of where each student is, in his head, on that first day. (Hentoff, 1989: 145)

Such an approach not only provides useful practical information to teachers about their students, but it has the added value of reflecting back to the child an enhanced sense of personal worth as the teacher acknowledges the worthiness of what the child says.

This teacher effectively fought the stigma of racism. Now how does one bottle the prescription for eliminating ghosts in the modern classroom?

REFERENCES

Abarry, Abu Shardow (ed.). 1990. "Afrocentricity." *Journal of Black Studies* 21 (December): 123–240.

Alterman, Eric. 1989. "Black Universities in Demand and in Trouble." *New York Times Magazine* (November 5): 60–63.

Armor, David J. 1989. "After Busing: Education and Choice." *Public Interest* (Spring): 24–37.

Bailyn, Bernard, et al. 1977. *The Great Republic.* Lexington, MA: D.C. Heath.

Bell, Derrick A., Jr. 1984. "The Remedy in *Brown* Is Effective Schooling for Black Children." *Social Policy* 15 (Fall): 8–15.

Berger, Joseph. 1988. "What Do They Mean by 'Black Learning Style'?" *New York Times* (July 6): 84.

Blackwell, James E. 1989. "Mentoring: An Action Strategy for Increasing Minority Faculty." *Academe* 75 (September–October): 8–14.

Blauner, Bob. 1989. *Black Lives, White Lives.* Berkeley: University of California Press.

Blits, Jan H., and Linda S. Gottfredson. 1990. "Equality or Lasting Inequality?" *Society* 27 (March/April): 4–11.

Braddock, Jomills Henry, II, Robert L. Crain, and James S. McPartland. 1984. "A Long-Term View of School Desegregation: Some Recent Studies of Graduates as Adults." *Phi Delta Kappan* 66 (December): 259–264.

Branch, Taylor. 1988. *Parting the Water: America in the King Years, 1954–63.* New York: Simon and Schuster.

Bunzel, John H., and Jeffrey K. D. Au. 1987. "Diversity or Discrimination? Asian Americans in College." *Public Interest* (Winter): 49–62.

Butterfield, Fox. 1990. "Harvard Law Professor Quits until Black Woman Is Named." *New York Times* (April 24): A1.

Coleman, James S., et al. 1966. *Equality of Educational Opportunity.* Washington, DC: U.S. Government Printing Office.

Coleman, James S., et al. 1982. *High School Achievement.* New York: Basic Books.

Cuban, Larry. 1989. "The 'At-Risk' Label and the Problem of Urban School Reform." *Phi Delta Kappan* 70 (June): 780–784.

DePalma, Anthony. 1991. "Separate Ethnic Worlds Grow on Campus." *New York Times* (May 18): 1.

Divoky, Diane. 1988. "The Model Minority Goes to School." *Phi Delta Kappan* 70 (November): 219–222.

Douglass, Frederick. 1968. *Narrative of the Life of Frederick Douglass.* New York: Signet Books. Originally published in 1845.

Epps, Edgar R. 1989. "Academic Culture and the Minority Professor." *Academe* 75 (September–October): 23–26.

Fine, Michelle. 1985. "Dropping Out of High School: An Inside Look." *Social Policy* 16 (Fall): 43–50.

Fiss, Irene. 1989. "Why Cold Spring School?"

Fitzpatrick, Joseph P. 1987. *Puerto Rican Americans: The Meaning of Migration to the Mainland.* Englewood Cliffs, NJ: Prentice-Hall. Second edition.

Fuchs, Estelle, and Robert J. Havighurst. 1972. *To Live on This Earth: American Indian Education.* Garden City, NY: Doubleday & Company.

Gallup, Alec. M., and Stanley M. Elam. 1988. "The 20th Annual Gallup Poll of the Public's Attitudes toward the Public Schools." *Phi Delta Kappan* 70 (September): 33–46.

Glenn, Charles L. 1989. "Just Schools for Minority Children." *Phi Delta Kappan* 70 (September): 777–779.

Grant, Carl A. 1989. "Urban Teachers: Their New Colleagues and Curriculum." *Phi Delta Kappan* 70 (June): 764–770.

Haberman, Martin. 1989. "More Minority Teachers." *Phi Delta Kappan* 70 (June): 771–776.

Hacker, Andrew. 1989. "Affirmative Action: The New Look." *New York Review of Books* 36 (October 12): 63–68.

Hale-Benson, Janice E. 1986. *Black Children: Their Roots, Culture, and Learning Styles.* Baltimore: Johns Hopkins University Press. Revised edition.

Henig, Jeffrey R. 1990. "Choice in Public Schools: An Analysis of Transfer Requests among Magnet Schools." *Social Science Quarterly* 71 (March): 69–82.

Hentoff, Nat. 1989. "Anonymous Children/Diminished Adults." *Proceedings of the Academy of Political Science* 37: 137–148.

Hirschman, Charles, and Morrison G. Wong. 1986. "The Extraordinary Educational Attainment of Asian-Americans: A Search for Historical Evidence and Explanations." *Social Forces* 65 (September): 1–27.

Holm, Agnes, and Wayne Holm. 1990. "Rock Point: A Navaho Way to Go to School: A Valediction." *Annals of the American Academy of Political and Social Science* 508 (March): 170–184.

Hsia, Jayjia. 1988. *Asian Americans in Higher Education and at Work.* Hillsdale, NJ: Lawrence Erlbaum Associates.

Jaynes, Gerald David, and Robin M. Williams, Jr. (eds.). 1989. *A Common Destiny: Blacks and American Society.* Washington, DC: National Academy Press.

Lang, Marvel. 1988. "The Black Student Retention Problem in Higher Education: Some Introductory Perspectives," pp. 3–11 in Marvel Lang and Clinita A. Ford (eds.), *Black Student Retention in Higher Education.* Springfield, IL: Charles C. Thomas.

Lukas, J. Anthony. 1985. *Common Ground.* New York: Alfred A. Knopf.

Marriott, Michel. 1990. "A New Road to Learning: Teaching the Whole Child." *New York Times* (June 13): A1.

Media General-Associated Press Poll. August 1988.

Morison, Sidney H. 1990. "A Spanish-English Dual-Language Program in New York City." *Annals of the American Academy of Political and Social Science* 508 (March): 160–169.

Ogbu, John U. 1990. "Minority and Literacy in Comparative Perspective." *Daedalus* 119 (Spring): 141–168.

Rosenthal, Robert, and Lenore Jacobson. 1968. *Pygmalion in the Classroom.* New York: Holt, Rinehart and Winston.

Rossell, Christine H. 1988. "Is It Busing or the Blacks?" *Urban Affairs Quarterly* 24 (September): 138–148.

Rothenberg, Paula S. (ed.). 1988. *Racism and Sexism: An Integrated Study.* New York: St. Martin's Press.

Simpson, George Eaton, and J. Milton Yinger. 1985. *Racial and Cultural Minorities.* New York: Plenum Press. Fifth edition.

U.S. Bureau of the Census. 1981. *Statistical Abstract of the United States: 1981.* Washington, DC: U.S. Government Printing Office. 102nd edition.

U.S. Bureau of the Census. 1991. *Statistical Abstract of the United States: 1991.* Washington, DC: U.S. Government Printing Office. 111th edition.

Wigdor, Alexandra K., and John A. Hartigan. 1990. "The Case for Fairness." *Society* 27 (March/April): 12–16.

Wilkerson, Isabel. 1988. " 'Separate and Unequal': A View from the Bottom." *New York Times* (March 1): A12.

Wilkerson, Isabel. 1990. "Racial Harassment Altering Blacks' Choices on Colleges." *New York Times* (May 9): A1.

Willis, Madge Gill. 1989. "Learning Styles of African American Children: A Review of the Literature and Interventions." *Journal of Black Psychology* 16 (Fall): 47–65.

Wong, Morrison G. 1990. "The Education of White, Chinese, Filipino, and Japanese Students: A Look at 'High School and Beyond'." *Sociological Perspectives* 33 (Fall): 355–374.

Chapter
7

All God's Children?: Minority Families

*O*n January 25, 1986, Bill Moyers, a well-known newsman, hosted a prime-time, two-hour CBS Special Report titled "The Vanishing Black Family: Crisis in Black America." Viewers were taken into a Newark, New Jersey, housing project for an intimate look at the alleged crisis in the modern African-American family. They saw black teenage welfare mothers with their babies and children, with young fathers sometimes located on the fringe. When asked about their lives, some conceded that if it weren't for welfare, they wouldn't keep having children. One young man who had fathered six children by four women and supported none of them said, "So what I'm not doing the government does." While interviewing, Moyers generally appeared reasoned and nonjudgmental, but several statements seemed to bring him close to losing his temper (Corry, 1986).

Jewell Handy Gresham suggested that beyond the already well-established conclusion that poor African-American families have significant problems, two themes emerged. First, "a picture of 'jungle' immorality and degeneracy" was reinforced. Middle-class, white viewers could look with horrified fascination at these blacks, readily forgetting about many political and economic leaders' well-publicized corruption and immorality, and conclude that these young people were alien and inferior. Second, there seemed to be such "pervasive pathology" that realistically it appeared no intervention could alter the situation. Contributing to this conclusion was a significant omission—the failure to consider the economic and political sources of family crisis among poor blacks. The difficulty, Moyers and others on the program suggested, lay within the African-American family itself. At the end of the program, an older African-American woman delivered the clincher when she said, "If Martin Luther King were alive, he would not be talking about the things I think he was talking about—labor and all that. He would be talking about the black family" (Gresham, 1989: 119).

For many observers of race and poverty in the United States, this CBS program produced a powerful sense of déjà vu. In this chapter we see that a celebrated government-sponsored report in 1965 offered similar conclusions. Neither then nor now have the facts cited about the black family been incorrect. Statistics and studies, to be sure, indicate that serious problems of poverty and fragmentation exist. An effective sociological approach, however, needs to provide a thorough analysis of the sources of these problems.

Treatises that focus on the degenerate quality of black families, or other minority-group families are racist in the tradition described by internal colonialism since they emphasize cultural inferiority of blacks' family structure and, as we see, because they fail to propose practical economic programs that would alleviate or eliminate the problems. The second major part of this chapter indicates that racism lies in both the dominant culture's outlook on racial minorities' families and in the steps taken to overcome crises associated with them.

But before confronting these issues, we briefly examine the history of minority-group families, which begins to reveal why current problems exist.

HISTORY OF RACIAL MINORITIES' FAMILIES IN THE UNITED STATES

Slaves could not enter into binding contractual relationships, and since marriage is a contract, so-called slave marriages were not marriages in a legal sense. These arrangements required their masters' approval, and the masters could also dissolve them. Masters preferred marriages between their own slaves. The primary reason masters encouraged these unions was to perpetuate the slave population, and an owner considered it a waste if his male slave impregnated a woman on another plantation. In addition, if slave marriages involved workers on different plantations, then valuable working time was lost if slaves spent time away from their home plantations. Thus slaves were encouraged to marry individuals on their own plantations, and when this was not possible, masters often sought to purchase the spouse or sell their slave to the spouse's owner.

Frequently slaveholders' economic situations, such as bankruptcy or need for funds, prompted the sale of a slave spouse or child. However, even some owners who were indifferent to their slaves' interests felt that if the slave family remained intact, the man would remain concerned about his family's welfare and was less inclined to rebel or attempt to escape.

The bearing of children was particularly difficult for slave women, who had little or no medical care during pregnancy, childbirth, and afterward. Furthermore they were required to work up to the moment they gave birth. During the week before childbirth, pregnant women picked three-quarters as much cotton as slave women of the same age who were neither pregnant nor nursing. Not surprisingly over half of slave infants died during the first year—about twice the mortality rate for Southern white infants. Survivors received little care from mothers who were kept busy in the fields or household. Until the age of 14, the death rate for slave children remained twice that of white children. In spite of brutal conditions, slave mothers did what they could to stabilize the family and fiercely resisted its division. J. W. Loguen's mother, for instance, had to be tied to a loom when her children were taken from her to be sold.

In slave families men also encountered many restrictions. Unlike free men they could not economically support or protect their families. Frequently masters physically or sexually abused slave wives, and a husband's effort to intervene invariably produced dire consequences, including the possibility of death. In spite of the danger, slave narratives indicate that husbands intervened on behalf of their wives many times.

During the slave era, there were about half a million free blacks. Because they could own property and enter a variety of jobs, including skilled positions, their economic prospects were fairly good and their families tended to be stable. While some of them owned slaves, most of the men were former slaves who had purchased their wives and children. From this group the African-American middle class began to develop.

Some historians suggested that slavery weakened the value of marriage for African-Americans. Once freed, however, they began to marry in large numbers, and in 1917, 90 percent of all black children were born in wedlock.

In the late nineteenth century, racial discrimination made it difficult for most black men to find jobs. For black women, however, less restriction existed, and so even though it was considered a mark of slavery for them to work, many did. In 1900 about 41 percent of African-American women were in the labor force compared to 16 percent of white women. In spite of their poverty, black families in the late nineteenth and early twentieth centuries tended to be stable, with men, especially unemployed men, taking a significant role in domestic tasks (Franklin and Moss, 1988: 127–128; Johnson, 1989: 53–54; Staples, 1984: 218–221). At all income levels, African-Americans endorsed stable, economically self-sufficient families (Parker and Kleiner, 1977; Staples, 1984). Later in the chapter, we examine the forces that have produced major problems in many current black families.

While Native Americans were not slaves, whites also drastically altered their family life. The Native Americans that the early settlers encountered often had considerable tolerance for diverse forms of marriage. Monogamy, polygyny (one man with two or more wives), and polyandry (one woman with two or more husbands) were all acceptable forms of marriage in most societies. Generally polyandry occurred because of unusual circumstances, such as the crippling of an older brother encouraging that man's wife to form an additional marriage with her husband's younger brother, who then served as her chief means of economic support. Polygyny, on the other hand, was fairly common, with more than 20 percent of the tribes of the Great Plains and the Pacific coast engaging in the practice.

Another significant difference between Native Americans and whites was their relationship to the kinship structure, with this issue playing a much larger part in Native Americans' lives. When Native Americans married, the union was more a contract between two kinship groups (clans) than between two people. In addition, the type of kinship system determined significant relatives in an individual's life. Among the Crow, Hopi, and Choctaw people, there was a matrilineal system, in which people traced descent through the mother's kinship structure and the mother's relatives were recipients of prominent rights and obligations. Thus within this system, a boy's father was not considered a significant relative. His mother's brother was his source of authority and instruction, and this man provided food, clothes, shelter, and eventually inheritance.

When European settlers encountered Native Americans, they readily adopted an internal-colonialist standard, designating their customs barbaric and inferior, seldom taking them seriously, and thus not understanding why Native Americans continued to follow cultural patterns that were distinctly non-European. For instance, nineteenth-century missionaries, teachers, and government agents were disturbed that among the Choctaw tribe, fathers seemed unconcerned about providing materially for their own children. When the whites learned that the source of fathers' outlook was the matrilineal system, in which fathers were not economically responsible for their own children but for their sisters', they simply abolished that system. Clans were broken down or eliminated, and the nuclear family became the dominant kinship unit. In addition, a patrilineal system of obligation and inheritance replaced its matrilineal predecessor.

Alien standards abruptly replaced kinship patterns and customs that had existed successfully for hundreds, even thousands of years. Christian morality became the norm for assessment: Government officials did not consider whether or not a custom had historically contributed to individuals' welfare and a tribe's stability. Thus all forms of plural marriage were eliminated, even though polyandry often provided economic provision for a woman or family that otherwise would have had no economic support. On the Pacific coast, the potlatch ceremonies, in which a lavish exchange of gifts occurred, were considered wasteful, heathen activities and were abolished even though these practices validated kinship titles and produced order among these groups (Price, 1984: 246–252).

Unlike African-Americans and Native Americans, Asian-Americans did not suffer forced change in family practices. They were neither slaves nor invaded people. However, their situation was often not easy.

The Chinese Exclusion Act of 1882, which restricted Chinese migrants who were competing against whites for jobs, also prevented Chinese men from bringing their wives and children to the United States. The Immigration Act of 1924 further contributed to the problem, making it impossible for Chinese-American men to have their spouses naturalized. Consequently Chinese men in the United States remained separated from their wives and children for many years (Daniels, 1988: 95–97; Li, 1982: 306).

In the early years of prejudice and isolation, the limited number of Chinese women meant that American Chinatowns largely contained single males. This situation remained until the 1940s when officials permitted Chinese to enter the country in larger numbers than during the previous 60 years.

In Chinese communities individuals or families did not have isolated lives. Most immigrant Chinese belonged to a family association (clan), which had been village-centered in China and originally involved real blood relationships. When the Chinese moved overseas, however, clans tended to broaden their memberships, and in the Chinese communities of many American cities, a single clan tended to dominate, with most residents obtaining membership in that clan and maintaining loyalty to it in exchange for protection and assistance at difficult or dangerous times. While other ethnic groups had organizations for their members, Chinese clans were more intense: Even though members were usually unrelated to each other, they considered these groups to be extended families, and all who belonged to an individual's association were designated "clan cousins" (Kitano and Daniels, 1988: 25–26). In an often violent new land, Chinese immigrants found their clans a major source of both psychological and practical support.

Early Japanese immigrants suffered similar discrimination, with a number of California newspapers agitating in 1905 for laws against their settlement in the United States. Three years later President Theodore Roosevelt negotiated the so-called "gentlemen's agreement," whereby the Japanese government agreed not to issue any more passports to laborers if Japanese-American children in San Francisco could enter the local public schools. The agreement between the two governments was deceptive in its representation of what was supposedly in American citizens' interest. In public statements Roosevelt had claimed that the result would be almost complete blockage of further Japanese immigration. Actually for the next 16 years, female Japanese continued to enter the United States, and by 1930 the female Japanese population, which in 1900 had been 3.9 percent of the Japanese total in the United States, had become 41.1 percent of that total (Kitano and Daniels, 1988: 55–57). Thus, compared to early Chinese communities, Japanese settlements had a smaller percentage of bachelors.

The Japanese, to be sure, suffered intense hardships. In the twentieth century, no other American ethnic or racial group experienced forcible relocation, which happened to Japanese-Americans when they were removed from the West Coast in 1942 and placed in ten so-called relocation centers (concentration camps) during the remainder of World War II. While research did not document systematically the impact of living in the camps on family life, it must have been considerable. Quarters were cramped, and centers were surrounded by barbed wire and patrolled by armed soldiers who in several cases shot and killed individuals they were guarding (Kitano and Daniels, 1988: 61–62).

One eloquent indication of the impact of camp life on individuals occurs when elderly Japanese-Americans living on the West Coast meet each other for the first time. Conversation often begins with the question, "What camp were you in?", and the discussion then proceeds with exchanges of personal camp experiences that are so intimate and detailed that all those who were not in the camps feel excluded (Ima, 1982: 266).

Like Asian-Americans the majority of Mexican-American families entered this country under harsh conditions. Spurred by poverty and political instability, about a half-million Mexicans immigrated to the United States between 1900 and 1930. Working as farm or factory laborers, their jobs were usually unstable and low paying; frequently they found themselves objects of racial hatred or exploitation; and their inability to speak English helped to isolate them (Maldonado, 1982: 172–173).

In this difficult situation, Chicanos tended to find the family a source of strength. One prominent factor encouraging this trend was Spanish culture, which has taught that close personal relationships are at the core of people's existence and that relationships establishing individuals' confidence, sense of security, and identity are those formed within the family. From Spanish tradition Chicanos also adopted the use of *compadres*— individuals who, whether related by blood or not, become ritualized kinship members after serving in ceremonies as godparents at a child's baptism or witnesses at a couple's wedding.

In modern times families play an important role in another way, with Mexican-Americans tending to migrate to areas where relatives live. As young adults Chicanos tend to have a wide range of kin in the vicinity— grandparents, parents, aunts, uncles, and cousins. Research has suggested that the higher the socioeconomic status, the more likely Mexican-Americans will retain close relations with kinship members. In general, however, Chicanos tend to remain in the same area for many years, thus keeping open the distinct possibility of maintaining close contact with relatives (Keefe and Padilla, 1987: 142–143).

Like Mexican-Americans Puerto Ricans use *compadres.* Among Puerto Ricans *compadres* have a deep obligation to provide economic assistance, emotional support and encouragement, and even criticism and suggestions for personal improvement. While the Spanish provided a tradition that helped to solidify family life, they also produced a distinctly negative influence on it. Between 1511 and 1873, Spanish rulers practiced slavery in Puerto Rico. Even though the treatment of slaves was less brutal than in the United States, owners responded to the same economic pressures as did their counterparts in the United States and thus bought and sold slaves with little or no regard for the impact on slave families (Fitzpatrick, 1987: 69–73).

Like African-Americans Puerto Ricans have suffered the economic legacy of slavery. Often caught in the vicious cycle of poverty, they have experienced substandard education, high unemployment, poverty, and family fragmentation. In 1988, 30.8 percent of Puerto Rican families were living below the poverty level compared to 28.2 percent for African-American families, and the proportion of single-parent families with children under 18 was almost the same—52.5 percent for Puerto Ricans and 51.9 percent for African-Americans (U.S. Bureau of the Census, *Statistical Abstract of the United States: 1990.* No. 45, No. 65, and No. 745).

We now move into the present, assessing major problems in minority families and the impact of racism on their development and perpetuation.

MINORITY FAMILIES AND RACISM

In this section we examine two issues that relate to racism: The first concerns a celebrated racist analysis of the minority—primarily black—family, and the second involves current racist outlooks on and programs for minority families.

The Moynihan Report

In 1965 a report titled *The Negro Family: The Case for National Action* appeared. While no individual was listed as author—the Office of Policy Planning and Research, United States Department of Labor received the designation—the public learned that the chief writer was Harvard professor, later New York senator, Daniel Patrick Moynihan.

The so-called Moynihan Report created a furor, because many readers considered it a simplistic indictment of the African-American family and thus African-Americans. William Ryan, whose concept of blaming the victim was discussed in Chapter 3, felt that the document served as a notable illustration of that process. Ryan wrote:

> Moynihan was able to take a subject that had previously been confined to the Sociology Department seminar room . . . and bring it into a central position in popular American thought, creating a whole new set of group stereotypes which support the notion that Negro culture produces a weak and disorganized form of family life, which in turn is a major factor in maintaining Negro inequality. (Ryan, 1976: 64)

Thus, the report emphasized, when African-American families were not economically or educationally successful, the major problem was deficiencies within the African-American culture. The victims—African-Americans—were designated as the source of their own failure. Once again we see the internal-colonialist perspective's emphasis on both a racial minority's supposed cultural inferiority and the necessity for its members to adopt standards of the dominant culture.

Since the Moynihan Report serves as the foundation for this section of the chapter, it seems reasonable to discuss the document in greater detail. The report contained five major conclusions.

First, it emphasized that while the white family had achieved a high degree of stability and was managing to maintain it, the black family, especially the lower-class black family, was highly unstable, with an increasing percentage of female-headed families and a sharp rise in welfare dependency.

Second, the report indicated that slavery had been a major influence on the development of the black family. Along with their cultural heritage and personal rights, slaves were deprived of the opportunity to produce and maintain a stable family. When slavery ended, blacks received liberty but not equality. In particular, black men, widely seen as threats by whites, were systematically deprived of rights, including the right to work. Thus black women became the breadwinners and also assumed the dominant role in family life.

Third, the Moynihan Report claimed that high levels of black unemployment, which have existed since the collection of unemployment data started in 1930, have contributed to the increasing fragmentation of African-American families—a growing proportion of illegitimacy and female-headed families.

Fourth, Moynihan indicated that "the tangle of pathology"—the combined impact of poverty, the absence of fathers, and exposure to delinquency and crime—make it impossible for poor black children, especially poor black males to perform effectively in schools and in the work place.

Fifth, the report concluded that "the case for national action" was clear. The United States needed an effective strategy, and because of the extent of current pathology in the black family, it could focus only one place. Moynihan wrote:

In a word, a national effort toward the problems of Negro Americans must be directed towards the question of family structure. The object should be to strengthen the Negro family so as to enable it to raise and support its members as do other families. (*Office of Planning and Research, United States Department of Labor,* 1965: 47)

At this point perhaps you are wondering why the Moynihan Report deserves so much attention. After all, you might be thinking, the document is now over a quarter-century old and probably forgotten by everyone except the fellow whose book I am presently reading.

Actually the last conclusion is wrong. Discussion—not mere mention but detailed analysis of the Moynihan Report—continues to appear in a variety of sources (See Besharov, Quin, and Zinsmeister, 1987; Blauner, 1989: 41; Brewer, 1988; Cockburn, 1989; Darity and Myers, 1984; Demos, 1990.)

But more significant than these references is the reason why writers on racism and the African-American family continue to provide such analyses. As the opening of this chapter suggests, the plight of poor black families has not improved in the past quarter century. In fact, as Table 7.1 indicates, over the past three decades, there has been an increase in the proportion of female-headed poor black families. Furthermore in 1985, 60.1 percent of newborn African-American children had unmarried mothers. All other major racial minorities had lower proportions of children born out-of-wedlock. For Chinese-Americans the figure was 3.7 percent, for Japanese-Americans 7.9 percent, for whites 14.5 percent, for Mexican-Americans 25.7 percent, for Native Americans 40.7 percent, and for Puerto Ricans 51.1 percent (U.S. Bureau of the Census, *Statistical Abstract of the United States: 1990.* No. 89).

Nobody disputes the statistics. At the national level, the practical necessity is to determine why minority family fragmentation has been so extensive, and then to figure out what measures can alleviate the destructive conditions imposed on black and other poor minority families.

But our agenda is more modest—simply to learn about the relationship between racism and minority families. One way to analyze this topic is to consider four major criticisms of the Moynihan Report. This approach not only provides information about current minority families but also points out the racism frequently found in official, government-sponsored investigations of racial issues.

Four Criticisms of the Moynihan Report and Their Application to Modern Minority Families

The four issues to be discussed are the report's analysis of fragmentation in black families; the role of welfare in the poor minority family; stereotyped minority; especially black families; and de-emphasis or omission of minority families' strengths.

Table 7.1   AFRICAN-AMERICANS VERSUS WHITES:
FAMILY FRAGMENTATION AND POVERTY

| | Female-headed families with children under 18 | |
	African-American	White
1960	22.4 %	8.7 %
1970	29.5 %	7.8 %
1980	46.9 %	13.4 %
1985	51.0 %	15.6 %
1988	48.2 %	15.3 %

| | Families below the poverty level | |
	African-American	White
1959	48.1 %	15.2 %
1966	35.5 %	9.3 %
1970	29.5 %	8.0 %
1975	27.1 %	7.7 %
1980	28.9 %	8.0 %
1985	28.7 %	9.1 %
1988	28.2 %	7.9 %

Note: In 1960 there were 14 percent more female-headed African-American families than female-headed white families. By 1988 the difference had increased to 33 percent. While from 1959 to 1988, the proportion of both African-American and white families below the poverty line declined, a significant gap between the two sets of families has remained.

Source: U.S. Bureau of the Census. *Statistical Abstract of the United States: 1961.* No. 34; U.S. Bureau of the Census. *Statistical Abstract of the United States: 1989.* No. 71 and No. 739; U.S. Bureau of the Census. *Statistical Abstract of the United States: 1990.* No. 43 and No. 748.

Fragmentation of Poor Minority Families   The Moynihan Report concluded that poverty produced "a tangle of pathology" that made it impossible for poor African-American children, especially male African-Americans, to function effectively in schools and in the work world. This image—a tangle of pathology—creates the same sense of jungle immorality and dire hopelessness that Jewell Handy Gresham associated with the 1986 CBS special report on the allegedly vanishing black family.

Besides its negative imagery, the phrase is vague. To understand fragmentation within the poor black family, the analyst needs to move beyond sloganlike phrases and examine concretely how economic conditions adversely affect poor African-Americans. Hopefully in the following pages, we can begin to untangle ideas related to the tangle of pathology.

A useful place to start is Elijah Anderson's study entitled "Sex Codes and Family Life among Poor Inner-City Youths." In a poor inner-city black area, Anderson interviewed prospective and present teenage parents as well as their family members in an effort to understand the process producing an increasing number of out-of-wedlock children.

Anderson suggested that for a young, inner-city black man, members of his peer group tend to be the most important people in his life. As in most young men's peer groups, there is a strong emphasis on obtaining high status. For these young men, good job prospects are remote or nonexistent, and so economic achievement and the status that goes with it are unrealistic. The most available means for achieving high status is sexual—the conquest of teenage girls.

So the teenage boy develops his sexual "game," focusing on his clothes, dancing ability, and, above all, his style of conversation or "rap." Whether the young man is a winner or loser in his peers' eyes depends on the number of sexual conquests he obtains.

If the teenage girl is inexperienced, the boy's game might fool her. But even if she is not fooled, she is vulnerable to his advances. She has her own agenda—the American dream of living with a loving husband and children in a nice house in a pleasant neighborhood. This dream has been nurtured by love songs that she has heard ever since her early childhood and by soap operas, which show affluent, comfortable middle-class housewives.

The dream is sufficiently powerful that when approached by the boy, the girl simply tends to fit him into the dream. If successful at playing the romantic game, the boy knows what is on the girl's mind and exploits the knowledge. He might take her for walks, visit her family, even go to church with her family to show that he is an upstanding young man.

At times even the boy might get caught up in the dream, but then he recalls job prospects for young African-American men in the inner city, and he rejects the idea of becoming the young woman's provider in the middle-class tradition. So he returns to the game, focusing on sexual conquest by playing the role of the "dream man," who appears to plan to marry the girl and live with her happily ever after. A 23-year-old respondent, who had become a single mother at 17, explained that the young man sometimes window shops with the young woman. He points

> in the window, "Yeah, I'm gonna get this. Wouldn't you like this? Look at that nice livin' room set." Then they want to take you to his house, watch some TV. Next thing you know your clothes is off and you in bed havin' sex, you know. (Anderson, 1989: 63)

Peers tend to accord high status to boys who can demonstrate extensive control or exploitation of their girlfriends. To achieve this, the boy is likely to try "to break the girl down" in front of his friends. The girl often accepts this treatment if she feels that it will help promote her dream of marriage and domestic happiness. On the other hand, if she believes that aggression or manipulation better serves her interests, then she follows an appropriate course of action. Each of them has a definite goal in mind and will do what is necessary to achieve it. As one respondent said:

> They trickin' them good. Either the woman is trickin' the man, or the man is trickin' the woman. Good! They got a trick. She's thinkin' it's [the relationship is] one thing, he playing another game, you know. He thinkin' she all right, and she doing something else. (Anderson, 1989: 64)

Ultimately the boy wants to demonstrate that he "has the girl's nose open"—that she is so sick in love with him that he has complete control.

Interestingly at the time when the boy believes that he is achieving this objective, the girl is likely to give up birth control. She accepts what he told her about taking care of her and believes that if she becomes pregnant he will marry her or at least take care of her. She thinks little about the job market or the boy's job prospects; she also underestimates the impact of his peer group. She is in love and the relentless dream of marriage and domestic happiness seems very close.

When the girl becomes pregnant, the boy faces a decision. Should he accept the peer-group ethic of "hit and run," or should he risk the loss of his friends' support by opposing the ethic? Actually he can usually maintain prestige in peers' eyes if he acknowledges the paternity but provides the amount of financial support that he, not the girl, considers appropriate. With the pregnancy the boy's economic situation becomes an even more critical reality. He recognizes that it is difficult simply to support himself. The prospect of maintaining at least two others seems difficult or impossible, especially in light of the peer group's ridicule of settling down.

The young man's economic situation also creates ambivalence for the young woman. Upon giving birth she must decide whether or not to depend wholly upon the father. She might decide that she would be better off financially receiving regular checks from the welfare office instead of occasional support from a young man who is irregularly employed.

Frequently the expectant father decides that his best interest involves leaving the pregnant girl, even if he knows that the baby is his own. His desire for freedom is very strong, and he receives peer-group support. In addition, in a modern economy offering few job prospects, the young inner-city black man is unlikely to have sufficient funds to give him leverage to control the domestic situation, permitting him to "play house" in what he considers an enjoyable way.

Mercer L. Sullivan's (1989) research provides consistent evidence. Sullivan studied young men living in three low-income neighborhoods in Brooklyn, New York. One area contained primarily white, Catholic, third- or fourth-generation descendants of immigrants from Italy and Poland; the people in this district were among the poorest non-Hispanic whites in New York City, but their average income was considerably higher than that of the other two groups. The second neighborhood had predomi-nantly black residents who were first- or second-generation immigrants from the southern United States. The final district was largely Puerto Rican, with a population whose members were first- or second-generation immigrants from Puerto Rico. In the latter two groups, about half the families were living below the poverty level and obtained Aid to Families with Dependent Children (AFDC), the largest government-subsidized welfare program. For the white group, about 12 percent of families were living below the poverty level, and less than 10 percent received AFDC.

Sullivan found that among young men in the three neighborhoods, economic prospects and culture combined to affect their responses to getting a young woman pregnant. Compared to young black men in the study, young white men who got young women pregnant were more likely to marry them. Better job possibilities seemed to be the major factor that produced the stronger inclination to accept marriage. Through family and neighborhood contacts—this is the issue of informal networks in-fluencing hiring discussed in Chapter 5—young white men tended to have fairly stable, decently paying blue-collar jobs that permitted them to set up independent households. In contrast, young black men lacked such contacts and the jobs produced by them, and so they were much less inclined than whites to marry the young women they made pregnant. In many cases, however, black fathers did provide some support for their children.

In addition, culture played a role. Puerto Rican men in the study were as poor as blacks and had equally unpromising job prospects, but coming from a cultural tradition that strongly emphasizes marriage, most of them married the young women they made pregnant. Because the majority were unlikely to find jobs that paid sufficiently well and were steady enough to maintain their families, it seemed likely that many of these marriages would soon end. Most Puerto Rican men, in fact, had come from homes where their fathers had employment difficulties and as a result had left the home when the research subjects were still young children. Earlier in this chapter we saw data on single-parent families that showed Puerto Ricans' rate running slightly ahead of blacks'. Probably over time the economic factor plays a larger role than the cultural one, causing Puerto Ricans' family fragmentation to be statistically similar to blacks'.

In a third investigation, Mark Testa et al. (1989) also found that the dominant issue affecting family fragmentation was the family's economic condition. Examining data from a survey of 2490 inner-city residents in Chicago, this team of researchers found that among African-American, white, Puerto Rican, and Mexican-American respondents the likelihood was almost twice as great that a single man eventually would marry the mother of his first child if he were employed than if he were unemployed. In addition, while researchers did not have income data, they learned that the higher the joint educational attainment of unmarried parents—and thus most likely the greater their combined income—the stronger the likelihood that they would marry. Testa and his colleagues concluded that "improvements in the economic status of both low-income men and women promise to enable most parents to marry and thus provide a financially and, it is hoped, socially better environment for themselves and their children" (Testa et al., 1989: 91).

A study of rates of murder and robbery in 150 American cities took the above conclusion a step further. Robert J. Sampson (1987) learned that as a result of a three-step process, African-American men had greater involvement in these two violent crimes than white men. Because their fathers were more likely than whites' fathers to have been unemployed, there was a higher likelihood that they came from single-parent families. As a result African-American males received less support, control, and supervision at home. Therefore they were more likely than white males to be vulnerable to involvement in delinquency and crime. Sampson concluded that to alleviate these problems, social policies need to address structural conditions that have maintained a high rate of joblessness among black men, encouraged the fragmentation of poor black families, and helped produce the high rate of violent crime among black men.

The following case study relates to the previous material on the relationship between African-American men's employment and family structure and activity.

Unemployed or Employed Father: Social Impact on the African-American Family

For most Americans there has been a strong expectation that husbands/ fathers will be breadwinners supporting their families. As Frank Casey's experience suggests, a black man whose chances to be an effective breadwinner have been limited by institutional racism in education and work is likely to suffer a diminished self-image that adversely affects not only him but also other family members.

During the 1960s Frank Casey was hired by a federally funded project called New Careers for the Poor, that trained low-income minority residents to fill positions in the schools, police departments, and other community organizations. Casey was a liaison between the primarily black parents and children and the largely white teachers and administrators. Previously he had worked irregularly, sweeping floors and cleaning streets, and sometimes he was on welfare.

Casey loved his new job. He felt a special relationship with the children—both African-American and white. There was something of the kid in him still, he told Bob Blauner. Blauner watched him dealing with the children. Casey was relaxed and easy and yet without blaming he'd get kids to explore the process that had produced problems with their teachers and brought them to his office.

Casey indicated that because the job permitted him to help others and also himself, it provided him with dignity. Most important of all perhaps, it gave Casey's children a positive image of their father.

A few years before, when he had either been working irregularly or was on welfare, Casey was at home a great deal. The children would see him when they left to go to school and then when they returned in the afternoon. They would look at him, Casey indicated, but "they wouldn't see anything." In the sense of a father providing a role model, he simply didn't exist. Casey explained that

> [A] father will go out with his lunch bucket and come back all dirty and tired. I wasn't that way, because I didn't have no job. And a whole lot built up within me that made me feel that I wasn't no father no more. I wasn't nothing but an empty shell. . . . And I couldn't even help them with homework—not that I didn't know how, but inside of me I felt that I couldn't. (Blauner, 1989: 151)

This was the situation, Casey indicated, that many African-American men he knew faced at home. They were trapped in the black urban underclass, but he wasn't. Now he had a good job, and the situation had changed dramatically. He was earning money that contributed to the family, and because of the money and the impact of what he was accomplishing with students at the school, his own children were much closer to him. Sometimes Casey's children warned him to watch what he said and not to insult the school administrators, because if he did, he could once more be out of a job and be back where he'd been—diminished in their eyes and in his own.

Casey was convinced that one of the most important reasons to hold on to his job was to provide a role model for his children. They needed to see their father as a breadwinner, contributing to the family income—proud and not stigmatized—and upon reaching adulthood they should expect to fill the same role, or marry someone who would.

Welfare's Effect on Poor Minority Families   Besides focusing on the supposed fragmented nature of African-American families, the Moynihan Report suggested that welfare plays a destructive impact on poor minority families. One can examine three possible ways welfare might negatively affect minority families.

First, there is the claim that AFDC and other welfare programs promote fragmentation. A review of research on the topic indicated that there is a statistically detectable but modest relationship between levels of welfare benefits that different U.S. states provide and the proportion of female-headed families (Jaynes and Williams, 1989: 531).

Second, the possibility exists that women on welfare are likely to have an increased number of illegitimate children. A review of studies on the subject concluded that there is no evidence to support such a claim (Hayes, 1987).

Third, perhaps AFDC lowers or even kills poor parents' work incentive. In research on black, female-headed poor families throughout the

United States, Jones (1987) found that higher proportions of these women were on welfare when the states in which they lived provided primarily low-paying clerical, service, and operative jobs to modestly educated black women. On the other hand, in states where jobs available to African-American female heads of poor families offered higher wages, the proportion of these women supported by welfare dropped.

Reading the preceding paragraph, you might feel that even if wages are low, people should have the pride to work instead of seeking welfare support. The problem is that welfare recipients lose nearly a dollar in benefits for each dollar earned, and in some states they also lose health benefits. In addition, while working, they often need to pay for a baby-sitter or a child-care program. These economic realities help to explain why among the poorest female-headed families, AFDC and other welfare subsidies tend to encourage women to stay out of the work force (McLanahan and Garfinkel, 1989).

Policy makers often ignore or gloss over such economic realities, focusing instead on what the Moynihan Report considered the tangle of pathology dominating the poor black family. In 1988 Moynihan and Senate colleague William Armstrong sponsored a bill, which claimed to represent welfare reform and was passed by the Senate. This legislation required all AFDC mothers with children over three to enter the labor force as cheaply paid workers. The bill simply failed to assess such practical problems as obtaining jobs in largely jobless areas, locating effective child-care personnel, and getting children to and from their caretakers.

Examining this legislation, a pair of writers wondered "how many of the men who sit in the halls of Congress have ever played a parenting role in which they had the opportunity to engage in such tasks for even, let us say, one week" (Wilkerson and Gresham, 1989: 128). Unfortunately politicians establishing welfare programs seem to maintain both sexist and racist outlooks.

Stereotypes of Minority Families   Consider two titles—*The Negro Family: The Case for National Action* and "The Vanishing Family: Crisis in Black America." These are the precise titles of the Moynihan Report and the CBS Special Report on black family problems. So what, you might say. The point is that in these two works, which appeared 21 years apart, the reference in the title is to *a family*—singular. The analysts suggest that blacks have a single family structure: A stereotype emerges—in particular, Moynihan's idea of "a tangle of pathology." This stereotype has continued to thrive.

A recent study of 25 textbooks in the sociology of the family indicated that nine of the books analyzed black families under headings suggesting deviance or inadequate functioning. There were statements that black families are more likely to be female-headed and to experience unemployment, illegitimacy, and break-up than white families. Such statements are factually correct, but without further explanation, they are misleading.

Useful discussion would indicate how factors besides race, such as poverty and unemployment, have come into play. (Our earlier discussion of fragmentation in the poor minority family used such an approach.) Otherwise readers are likely to receive the impression "that black families are innately problem-ridden or dysfunctional" (Bryant and Coleman, 1988).

A review of the 283 data-based articles about black Americans published in the *Journal of Marriage and the Family* between 1939 and 1987 revealed a declining tendency over time to present a distinctly problematic, pathological image of the black family. However, research-related factors have contributed to a somewhat negative image of black families in this journal's articles. Since the early 1960s, the analysis indicated, articles published about black families in *Journal of Marriage and the Family* were more likely than in earlier years to have been quantitative studies conducted by researchers at large, primarily white universities and subsidized by government grants. These studies tended to present an abstract sense of black family issues, failing to represent respondents' point of view and often, with little or no justification for claims of their significance provided, highlighting statistical information indicating that blacks are more deviant or less successful than whites. Tendencies for this research to have been conducted at white universities and to have received government support have been consistent with this quantitative trend. White universities can best afford the mainframe computers necessary for this type of investigation, and government sponsors have been more inclined to fund large quantitative projects than qualitative studies. In short, all three trends have dovetailed in support of published studies that present an abstract, somewhat negative view of the black family (Demos, 1990). It would be instructive to know whether other prominent social-scientific journals with articles on minority families have produced similar results.

Some researchers have directly confronted stereotypes of the African-American family. In *A New Look at Black Families,* Charles Willie suggested that his study of black families indicated that they roughly divide into three categories—affluent or middle-class, working-class, and poor.

Affluent black family members tend to be well educated, with one or both spouses college graduates. The adults generally work hard, obtaining positions in the public sector, industry, education, and in private business. Work is often a consuming experience; little time remains for recreation and other kinds of activities, with the possible exception of regular church attendance. Because of the income limitations of jobs available to blacks, wife and husband usually both work and as a result produce a total income at or above the national median. A recent study of 41 black professional couples concluded that while the respondents considered work a significant part of their lives, they heavily depended upon their marriages for happiness and psychological well-being (Thomas, 1990).

Middle-class African-American families want the home to be a pleasant, often elegant place to live—"their home is their castle" Willie indicated—and so affluent blacks emphasize modern furnishings and appliances.

Affluent African-Americans tend to have two or fewer children and to encourage them to go to college directly after high school. The parents hope that their children will have more opportunities than they did, and they consider a college degree important for success in the work world. In their children middle-class African-Americans try to develop the same positive emphases toward work and thrift that dominate their own lives.

Among working-class black families, life is a struggle requiring cooperative activity among all family members. Both spouses tend to be employed, with husbands sometimes maintaining two jobs. The sense of unity in this type of family is often less the result of understanding and tenderness than of the joint effort to avoid major economic hardship. Because their salaries tend to be low, working-class black families find that any reduction in the overall income is likely to push them below the poverty level.

Working-class African-Americans consider children their special contribution to society, and they tend to have more of them than do affluent African-Americans—sometimes five or even more. While these parents value education, they generally draw the limit at high-school graduation. Job expectations for their children are those requiring no more than a high-school or junior-college education—for instance, employment as a secretary, nurse, or skilled manual worker.

The third category—poor black families—has already been discussed. As we have noted, these families have various problems rooted in poverty. Willie indicated that sometimes poor African-American families are rebellious, rejecting the society that has rejected them, trusting few, if any, outsiders and appearing uncommitted to anyone or anything. However, mothers remain loyal to their children, and brothers and sisters generally accept the obligation to help each other (Willie, 1981: 56–57).

Table 7.2 provides economic data on African-American, Puerto Rican, Mexican-American, and white families. Like the previous discussion, it suggests that all three sets of families are too diversified in income to fit an economic stereotype.

De-emphasis or Omission of Minority Families' Strengths Stereotypes are negative, failing to consider possible positive qualities in a group. For the black family, Moynihan's "tangle-of-pathology" perspective is invariably negative. In contrast, research has suggested positive qualities about minority families.

A study of 41 black families that were poor, urban, and intact found that the husband played a prominent role. In at least seven out of ten cases, the husband was the main provider and an active decision maker in such issues as choosing household appliances and selecting the residence (Robinson, Bailey, and Smith, 1985).

Recent research has indicated that for many African-Americans, fam-

Table 7.2   BLACK, PUERTO RICAN, MEXICAN-AMERICAN, AND WHITE FAMILY
INCOME LEVELS: 1989

	Percentage in each income category			
	African-American families	Puerto Rican families	Mexican-American families	White families
Under $9,999	27.3	29.2	20.1	8.5
$10,000–$24,999	33.3	33.1	37.5	25.8
$25,000–$49,999	26.7	27.1	32.6	38.4
$50,000 or more	12.6	10.7	9.9	27.4
Median income	$19,329	$18,932	$21,025	$33,915

Note: While black, Puerto Rican, and Mexican-American families are less affluent than white families, a fairly broad distribution of income exists within each type.

Source: U.S. Bureau of the Census. *Statistical Abstract of the United States: 1991.* No. 43 and No. 45.

ily members frequently lived close by and often served as a source of emotional or financial support. A large investigation revealed that when African-Americans faced a serious emergency, eight out of ten had either a relative or friend available to help: 24 percent of the respondents turned to parents or siblings, 21 percent to friends, 12 percent to their children, and 10 percent to in-laws (Taylor, Chatters, and Mays, 1988). A study of poor African-American families indicated that resident grandmothers' parenting activity was substantial, second only to mothers in areas of control, punishment, support, and presence at bedtime (Pearson et al., 1990).

Native Americans also can often rely on support from a variety of relatives. In spite of government officials' historical efforts to undermine traditional family structures, many modern Native Americans continue to emphasize extended family ties. Sometimes young people leave their parents' home and move in with other relatives. They do not need to pay rent, nor must they suffer inquiries about when they plan to leave. One Native-American analyst noted that relatives accept that "the child will decide when it is right for him or her to go home" (Edmo, 1990: 3).

Findings on the Puerto Rican family suggest that when influenced by the desire for economic advancement on the mainland, second-generation adults are less familistic than parents who were born on the island and migrated to the United States. Such a comparison can be misleading, however, because even adult children who de-emphasize family ties tend to turn to their parents for assistance when emergencies strike (Zayas and Palleja, 1988).

A recent analysis concluded that for all the minority families examined in this chapter—African-American, Native-American, Chinese-American, Japanese-American, Mexican-American, and Puerto Rican—the extended

---

Box 7.1 **MAJOR CONCLUSIONS ABOUT THE ANALYSIS OF MINORITY FAMILIES**

1. Family fragmentation: that limited educational and occupational opportunities have made a major contribution to this problem

2. Welfare impact: that analysts and policy makers often fail to assess effectively the complex effect on poor minority families of being on welfare

3. Stereotypes of minority families: that many investigations, particularly large studies, tend to present a negative or abstract image of minority families; that analyzed by income level, black families divide into three broad types

4. De-emphasis or omission of minority families' strengths: that racial minorities' relatives provide considerable extended family support

---

family has been both a problem-solving and stress-coping system (Harrison et al., 1990).

In this section we have examined the complex, primarily economic factors affecting minority families. We have also considered the role of racist, victim-blaming official outlooks on and policies toward minority families. Box 7.1 summarizes significant points about minority families raised in this section. For the next issue, similar themes arise once again.

MINORITY CHILDREN AT RISK

Recent statistics are impressive. Compared to white children, African-American children are twice as likely to have been born prematurely, to have substandard birth weight, to live in inferior housing, and die in the first year. Compared to white children, black children are three times as inclined to be poor, to live in a female-headed household, to have no employed parent, and to be murdered between the ages of five and nine. Finally, compared to white children, African-American children are five times more likely to be dependent on welfare and nine times more inclined to live with a parent who had never been married (Edelman, 1989: 22; Taylor, 1990: 5–6). Thus it is no exaggeration to conclude that in various life-threatening or life-diminishing ways, black children are at greater risk than their white counterparts. Poor Puerto Rican and Native-American children also experience a highly disproportionate exposure to life-threatening or life-diminishing circumstances.

Besides South Africa, the United States is the only major industrialized nation that does not provide financial or medical aid when the birth or major illness of a child occurs (Rosewater, 1989: 11). Since African-Americans, Puerto Ricans, and Native Americans are disproportionately poor, this omission clearly suggests institutional racism in government practice: The policy, or absence of a policy, systematically discriminates against a greater proportion of minority children than white children.

The relationship between family income and race also affects child-care programs. Because of poverty, low-income parents, who are disproportionately members of racial minorities, must send their children to governmentally subsidized child-care programs. Middle- and upper-income parents enroll their children in fee-based services. The result is that in many residential areas, child-care programs are racially segregated. Because of the Supreme Court decision in *Brown* v. *Topeka Board of Education,* segregation of schools has been under attack since 1954. However, a similar concern has not developed for preschool child-care programs (Kagan, 1989: 77).

A situation that produces major difficulties for some children is homelessness. Among the hundreds of thousands of homeless American children, there are both whites and members of racial minorities. Because of more widespread poverty, minority youth—African-American, Puerto Rican, and Native-American children—are disproportionately represented.

In 1980 homeless children were rare, but three factors have altered that situation. First, as we noted in Chapters 3 and 5, economic downturns, especially when exacerbated by residential segregation, produce significant neighborhood deterioration. Homelessness is one possible outcome: In deteriorating areas housing officials declare that because of an excess of code violations, many houses and apartment buildings are uninhabitable; poor residents must leave and sometimes cannot find affordable housing. Second, starting in the late 1970s, millions of dollars in public funds helped convert urban low-cost housing into residences for affluent, middle-class citizens. While gentrification has bolstered cities' tax base and rejuvenated many inner-city areas, it has helped to make cheap housing scarce. Third, during the Reagan years, federal funds allocated for low-income housing were cut by about 80 percent. Because of these three factors, poor families have increasingly faced homelessness (Hayes, 1989: 60–61). Policy makers and politicians often fail to assess the impact of these conditions on homelessness. They are more inclined to take a blaming-the-victim approach as the following account suggests.

On March 6, 1986, David Bright, a ten-year-old, homeless black boy from New York City, testified before the House Select Committee on Hunger in Washington, D.C. When he grows up, David explained, he wants to become president so that he can make certain that "no little boy like me will have to put his head down on his desk at school because it hurts to be hungry" (Hayes, 1989: 58).

David's statement left few dry eyes in the hearing room. From Mayor Edward Koch, however, it aroused an angry reply. Koch indicated that

David's testimony "simply doesn't reflect reality. New York does more for the homeless than any other city in America" (Rimer, 1986: 42). Koch took further action. Trying to prove that David's mother was directly responsible for her son's hunger, Koch had a spokesperson, whom he later appointed a judge of the New York Family Court, leak to the press confidential information from the Bright family's records about the mother's suspected drug abuse.

David Bright took the developing feud in stride, saying that the root of the problem might be jealousy produced by the fact that "I've got hair, and he doesn't." David's school principal declared that while Koch had an effective public presence "he's no match for this kid" (Rimer, 1986: 42).

Although David Bright had his moment in the sun, much of his life has been dreary and painful. At the time of the hearing, he was living with his mother and three siblings in two small rooms in New York City's crowded Hotel Martinique, along with 1500 homeless children and their families. Sometimes his mother would become so depressed that she would tell the children to leave her alone in one room so that she could cry.

But while adults suffer because of homelessness, children perhaps suffer more. There is no physical stability—no place, even though it might fall short of ideal—that provides a basic sense of stability, a home, during their early years. As one writer indicated, homelessness destroys "the inner beauty of a child" (Hayes, 1989: 66).

CONCLUSION

Throughout this chapter we have repeatedly encountered two points. First, minority families are often the victims of institutional racism, disproportionately suffering more limited educational and occupational opportunities and thus encountering a greater risk of poverty and its associated problems than white families. Second, in the tradition of the Moynihan Report, a victim-blaming strategy has prevailed. These approaches emphasize that the source of serious problems with African-American and other minority families resides in the family itself. If one focuses on the "tangle of pathology" or other supposed indicators of what internal colonialism labels racial minorities' cultural inferiority, then one can overlook the economic and political roots of minority families' problems. To date this racist strategy has remained alive and well.

REFERENCES

Anderson, Elijah. 1989. "Sex Codes and Family Life among Poor Inner-City Youths." *Annals of the American Academy of Political and Social Science* 501 (January): 59–78.

Besharov, Douglas J., Alison Quin, and Karl Zinsmeister. 1987. "A Portrait in Black and White: Out-of-Wedlock Births." *Public Opinion* 10 (May/June): 43–45.

Blauner, Bob. 1989. *Black Lives, White Lives.* Berkeley: University of California Press.

Brewer, Rose M. 1988. "Black Women in Poverty: Some Comments on Female-Headed Families." *Signs* 13 (Winter): 331–339.

Bryant, Z. Lois, and Marilyn Coleman. 1988. "The Black Family as Portrayed in Introductory Marriage and Family Textbooks." *Family Relations* 37 (July): 255–259.

Cockburn, Alexander. 1989. "Beat the Devil." *Nation* 249 (July 24/31): 113–114.

Corry, John. 1986. "TV: 'CBS Reports' Examines Black Families." *New York Times* (January 25): 49.

Daniels, Roger. 1988. *Asian Americans: Chinese and Japanese in the United States since 1850.* Seattle: University of Washington Press.

Darity, William A., Jr., and Samuel L. Myers, Jr. 1984. "Does Welfare Dependency Cause Female Headship? The Case of the Black Family." *Journal of Marriage and the Family* 46 (November): 765–779.

Demos, Vasilikie. 1990. "Black Family Studies in the *Journal of Marriage and the Family* and the Issue of Distortion: A Trend Analysis." *Journal of Marriage and the Family* 52 (August): 603–612.

Edelman, Marian Wright. 1989. "Children at Risk." *Proceedings of the Academy of Political Science* 37: 20–30.

Edmo, Ed. 1990. "Cradleboards and Development." *American Indians for Development Newsletter* 5 (May/June): 2–3.

Fitzpatrick, Joseph P. 1987. *Puerto Rican Americans: The Meaning of Migration to the Mainland.* Englewood Cliffs, NJ: Prentice-Hall. Second edition.

Franklin, John Hope, and Alfred A. Moss, Jr. 1988. *From Slavery to Freedom: A History of Negro Americans.* New York: Alfred A. Knopf. Sixth edition.

Goffman, Erving. 1974. *Stigma: Notes on the Management of Spoiled Identity.* New York: Jason Aronson.

Gresham, Jewell Handy. 1989. "White Patriarchal Supremacy: The Politics of Family in America." *Nation* 249 (July 24/31): 116–122.

Harrison, Algea O., et al. 1990. "Family Ecologies of Ethnic Minority Children." *Child Development* 61 (April): 347–362.

Hayes, Cheryl D. 1987. *Risking the Future: Adolescent Sexuality, Pregnancy, and Childbearing.* Washington, DC: National Academy Press.

Hayes, Robert M. 1989. "Homeless Children." *Proceedings of the Academy of Political Science* 37: 58–69.

Ima, Kenji. 1982. "Japanese Americans: The Making of 'Good' People," pp. 262–302 in Anthony Gary Dworkin and Rosalind J. Dworkin (eds.), *The Minority Report.* New York: Holt, Rinehart and Winston. Second edition.

Jaynes, Gerald David, and Robin M. Williams, Jr. (eds.). 1989. *A Common Destiny: Blacks and American Society.* Washington, DC: National Academy Press.

Johnson, Michael P. 1989. "Upward in Slavery." *New York Review of Books* 36 (December 21): 51–55.

Jones, John Paul, III. 1987. "Work, Welfare, and Poverty among Black Female-Headed Families." *Economic Geography* 63 (January): 20–34.

Kagan, Sharon L. 1989. "The Care and Education of America's Young Children: At the Brink of a Paradigm Shift?" *Proceedings of the Academy of Political Science* 37: 70–83.

Keefe, Susan E., and Amado M. Padilla. 1987. *Chicano Ethnicity.* Albuquerque: University of New Mexico Press.

Kitano, Harry H. L., and Roger Daniels. 1988. *Asian Americans: Emerging Americans.* Englewood Cliffs, NJ: Prentice-Hall.

Li, Wen Lang. 1982. "Chinese Americans: Exclusion from the Melting Pot," pp. 303–328 in Anthony Gary Dworkin and Rosalind J. Dworkin (eds.), *The Minority Report.* New York: Holt, Rinehart and Winston. Second edition.

Maldonado, Lionel A. 1982. "Mexican-Americans: The Emergence of a Minority," pp. 168–195 in Anthony Gary Dworkin and Rosalind J. Dworkin (eds.), *The Minority Report.* New York: Holt, Rinehart and Winston. Second edition.

McLanahan, Sara, and Irwin Garfinkel. 1989. "Single Mothers, the Underclass, and Social Policy." *American Academy of Political and Social Science* 501 (January): 92–104.

Office of Policy Planning and Research, United States Department of Labor. 1965. *The Negro Family: The Case for National Action.* Washington, DC: United States Department of Labor.

Parker, Seymour, and Robert J. Kleiner. 1977. "Social and Psychological Dimensions of the Family Role Performance of the Negro Male," in Doris Y. Wilkinson and Ronald L. Taylor (eds.), *The Black Male in America: Perspectives on His Status in Contemporary Society.* Chicago: Nelson-Hall.

Pearson, Jane L., et al. 1990. "Black Grandmothers in Multigenerational Households: Diversity in Family Structure and Parenting Involvement in the Woodlawn Community." *Child Development* 61 (April): 434–442.

Price, John A. 1984. "North American Indian Families," pp. 245–268 in Charles H. Mindel and Robert W. Habenstein (eds.), *Ethnic Families in America: Patterns and Variations.* New York: Elsevier. Second edition.

Rimer, Sara. 1986. " 'Hotel Kid' Becomes Symbol for the Homeless." *New York Times* (March 6): 42.

Robinson, Ira E., Wilfrid C. Bailey, and John M. Smith, Jr. 1985. "Self-Perception of the Husband/Father in the Intact Lower Class Black Family." *Phylon* 46 (June): 136–147.

Rosewater, Ann. 1989. "Child and Family Trends: Beyond the Numbers." *Proceedings of the Academy of Political Science* 37: 4–19.

Ryan, William. 1976. *Blaming the Victim.* New York: Vintage Books. Revised edition.

Sampson, Robert J. 1987. "Urban Black Violence: The Effect of Male Joblessness and Family Disruption." *American Journal of Sociology* 93 (September): 348–382.

Staples, Robert. 1984. "The Black American Family," pp. 217–244 in Charles H. Mindel and Robert W. Habenstein (eds.), *Ethnic Families in America: Patterns and Variations.* New York: Elsevier. Second edition.

Sullivan, Mercer L. 1989. "Absent Fathers in the Inner City." *Annals of the American Academy of Political and Social Science* 501 (January): 48–58.

Taylor, Robert Joseph, Linda M. Chatters, and Vickie M. Mays. 1988. "Parents, Children, Siblings, In-laws, and Non-kin as Sources of Emergency Assistance to Black Americans." *Family Relations* 37 (July): 298–304.

Taylor, Ronald L. 1990. "Black Youth: The Endangered Generation." *Youth and Society* 22 (September): 4–11.

Testa, Mark, et al. 1989. "Employment and Marriage among Inner-City Youths." *Annals of the American Academy of Political and Social Science* 501 (January): 79–91.

Thomas, Veronica G. 1990. "Determinants of Global Life Happiness and Marital Happiness in Dual-Career Black Couples." *Family Relations* 39 (April): 174–178.

U.S. Bureau of the Census. 1989. *Statistical Abstract of the United States: 1989.* Washington, DC: U.S. Government Printing Office. 109th edition.

U.S. Bureau of the Census. 1990. *Statistical Abstract of the United States: 1990.* Washington, DC: U.S. Government Printing Office. 110th edition.

Wilkerson, Margaret, and Jewell Handy Gresham. 1989. "Sexual Politics of Welfare: The Racialization of Poverty." *Nation* 249 (July 24/31): 126–130.

Willie, Charles Vert. 1981. *A New Look at Black Families.* Bayside, NY: General Hall. Second edition.

Zayas, Luis H., and Josephine Palleja. 1988. "Puerto Rican Familism: Considerations for Family Therapy." *Family Relations* 37 (July): 260–264.

Chapter
8

Distorted Image: Racial Minorities in the Mass Media

*S*pike Lee, the producer, director, writer, and star of the celebrated film *Do the Right Thing,* developed the idea for the movie when white youths attacked three black men in Howard Beach, Queens, and one was killed by a passing car as he sought to flee from his assailants.

Lee didn't simply tell the story of the Howard Beach killing. Fiction, he felt, provided greater possibility than reality for representing complexities of race relations. It was the first time that Lee, already a successful film maker, depicted white characters. In fact, the first character Lee began to sketch out was Sal, the white owner of the pizzeria that dominated street life in the primarily black neighborhood. Sal and his two sons had diverse feelings toward blacks, ranging from polite respect to fear and hatred. Commenting on the complexity of his white characters, Lee said, "After all, we know more about white culture than whites do about black culture" (Kaufman, 1989: 20).

In two respects *Do the Right Thing* represents a departure from

African-Americans' traditional relationship to popular mass media. The central person in its production is African-American; ordinarily control of prominent films has been in whites' hands. In addition, characters and situations represented in the movie are diversified and complex—not the standard stereotypes that have dominated African-Americans' and other racial minorities' depictions in the mass media. *Do the Right Thing* is an unusual film. While racial minorities' relationship to films and other mass media has been changing, minority-group members often play a modest role, or none at all, in important decisions involving their production and also receive stereotyped representations. We examine these two issues in this chapter.

The central subject in this chapter is the **mass media,** which is comprised of the instruments of communication that reach a large audience without any personal contact between senders and receivers. Books, records, newspapers, radio, television, and movies are the most significant mass media.

Prominent in these discussions is a concept we have already used extensively. A stereotype is a highly exaggerated, greatly oversimplified image, maintained by prejudiced people, of the characteristics of the group members against whom they are prejudiced.

In this chapter we discuss mass media from the internal-colonialist perspective. Then we consider the impact of mass media on racial minorities.

MASS MEDIA AND INTERNAL COLONIALISM

Three tenets of internal colonialism apply to racial minorities' relationship to the mass media. The colonial-labor principle is relevant: Members of racial minorities tend to be kept out of powerful, desirable jobs, with few Spike Lees—minority-group members in leadership positions in the popular mass media. The second principle of internal colonialism is restriction of racial minorities' freedom of movement. In this chapter we see how minorities' stereotyped portrayal in the mass media has helped impose restrictions on them. Finally stereotyped representations of racial minorities in the media have served to represent them as culturally and even genetically inferior.

Racial Minorities' Participation in Mass Media

The number of blacks who have been able to enter white-owned print media has been small. In 1983 the nation's daily newspapers employed about 50,000 people, but only about 2800 (5.6 percent) belonged to racial minorities, who then composed about 20 percent of the population. In addition, about 60 percent of American dailies employed no minority-group members.

Statistics also show that blacks are underrepresented in the broadcast industry and cable television. While blacks comprised nearly 12 percent of the population in 1983, they held 8.9 percent of the broadcast jobs and 7.6 percent of the cable-television positions.

Throughout all mass media, African-Americans and other minority-group members have had low representation in leadership positions—such as editors, managers, and, in particular, owners. In 1983 African-Americans owned less than 2 percent of licensed and operating radio and television stations. Obstacles to black media ownership include high-entry costs, discrimination by some advertisers, and, in the broadcast media, the scarcity of stations and the abandonment of rules created to prevent ownership concentration (*Crisis*, 1985). In spite of such limitations, there have been some successful black owners of broadcast media. Most notably Inner City Broadcasting Corporation, which owns Harlem's legendary Apollo theater, numerous radio stations, a cable network, a magazine, a music company, a theater syndication, and various other business interests, secured $28 million in revenues in 1988 (Edmond, 1989).

Since the 1940s there has been a number of African-American novelists, playwrights, and poets whose works have been published or produced widely. Following World War II, talented and versatile blacks actors have performed on the stage and on the screen, and since the 1940s black actors have appeared on television, starting to play major characters in situation comedies during the early 1950s. By the late 1980s, Bill Cosby and Oprah Winfrey were the highest paid entertainers on television.

Perhaps African-American artists have been best known in popular music. During the 1950s a number of African-American singers and singing groups were commercially successful. In the past three decades, such performers as Ray Charles, Stevie Wonder, Diana Ross, and Michael Jackson have achieved the "crossover" effect, becoming as popular with white as with African-American audiences (Abarry, 1990; Franklin and Moss, 1988: 374–375; 431–432; Jaynes and Williams, 1989: 101–102). But the number of successful African-American singers and entertainers is relatively small.

Other racial minorities have also had limited prominence in the major mass media—for instance, Asian-Americans. In such low-budget movies as *Dim Sum, Chan Is Missing,* and *Hito Hata,* Asian-American filmmakers have had some popular and commercial success portraying the Asian-American experience. It appears, however, that most white Americans do not want Asian-Americans represented in dominant roles in the popular media (Kitano and Daniels, 1988: 176).

Even when they are successful, some minority artists face an indifferent, even hostile commercial world. Rudolfo Anaya's novel, *Bless Me, Ultima,* was first published in 1972, selling over 250,000 copies and still producing 13,000 sales annually. While the book remains popular among Mexican-Americans, no major publisher has issued a mass-market edition. John Randall, who runs a bookstore featuring Chicano and Native-American material, feels that censorship is common with writers like Anaya whose writings help members of their racial group understand and rebel against political and economic oppression. Referring to Chicano writers breaking into mainstream publishing, Anaya said, "It's just that we see how important it is for the culture that our voices be heard and known to a wider readership. So while we're struggling to maintain our culture, lack of attention to it helps ensure that cultural genocide goes on" (Margaret Jones, 1990: 30).

The relevance of the colonial-labor principle to racial minorities in the mass media concerns not simply their extent of participation in the mass media but also their portrayal. Consider the following television advertisement that was prominent in 1989 and 1990. The ad, which involved a major airline, showed a black airline attendant suddenly realizing that his last customer, a well-dressed white businessman, had left his briefcase at the check-in counter. Grabbing the briefcase, the attendant took off at full speed, skirting people, vaulting over chairs and other obstacles, and showing, the narrator informed the viewers, the moves he displayed as a first-string halfback. Just as the passenger reached the gate, the attendant handed him the briefcase. They exchanged smiles—they didn't shake hands, which would have emphasized their equality—the white man thanked the black man, and the black man, still smiling but breathing heavily, said "Piece of cake."

Now there is nothing racist about this situation, you might be thinking: It just represents one person helping another. But the core issue concerns how the people, especially the black man, are portrayed. With a great display of physical energy and grace—the area of physical prowess has often been reserved for blacks since the days of slavery—the black employee exerted himself on behalf of the white man, who needed to make no special effort, and then the black man downplayed the contribution he made—a modesty that implicitly undercut his own significance. What would have been the public reaction, one might wonder, if the roles had been reversed?

The colonial-labor principle has another, somewhat different application to the mass media (defined in this case somewhat more broadly than is usual). Steven C. Dubin (1987) studied African-Americans' representation on objects like salt and pepper shakers, cookie jars, lawn statues, and ashtrays. These media often portray African-Americans with grossly distorted features and dressed like slaves ready to perform menial domestic tasks. Dubin described the representations as "symbolic slavery." Such a designation conveys a sense of the colonial-labor principle: that the purchasers would be comfortable with a world where blacks and members of other racial minorities were restricted to menial, slavelike jobs. Such stereotyped images on objects were most popular from the 1890s to the 1950s and have become much less prevalent in the past three decades as whites have realized that they are insulting to blacks.

Many of us have observed that over the past quarter-century suburbanites with lawn statues of black lackeys have either removed them or painted the face white, thereby preserving the statue and a sense of the elitest life-style it implies. The latter action seemed to represent such people's sensibility about racism—that all that's needed to remove racism is a symbolic coat of paint.

Media Stereotypes and Restriction of Minorities' Activity

Why have stereotypes been used in the mass media? One answer is that through the centuries their use has proven to be profitable (Clifton, 1990: 19–20). By the middle of the nineteenth century, writers learned that they could become wealthy writing Indian-captivity narratives, which barraged readers with sensationalized accounts of tortures and sexual abuse inflicted on captives, especially female captives (VanDerBeets, 1984).

Early films about Native Americans grew out of this tradition, recognizing that lurid, blood-thirsty sensationalism would bring patrons streaming into the theaters just as it had sent them running to the bookstores. Once filmmakers obtained proof that flaming arrows, burning forts and wagons, and screaming, soon-to-be-raped white women would effectively sell tickets, they gave up efforts to produce historically accurate portraits of Native Americans. Sensationalism in these films caught on so quickly, in fact, that in 1911 members of four Western tribes traveled to Washington, D.C., to protest their treatment in films to Congress and to President William Howard Taft (Stedman, 1982: 157–158).

Certainly stereotyped media representations can make fortunes. But we look further and speculate about what conditions in American society encourage support for stereotypes. Once more the internal-colonialist perspective seems relevant: Stereotypes prove useful in rationalizing limits imposed on racial minorities' activities.

The mass media, especially written accounts, played a role in this endeavor. Mary Rowlandson, a seventeenth-century homemaker, authored the earliest effort. Captured during a raid in 1675, Rowlandson was held by her captives for 12 weeks, then released after a ransom payment. Rowlandson's book described the atrocities she supposedly observed—the torture and killing of numerous white women and children. For decades the book was reprinted, and it became the prototype for later Indian-captivity novels. Unlike later fictionalized victims, Mary Rowlandson apparently was not sexually violated by her captors. Nonetheless, Raymond William Stedman indicated, even modern readers have found her account gruesome and terrifying.

> How much more unsettling it must have been when the depicted menaces were still only a night's march away from frontier cabins. It is well to remember that for two centuries and more the Rowlandson capture reflected ele-

ments of actual threat to many Americans—and a convenient excuse for land grabbing and Indian damning to others. (Stedman, 1982: 75)

Indian attacks ceased about a century ago. Undoubtedly African-Americans have been the source of contemporary white Americans' greatest racial fears. Sometimes those fears have been so great that they have even affected whites trained to provide calm, objective analysis. During the 1960s urban riots, many journalists claimed that strategically placed snipers launched carefully planned and coordinated attacks on whites. Professional investigators looked into 25 such reports and found little or no supportive evidence. This research, however, received almost no publicity. The press's accounts of systematic insurrection carried the day and contributed substantially to a stereotype of brutal blacks dedicated to the systematic murder of whites (Hartmann and Husband, 1974: 156). Obviously the idea that such people had to be controlled by any means necessary was readily forthcoming. The same implication applies to the following situation.

In late 1989 in Boston, a highly publicized murder occurred. Carol Stuart, a pregnant white woman, was shot and Charles Stuart, her white husband, was wounded. Stuart claimed that the assailant had been black. The police systematically searched an African-American neighborhood where Stuart claimed the assailant had forced him to drive before shooting Stuart and his wife. Even though Stuart's story had suspicious overtones, journalists accepted his account, not following the standard procedure of verifying sources. One reporter indicated that press coverage was "voluminous and dramatic" (Alex S. Jones, 1990: A21). On its front page, the *Boston Globe* published a picture of Mrs. Stuart's shattered head, and local radio and television kept replaying Mr. Stuart's desperate conversation with the police dispatcher, a conversation in which he referred to an unknown black assailant. Eventually evidence made it clear that Stuart should be the chief suspect, and at this point, he committed suicide. African-American leaders were enraged that the police and the press so readily mobilized to seek a black suspect when there was ample reason from the beginning to regard Stuart suspiciously (Butterfield, 1990). The incident suggests that with only flimsy evidence, many journalists are still inclined to represent African-Americans as a major source of threat, which implicitly must be controlled.

Other evidence has addressed the issue of controlling racial minorities, albeit in a more subtle manner. A study of African-Americans' portrayal in popular magazines' advertisements produced between 1950 and 1982 found that whites and African-Americans were much more likely to appear together on equal social terms in later ads. However, even recently the chances were substantially greater that the people in the pictures would be interacting with each other if all were white than if they were both black and white (Humphrey and Schuman, 1984). Thus in the course of three decades, advertising specialists have concluded that popular magazines' primarily white audiences have been increasingly willing to support African-Americans' entrance into their social world but have continued to want limited interaction with them.

Media Stereotypes of Racial Minorities' Cultural Inferiority

In a history of the relationship between American blacks and television, J. Fred MacDonald wrote, "In terms of utilization of black professional talent, and in the portrayal of Afro-American characters, TV as a new medium had the capability of ensuring a fair and equitable future" (MacDonald, 1983: 21).

So far it has produced limited success in this regard. In the late 1940s, as TV became popular, African-Americans appeared in very selected roles as singers, dancers, and clowns. One of the most popular programs was "Amos 'n' Andy," a televised re-creation of a radio show that had been very popular in the 1920s and 1930s with both black and white audiences. In spite of NAACP protests, the program premiered on CBS television in June 1951, bringing "the old minstrel stereotype of blacks as slow, foot-shuffling, fun-loving, slightly dishonest people from the radio to television for all the world to see" (Staples and Jones, 1985: 12).

As a child I sometimes watched the show, and the character who most vividly comes to mind is George "Kingfish" Stevens, a clumsily deceitful man who inevitably managed to trick Andy and all the other dumb nice guys portrayed on the program. I can remember thinking that if this slow-talking lightweight could outwit the others, then they must be dense indeed. It didn't consciously come to mind that these characters might be considered representative of all African-Americans, but psychologically speaking that idea couldn't have been very far away.

During the 1950s African-Americans were generally limited to small roles on television. As an exception Ethel Waters and later Louise Beavers starred in "Beulah," which started in 1950 and was the first television program with a black actor in the lead. The show contained many stereotypes. Beulah was a maid for a prosperous white family and in that role she served as an update of the Southern domestic slave—the "mammie" who was warm, loving, dedicated, and so accepted in her role that she could scold and lecture the children. In 1956 the "Nat King Cole Show" premiered on NBC. It was the first time that an African-American appeared on television in a dignified, unstereotyped way, and the program never did well, expiring in 1957 when it could no longer obtain sponsors. Apparently the American public simply was not ready to accept an African-American entertainer in anything but stereotyped roles.

Bill Cosby was the first person to break that particular barrier on television. In 1965 he starred with Robert Culp in "I Spy," playing a basically nonstereotyped role in a successful, three-year program where race was not the central issue. Racist overtones to the role did exist, however. As a spy, Cosby's cover was as a trainer for a tennis player, casting him in a subordinate role within one of blacks' traditional realms— sport. Furthermore the show's producers permitted Cosby no explicit romantic involvement, thereby reducing whites' possible anxieties about displaying a black man's sexual activities.

Perhaps the late 1960s was the heyday of African-Americans' prominence on television. Diahann Carroll, Teresa Graves, Leslie Uggams, and Flip Wilson obtained their own shows, and a host of other programs had African-Americans in supporting roles. While the percentage of black actors never approached their proportion of the population, they had an unprecedented chance to display their abilities relatively unhampered by stereotyped roles.

By the early 1970s, however, the civil-rights movement was in decline, and most Americans appeared to return to the asocial outlook of the 1950s and early 1960s. The situation comedy, with its trivialization of social issues and barrage of one-liners, became the rage and has remained prominent to the present day. Following the success of a number of all-white shows, there appeared such all-black or black-dominated shows as "The Jeffersons," "Good Times," "What's Happening," "In Living Color," and "Fresh Prince of Bel Air." Many African-American analysts have widely criticized these shows, suggesting that the actors' style, particularly their use of "black humor," presents the same kind of witless and deceitful stereotypes of blacks found 30 or 40 years earlier on "Amos 'n' Andy."

An exception has been the "Cosby Show." It is a program featuring black actors, but it does not display traditionally black-stereotyped situations—no ghetto, no drugs, an intact family. The variety of struggles and encounters involving Dr. and Ms. Huxtable and their children are typically American, not African-American. Some critics have pointed out that the show does not address poverty and racism, issues of extreme importance to many blacks, but its significance lies elsewhere: It has presented a middle-class black family in nonstereotyped roles, and it has been a resounding success.

The "Cosby Show" is a clear illustration that African-Americans can break long-accepted stereotypes and still be successful. Circumstances surrounding the program, however, are instructive. Selling his show to NBC, Cosby had the distinct advantage of being a very popular, successful entertainer, who was dealing with a network that at the time was dead-last in the ratings (Staples and Jones, 1985). The circumstances producing the success of the "Cosby Show" are unusual, and thus it is reasonable not to expect a great flood of nonstereotyped black shows. Nonetheless black entertainers will probably be able to find some opportunities to step outside narrow roles. In recent years "The Oprah Winfrey Show" has become very successful, convincing the American public that an intelligent, quick-witted, outgoing black woman can be an effective talk-show host.

In the future how extensive will be African-Americans' stereotype-breaking roles on television? While that's impossible to answer precisely, it probably is useful to remember what playwright Charles Fuller has said: "Americans trust black people when we sing, dance, or tell jokes. It's when we stop laughing that people get itchy" (*Time,* October 1, 1984: 76).

Like African-Americans and Native Americans, Asian-Americans have had stereotyped roles in the visual media. One analysis indicated that in films, "The evil Jap of World War II and the Communist gooks in Korea, China, and Vietnam—faceless, fanatic, maniacal, willing to die because life is not valued—are endlessly recycled with changes in nationality as our foreign policy changes" (Kitano and Daniels, 1988: 176). Less politically explicit, the karate films, that became commercially successful in the 1970s, provided similar stereotypes. In 1988 ABC television offered a short-lived series titled "Ohara," which starred Pat Morita, a Japanese-American in the lead role. Ohara was a small, elderly Japanese-American, behind whose unassuming bearing lurked an endless series of one-line putdowns reminiscent of the pre-World-War-II "Charlie Chan" films, along with, of course, the full martial-arts package. It was hardly the series to challenge prevailing stereotypes of Asian-Americans developed in films.

Since the Mexican War in the 1840s, white Americans have maintained stereotypes of Mexican-Americans. The contemptuous term "greaser" appeared at that time, probably because some Mexicans worked to grease wagon axles. The image that Mexicans were lazy, immoral, untrustworthy, stupid, and dirty was well-established by the time films started. The visual media sustained the stereotype. In movies Mexicans were often portrayed as bandits. In the case of the famed Pancho Villa, who conducted raids into Texas, his violence and criminality were emphasized, but films failed to show that white settlers' exploitation of Mexicans motivated the raids. On television Mexican or Mexican-American men were generally presented as lazy, fat, carefree, and immoral and women as flirtatious and promiscuous. Media advertising has also contributed to the Chicano stereotype. Frito commercials represented Mexicans as criminals ("Frito Banditos"), and a deodorant advertisement showed a grubby-looking Mexican bandit with the caption, "If it works for him, it will work for you" (Feagin, 1989: 261–263; Maldonado, 1982: 193).

About two-thirds of Puerto Rican characters on television are criminals (Staples and Jones, 1985: 15). Undoubtedly the best known entertainment feature involving Puerto Ricans has been *West Side Story,* first a Broadway musical and later a successful film. While one might concede that it presented a moving Romeo-and-Juliet-type story and appealing music, it clearly supported prevailing stereotypes of Puerto Rican men as violent, vicious gang members who physically intimidate and dominate their girlfriends.

In his book *A Puerto Rican in New York,* Jesus Colon noted that Puerto Ricans are frequently stereotyped by the mass media, which harp on "what is superficial and sentimental, transient and ephemeral, or bizarre and grotesque in Puerto Rican life" (Colon, 1961: 9).

Majority-group members often enjoy stereotypes of racial minorities' cultural inferiority, finding that they make them feel amused and superior. Whether intended or not, the suggestion of cultural inferiority supports a contention discussed in several chapters, especially the family chapter— that racial minorities' personal inadequacies and not economic, political, and social conditions outside of them are responsible for their lack of success. As we have seen, this blaming-the-victim perspective supports government programs forcing racial minorities to adopt the majority group's cultural standards after rejecting their own. Only then do they have a chance of receiving full acceptance and associated rewards within the society. Box 8.1 summarizes major conclusions from this section.

The present differs somewhat from the past, and in some modern media, representations of racial minorities appear more sympathetic. The following illustration is a case in point.

Breaking the Film Stereotype of Native Americans as Savages

Writing about stereotyped individuals, Erving Goffman suggested that they can employ different techniques in an effort to influence people's views about their status. For instance, an individual can attempt to conceal the status designated as inferior or try to pass off one status as another which is less undesirable—such as mental retardation represented as mental illness (Goffman, 1974: 93–94).

Goffman does not address the possibility that individuals who have been widely stereotyped—Native Americans, for example—simply can reject traditional stereotypes and seek to convey a positive image to others

---

Box 8.1 **MASS MEDIA AND INTERNAL COLONIALISM**

Tenet of Internal Colonialism	Example
1. Colonial-labor principle	Blacks' limited participation in newspapers and television
2. Restriction of minorities' activities	Response to the sense of threat created by Mary Rowlandson's book and Indian-captivity novels
3. Racial minorities' supposed cultural inferiority	Past and present television representation of stereotyped black, Japanese-American, Native-American, Mexican-American, and Puerto Rican characters

---

about what has widely been considered a racially inferior category of people.

In 1989 Gary Farmer, a Mohawk and an actor, starred in *Powwow Highway.* It is the story of two Native-American men who buy an old car, then take tribal funds that are supposed to be used to purchase bulls, and start a long drive from Montana to Sante Fe, where the sister of one of the men is held on a drug charge. At this point the precedent set by recent films about Native Americans would suggest that the two men would make a grand tour of seedy reservation bars, drifting from one drunken brawl or womanizing incident to another until the money ran out. The basic sense conveyed in such a film is that modern Native Americans are simply updated versions of their savage ancestors. In films made between the 1930s and late 1960s, Native Americans didn't even engage in riotous living. They were emotionless, savage characters, seldom expressing more than a few grunted phrases of pidgin English.

Powwow Highway, however, opposes such stereotypes. Its focus is Philbert Bono's spiritual search. Bono, played by Gary Farmer, is a six-foot-three-inch, 260-pound man. Bono is quiet, gentle, and carefully observant, and when in tight situations, he is decisive and reliable. While practical and down-to-earth, he also relies heavily on the time-tested lore and medicines he obtained from tribal elders.

One way the film offsets traditional stereotypes is its representation of Native Americans as diversified personalities. Consider the following incident. The two travelers stop to buy a stereo for their car. The salesman in the audio store is clearly a racist, not believing that they would have enough money to buy first-rate equipment. He urges them to buy a cheap model. When the stereo is installed, it doesn't work. Bono's companion, Buddy Red Bow, has a short fuse, and the dealings with the salesman have infuriated him. Convinced that the equipment has been incompetently installed, he begins to trash the store. Meanwhile, ignoring his friend, Bono carefully reads the directions. After making a few adjustments in the equipment, he turns on the stereo, and it works perfectly. This incident sets the behavioral pattern for the two central characters—Red Bow, constantly angry or frustrated about something and very touchy about criticisms of Native Americans, and Bono, continuously reading signs, looking to the Great Spirit for direction, and serving as the anchor for both of them during their physical and spiritual journey.

Throughout the film Bono gently but forcefully tries to teach Red Bow how the "old ways" can uplift modern Native Americans, permitting them to deal peacefully but forcefully with events as they develop. Standing in a cold river at dawn, Bono sings a greeting to the morning sun, just as his people have done for centuries. Typically distrustful, Red Bow wades into the water. But the power of the song overtakes him, and meekly, without knowing the words, he tries to sing along.

A reviewer of the film indicated that it provides an uplifting experience for Native Americans, who can leave the theatre without anger, fear, or frustration. In this one, the Indians win. The battle is over beliefs. *Powwow Highway* lets us all share in that victory, for seeing that there is a place for Indian spirituality in the modern world is a victory for all of us. (King, 1989: 17)

The film, in short, rejected an internal-colonialist perspective on both the inferiority of a central Native-American cultural element—spiritual beliefs—and the necessity to remove those beliefs from their lives. Will such stereotype-free films featuring nonstereotyped Native-American characters continue to appear in the future?

Having analyzed the treatment of racial minorities by the mass media, we can examine some effects of that treatment.

EFFECTS OF MASS MEDIA ON RACIAL MINORITIES

We discuss two issues—the impact on racial minorities of stereotypes in the mass media and actions taken by minority groups to offset discrimination in the media.

Stereotypes and Other Distortions: Impact of Media Representations on Minority-Group Members

One particularly troubling aspect of black stereotyping in the media is children's television programming. African-American children watch television extensively. A number of studies have suggested that when family-income level is held constant, African-American children tend to watch more television than their white age mates. What they see presents blacks neither extensively nor positively. In children's shows blacks are represented well below their proportion of the population, constituting about 7 percent of the characters in weekend programming and about 3 percent in after-school shows. Furthermore African-Americans presented are much more likely than whites to be poor, jobless, or in low-status jobs. Such results certainly justify many black parents' and professionals' concern that limited and stereotyped roles for African-Americans on television are likely to promote low self-concepts and negative views toward African-Americans in general (Stroman, 1984).

In addition, Henry Taylor and Carol Dozier (1983) suggested that commercial television has developed a fairly new stereotyped black character—the black superhero. This person is a policeman or other upright citizen, cut very much in the mold of white counterparts, and he tirelessly and often violently enforces order and keeps society safe for the good, law-abiding people of all races. Such programming both legitimates violence when used by law-enforcement officers and encourages young African-Americans to join the police and pursue the same violent agenda.

Television viewing can produce other distorted impressions. A study of 161 adult African-Americans concluded that heavy viewers were more inclined than light viewers to have the mistaken impressions that racial integration is extensive and that blacks are primarily middle-class members. The author argued that when exposed to a glut of commercial television, African-Americans readily obtain the false sense that an effective confrontation of racism now occurs and that political activism demanding social justice and equality no longer remains necessary (Matabane, 1988).

Sometimes the potential impact of blacks' representation on television is complex. As we noted, the "Cosby Show" has avoided the stereotyped African-American characters of the past. Dr. Cliff Huxtable and his family are successful, upper-middle-class people. They are much more successful than most blacks, and as a result the socioeconomic world in which they live and the challenges and problems they face are as remote to the majority of African-Americans as if the program focused on a white, upper-middle-class family. The Huxtables, in fact, are in most regards like successful whites. It appears that one of the reasons that the program has become so popular is that it never addresses tough issues related to race— in particular, political and economic conditions that have promoted limited opportunities for many blacks since the days of slavery. With these issues unaddressed, the "Cosby Show" and the steady flow of other sitcoms featuring middle-class blacks imply that blacks who are not economically successful are personally responsible for their situation (Gates, 1989).

A recent journal article indicated that popular commercial television programs featuring black characters seldom provide significant commentary on the issue of racial identity. When one or more characters start to explore this topic, they tend to do it in a highly specific but nonconducive context—in a comedy situation involving black children located in a largely white environment. Seldom does the program examine the issue in depth, and usually the conclusion emerges that either it is not productive to pursue the search for black identity or, if it appears that this is a positive course of action, viewers obtain little sense of how to go about the search (Peterson-Lewis and Adams, 1990).

Do Your Own Thing

In early 1985 at the University of California at Santa Barbara, there was a symposium on news-media coverage of black America. One of the participants was James Cleaver, executive editor of the *Los Angeles Sentinel,* an African-American newspaper. Not only are African-Americans and other racial minorities underrepresented in the mass media, Cleaver pointed out, but a more important issue, regardless of whether reporters are black or white, involves the presentation of topics about blacks. Unless black reporters have lived and worked in black communities, they are unlikely to be sensitive to urban black residents. Cleaver analyzed a recent story in the *Los Angeles Times,* a major white-owned newspaper. It discussed African-Americans' criminal activities in white residential areas. The factual material was accurate, Cleaver conceded. However, he noted that "the manner in which this was presented led the reader to believe that every person in the black community was a criminal. It led people to believe that they could not be safe in the black community" (*Center Magazine,* 1983: 9). To present African-Americans positively, Cleaver concluded, African-American mass media must continue to exist.

Certainly there is historical precedent for this position. Often African-Americans have not been permitted to participate extensively in the mass media, and they have not been represented effectively in them. Their alternative has been to found their own media. In the middle of the nineteenth century, Frederick Douglass's *North Star* condemned slavery, and late in that century, T. Thomas Fortune's *New York Age* blasted African-Americans' treatment as second-class citizens. In the twentieth century, African-American newspapers in many cities became vehicles operating on behalf of African-Americans. During World War I, they encouraged many readers to move to industrial centers for jobs. While supporting the war, African-American newspapers urged the complete integration of African-Americans into American life. Many of the newspapers prospered, with several having weekly circulations of over 100,000 by 1920 and more than 200,000 20 years later. Large black papers published several editions to service different sections of the country, and a few were sufficiently prosperous to form chains in various cities.

During the late nineteenth and early twentieth centuries, no black journalist was more celebrated than Ida B. Wells, who dedicated her life to fighting racism. Just recently her remarkable achievements have started to receive public attention, and it seems fitting to summarize them here.

Wells's first public action involving racism occurred when at the age of 22, she sat in the all-white "ladies car" of a train and refused to move when ordered to do so; she was removed forcibly from the train. Wells's articles about her protest led to her entrance into journalism, and she soon became the editor and co-owner of the *Memphis Free Speech.*

As a journalist Wells condemned the lynching of three black friends whose grocery store had successfully competed against a white-owned store. Lynchings became Wells's chief target, and she believed that the only effective way to convince whites to stop killing blacks was to punish the oppressors economically—to deprive them of black workers. Wells wrote editorials urging blacks to pack up and move to the newly opened Oklahoma Territory, and thousands went. Analyzing sources of white violence toward African-Americans, Wells wrote that sometimes there seemed to be an intense attraction between white women and African-American men. Whites were infuriated and stormed her newspaper, destroying the presses.

Wells, who was in the North at the time, was forced into exile and threatened with death if she ever returned to the South. First in New York

City and then in Chicago, Wells worked as a journalist for African-American newspapers in an effort to alleviate violence against African-Americans and to promote African-Americans' basic rights. Continuing to believe that economic pressure was the most effective means of ending lynching, she traveled to England, which was a major market for Southern cotton. She spoke with prominent individuals and lectured to groups, providing detailed information about the torture and killing of Southern blacks and seeking to convince the English to boycott Southern cotton if lynching continued. As a result of Wells's action, the English applied some pressure on Southern business people.

At the age of 60, Wells risked death by returning to the South for the first time in 30 years. Unrecognized by white authorities, she managed to interview 12 black farmers who had been sentenced to death for defending themselves against a white mob. Back in Chicago Wells wrote a pamphlet describing the case in detail and demanding the men's freedom. Largely because of Wells's effort, the prisoners were released (*Public Broadcasting System,* 1989).

While the largest black newspapers have lost circulation in recent years, there is still a substantial number of black print media. In 1979 there were over 350 black newspapers, magazines, and bulletins published on a regular weekly, monthly, or quarterly basis. The most recent growth has involved monthly or quarterly magazines such as *Ebony* and *Jet; Tuesday,* a Sunday supplement in many white newspapers; and *Monitor,* a supplement in many African-American weeklies. At present there are only two African-American newspapers published daily (Franklin and Moss, 1988: 379; Jaynes and Williams, 1989: 171).

Like African-Americans other racial minorities are significantly underrepresented in the mass media. Some Native Americans have followed blacks' lead, realizing that the only way to publicize their interests effectively is to establish their own newspapers. For instance, *Daybreak* is a quarterly publication, and its editorials and articles discuss historical and contemporary Native-American cultures and activities, and, in particular, racist oppressions. Next to the paper's masthead is a statement with a distinctly antiinternal-colonialist tone: "*Daybreak* is written by contemporary Indians to reflect ancient tribal values in new ways, to transfer knowledge to the future generations. Join us today and enjoy our insights about Indian realities" (*Daybreak,* 1989: 3).

Like African-Americans and Native Americans, Puerto Ricans have limited exposure in popular mass media. Newspapers, which have served a prominent role for blacks, have had a less significant impact on Puerto Ricans. In New York City, for example, Spanish-language papers have not been owned by Puerto Ricans and have not focused on their interests and problems. While generally not concentrating on Puerto Ricans, Spanish-language radio and television stations have provided music, news, and entertainment that have helped give Puerto Ricans a sense of being "at home" in a strange land (Fitzpatrick, 1987: 59–60).

REFERENCES

Abarry, Abu Shardow. 1990. "The African-American Legacy in American Literature." *Journal of Black Studies* 20 (June): 379–398.

Butterfield, Fox. 1990. "Boston in Uproar over Murder Case." *New York Times* (January 8): A12.

Center Magazine. 1983. "American Blacks as Seen by the Media: Getting the Story Straight." 16 (January/February): 8–15.

Clifton, James A. 1990. "Cultural Fictions." *Society* 27 (May/June): 19–28.

Colon, Jesus. 1961. *A Puerto Rican in New York.* New York: Mainstream Publishers.

Crisis. 1985. "Blacks & Mass Media: Where Do We Stand?" 92 (June/July): 27–31.

Daybreak. 1989. "Masthead Statement." 3 (Spring): 3.

Dubin, Steven C. 1987. "Symbolic Slavery: Black Representations in Popular Culture." *Social Problems* 34 (April): 122–140.

Edmond, Alfred, Jr. 1989. "It's Showtime!" *Black Enterprise* 19 (April): 46–48.

Feagin, Joe R. 1989. *Racial & Ethnic Relations.* Englewood Cliffs, NJ: Prentice-Hall. Third edition.

Fitzpatrick, Joseph P. 1987. *Puerto Rican Americans: The Meaning of Migration to the Mainland.* Englewood Cliffs, NJ: Prentice-Hall. Second edition.

Franklin, John Hope, and Alfred A. Moss, Jr. 1988. *From Slavery to Freedom: A History of Negro Americans.* New York: Alfred A. Knopf. Sixth edition.

Gates, Henry Louis, Jr. 1989. "TV's Black World Turns—But Stays Unreal." *New York Times* (November 12): Sec. 2, 1.

Goffman, Erving. 1974. *Stigma: Notes on the Management of Spoiled Identity.* New York: Jason Aronson.

Hartmann, Paul, and Charles Husband. 1974. *Racism and the Mass Media.* Totowa, NJ: Rowman & Littlefield.

Humphrey, Ronald, and Howard Schuman. 1984. "The Portrayal of Blacks in Magazine Advertisements: 1950–1982." *Public Opinion Quarterly* 48 (Fall): 551–563.

Jaynes, Gerald David, and Robin M. Williams, Jr. (eds.). 1989. *A Common Destiny: Blacks and American Society.* Washington, DC: National Academy Press.

Jones, Alex S. 1990. "Bias and Recklessness Are Charged in Boston Reporting of Stuart Slaying." *New York Times* (January 14): A21.

Jones, Margaret. 1990. "Salt of the Earth Books." *Publisher's Weekly* 237 (October 12): 29–30.

Kaufman, Michael T. 1989. "In a New Film, Spike Lee Tries To Do the Right Thing." *New York Times* (June 25): Sec. 2, 1.

King, Bruce. 1989. "*Powwow Highway:* Gary Farmer on the Road to Stardom." *Daybreak* 3 (Spring): 16–17.

Kitano, Harry H. L., and Roger Daniels. 1988. *Asian Americans: Emerging Minorities.* Englewood Cliffs, NJ: Prentice-Hall.

MacDonald, J. Fred. 1983. *Blacks and White TV: Afro-Americans in Television since 1948.* Chicago: Nelson-Hall.

Maldonado, Lionel A. 1982. "Mexican Americans: The Emergence of a Minority," pp. 168–195 in Anthony Gary Dworkin and Rosalind J. Dworkin (eds.), *The Minority Report.* New York: Holt, Rinehart and Winston. Second edition.

Matabane, Paula W. 1988. "Television and the Black Audience: Cultivating Moderate Perspectives on Racial Integration." *Journal of Communication* 38 (Autumn): 21–31.

Peterson-Lewis, Sonja, and Afesa Adams. 1990. "Television's Model of the Quest for African Consciousness: A Comparison with Cross' Empirical Model of Psychological Nigrescence." *Journal of Black Psychology* 16 (Spring): 55–72.

Public Broadcasting System. 1989. "Ida B. Wells: A Passion for Justice." (December 19).

Staples, Robert, and Terry Jones. 1985. "Culture, Ideology and Black Television Images." *Black Scholar* 16 (May/June): 10–20.

Stedman, Raymond William. 1982. *Shadows of the Indian: Stereotypes in American Culture.* Norman: University of Oklahoma Press.

Stroman, Carolyn A. 1984. "The Socialization Influence of Television on Black Children." *Journal of Black Studies* 15 (September): 79–100.

Taylor, Henry, and Carol Dozier. 1983. "Television Violence, African-Americans, and Social Control, 1950–1976." *Journal of Black Studies* 14 (December): 107–136.

Time. 1984. "Blues for Black Actors." (October 1): 76.

VanDerBeets, Richard. 1984. *The Indian Captivity Narrative.* Lanham, MD: University Press of America.

Chapter
9

South Africa and Brazil: Comparative Contexts of Racism

*J*oseph Lelyveld, an American journalist, was driving through heavy traffic in Johannesburg, the largest city in South Africa. It was night and raining heavily, and as he pulled away from a light, Lelyveld heard a scream, then a thud, and his windshield was smashed.

A black man wearing black trousers and jacket was lying on the pavement a few feet from the car. Lelyveld left his car and checked the man's pulse, which was strong. Then he covered him with a blanket and tried to direct traffic around him. White bystanders approached Lelyveld to learn whether he was all right and to assure him that they had seen the man dart out between parked cars; some even pressed little pieces of paper with their addresses into his hand, assuring him that they would be happy to testify on his behalf. Black bystanders stood at a distance, silently watching.

Meanwhile nobody was paying much attention to the figure under the soggy blanket. Lelyveld covered him again, this time with his raincoat, and found a policeman sitting nearby in his car reading a comic book. Lelyveld asked the policeman to please call an ambulance. It had already been called, the policeman said. The man would die of pneumonia before it arrived, Lelyveld asserted. It would arrive soon, the policeman said. Had the man been white the ambulance would have been there in minutes. But in South Africa, where nearly everything is segregated, Saturday nights are a particularly busy time for ambulances attending blacks, and it was an hour and a quarter before one arrived.

An hour later Lelyveld phoned the hospital and was told that the injury was nothing serious, just a bump on the head. He asked for the patient's name and learned it was Clifton Roche. The next morning Lelyveld planned to have a good neurologist examine the injured man.

But the next morning, nobody at the hospital had heard of Clifton Roche. Lelyveld went to police headquarters and was told that this wasn't unusual—that hospitals would release black patients shortly after accidents and then they'd sometimes be found dead a few days later. The policeman was courteous and promised to see if he could find out anything about Clifton Roche. For days Lelyveld called but was told each time that "your Bantu has not been found." Lelyveld left South Africa briefly, and then on his return he went to the hospital to search its records. There was no trace of Clifton Roche. The last time he phoned police headquarters Lelyveld was told, "You don't have to worry. No action will be taken against you."

This was Lelyveld's initiation into South African society, where what happened to blacks was a source of indifference to whites, unless, of course, the blacks did something directly affecting their welfare. What would have happened if he, Lelyveld, had stepped out between the cars and Clifton Roche had knocked him down? (Lelyveld, 1985: 11–13).

For this chapter South Africa provides one comparative case study and Brazil the other. Stepping outside our own cultural boundaries, we can get different perspectives on how racism affects human relations. On the surface, certainly, South Africa offers a far more devastating racism than the considerably milder picture in the United States and Brazil. At the end of the discussion, will we have new insights about whether, as we noted in Chapter 1, race is a "persistent category of advantage and privilege." Let's wait and see.

THE SOUTH AFRICAN CASE

We begin with a look at the country's history, then discuss current racial policies, and finally consider its future.

The Development of *Apartheid*

At the end of the eighteenth century, four large black groups dominated what would eventually become the Republic of South Africa. Conflict among these groups was frequent, including a series of bloody wars in the 1820s known as the *difaqane.* One significant impact of these wars was that many black tribal settlements were disrupted, making it much easier for recently arrived white immigrants to occupy unchallenged large sections of land.

In the 1650s white settlement started with Dutch immigrants brought over by the Dutch East India Company. During the 1820s over 3000 British citizens arrived in the Cape Colony, and for the rest of the century, thousands of European immigrants settled in that area. Beginning in the late 1830s, about 15,000 primarily Dutch-speaking whites, who were dissatisfied with British rule and seeking more land, left the Cape Colony and spread into the interior in what became known as "the Great Trek." When white settlers encountered blacks, they either expelled or conquered them. Conflicts between British and Dutch-speaking settlers (Afrikaners) frequently occurred over land or other natural resources, and eventually the Anglo-Boer War of 1899 produced the British conquest of what had been two independent Boer states. Afrikaners were defeated but not subdued. They produced an Afrikaner version of South African history, celebrating its central events, heroes, and martyrs. These people stressed that theirs was a divine destiny—to lead the way to wealth and prominence in a white supremacist nation (Oberholster, 1988; Thompson, 1990).

British rule was brief. Afrikaners outnumbered the British, and in 1948 their political party—the National Party—won control of the government and has maintained it ever since. Shortly afterward the policy of *apartheid* began. *Apartheid,* which means separate development, is a government policy involving racial segregation of major facilities—residential areas, hotels, restaurants, buses, work locations, and even staircases and toilets. *Apartheid* represents the implementation of internal colonialism on a scale never attempted in the United States since the slavery era. To many modern Americans, *apartheid* has become a term suggesting hatred and bigotry, the epitome of racism, but precisely what the policy involves is not well known. Let's examine it.

In the 1950s the winds of change were sweeping across Africa, and a host of new nations emerged from what had been former European colonies. Hendrik Verwoerd, the prime minister of South Africa, recognized that in this social climate Great Britain would be unwilling to agree to a long-time South African request that three British territories bordering on South Africa be incorporated by it. Acknowledging Britain's outlook, Verwoerd declared that he would set aside his country's previous position and encourage Great Britain to permit these territories to become independent.

On the surface Verwoerd's decision might have seemed progressive, even humane. Actually because of the poverty dominating these areas, the proposed course of action, which Britain quickly accepted, simply assured South Africa's legal separation from land and people that represented an economic liability. These black nation states and other African homelands tend to be overcrowded with no mining, very little manufacturing, and hardly any arable land. There are ten of these territories. Four have become independent, and the other six, though maintaining some degree of autonomy, remain part of the Republic of South Africa unless they decide to choose the highly questionable option of independence.

To survive, many blacks leave independent states and impoverished rural homelands within South Africa itself and migrate into South African cities. Often men go alone, living in barracks and leaving their families behind. Or, blacks settle in the sprawling black communities on the out-skirts of cities. In either case, because of *apartheid*'s requirement that races remain residentially separated, they seldom can avoid long com-mutes to work.

With a surplus of cheap labor available, whites have been systemati-cally making it more difficult for blacks to move into the cities. The domi-nant group has used two major techniques. First, since the middle 1960s, the central government has deliberately slowed and in some cases even stopped construction of African housing in cities. Second, there has been the outright destruction of black communities; in several instances bulldozers have flattened shelters and huts housing 10,000 to 15,000 peo-ple (Badsha, 1986: 10–14). It is apparent, in short, that under *apartheid* white leadership has harshly applied the internal-colonialist principle of restricting racial minorities' activity, including residential location.

These are some brutal historical realities of South Africa, and they continue to dominate the lives of blacks in that society. And yet while *apartheid* exists, the current leadership has learned to temper its restric-tions, allowing some actions that might strike the outside observer as surprising. For instance, authorities have relaxed extensive censorship. In the record section of the O.K. Bazaar, a big department store in Cape Town, an American woman heard Stevie Wonder's "Master Blaster," a song celebrating the independence of neighboring Zimbabwe. Among the white elite, there have been a host of encounter groups in which the participants, including a few members of racial minorities, have discussed and even debated the country's future.

But, historically, most apparent softenings of *apartheid* have had an underside. At the very moment "Master Blaster" was heard in the O.K. Bazaar, South African undercover units were taking steps to overthrow the black government in Zimbabwe. And while a few members of racial minorities took part in elites' encounter groups, these participants were carefully chosen "responsible" individuals who were considerably less militant than thousands of other possible spokespeople for racial minori-ties (Lelyveld, 1985: 29–31). The South African government, in short, has permitted some activities that have offset the harshness of *apartheid,* but the policy itself has remained a daily reality.

RACISM IN CONTEMPORARY SOUTH AFRICA

We look briefly at prominent South African institutions and then, to make the reality of what's being discussed more vivid, examine *apartheid* in everyday life. First, though, as a background for this discussion, we briefly examine the size of different racial groups.

South Africa's Racial Composition

In 1985 the population of the Republic of South Africa was 23,385,645. Of the total, 4,568,739 people (19.5 percent of the population) were white, with nearly twice as many Afrikaners as whites of British descent. The Coloreds, who are of mixed white, black, and sometimes Malay ancestry, were 2,832,705 in number (12.1 percent). Indians, who arrived in nineteenth-century South Africa to work on sugarcane plantations, comprised 821,361 individuals (3.5 percent). Finally blacks were the largest group, with 15,162,840 people (64.8 percent) (South African Foundation, 1988: 5).

A feature of South Africa which has made it unique among African territories located south of the Sahara desert is that for over a century-and-a-half, it has contained a relatively large white group, which has made the country its homeland and has committed itself to maintaining its position of dominance and privilege. Most sub-Saharan African territories were former European colonies that contained a small resident white contingent, often less than 1 percent of the country's total population. Zimbabwe, formerly Southern Rhodesia and located directly north of South Africa, was once controlled by its white settler class, but eventually the whites stepped down when a black ticket headed by Robert Mugabe won at the polls. Now both extensive verbal and guerrilla attacks against the South African ruling class originate from Zimbabwe.

As we look at institutional structures in South Africa, we begin to obtain a more detailed sense of how the ruling whites have imposed their control on racial minorities.

Racism in South Africa's Major Institutions

In Western democracies people grow to adulthood believing that with the inalienable right to vote in free and open elections, they participate in the process of choosing their rulers. In spite of possessing this right, they realize that tyranny can occur; without it, however, tyranny is almost inevitable.

In 1984 the South African government adopted a new constitution after a two-thirds majority of the white electorate had approved it the previous year. This document made some concession to the existing policy excluding all minority-group members from national elections. Now, along with whites, Coloreds and Indians could choose their own representatives. Each racial group would elect members to its own parliamentary house, which was proportional to its size in the population—thus 4:2:1 for whites, Coloreds, and Indians respectively (South African Foundation, 1988: 16–17).

Opponents to this "reform" pointed out that with exclusion of blacks, whites' supremacy was assured. But the supporters of the new plan were quick to emphasize that blacks were permitted political participation: They could elect representatives within their own townships. Most blacks have not bought this idea, boycotting all-black elections, which in their eyes can do nothing or almost nothing to alleviate the crushing oppression produced by *apartheid*. Furthermore both Coloreds and Indians have also turned out for elections in small numbers, realizing that with continued white control they inevitably remain second-class citizens.

Above all, constitutional reform has not changed the economic picture for racial minorities. In 1985 the average monthly earnings for the four racial groups were R418 (418 Rands) for blacks, R561 for Coloreds, R770 for Indians, and R1561 for whites (South African Foundation, 1988: 18–19). In South Africa an average African wage earner receives about 26.7 percent—barely a quarter of what an average white person makes.

This is a pretty grim picture, but it becomes even grimmer when one considers that it does not include the vast number of unemployed South Africans, who are primarily Africans. One can be working and still remain poor, but one is infinitely poorer without any economic resources. South Africa has no accurate figures on unemployment, but it is certain that large numbers of blacks forced out of farms, towns, and villages all over the country and onto the overcrowded reserves are without employment and also without prospect of finding any. One indication of the terrible poverty many Africans face is the estimate that in a given year about 50,000 black children die of malnutrition and other related diseases (Badsha, 1986: 7).

A relationship among political power, income, and education exists in all countries. Not surprisingly whites, who have the lion's share of power and income in South Africa, also have the best educational opportunities. In 1987 the average per capita governmental expenditure for whites for education was R2160; for Indians it was R1450; for Coloreds R818; for blacks it was R368, or about 17 percent the per capita government expenditure just for whites. Inevitably the overall quality of children's educational experience corresponds with the expenditure. For instance, the teacher-pupil ratio for white students was one teacher to every 19 students, and for blacks it was one teacher for every 41 students (South African Foundation, 1988: 56–62). Such a situation represents a perpetuation of internal colonialism's colonial-labor principle, with racial minorities' limited educational opportunities keeping them restricted to low-paying jobs that primarily benefit the white controllers.

Those with power and wealth are best situated to obtain quality education, and, in turn, superior education helps them maintain their dominance. In South Africa, of course, whites are decisively helped in this regard by the *apartheid* system, which, as we see in the following pages, promotes their dominance with a variety of very concrete, drastic measures.

The Maintenance of *Apartheid* in Everyday Life

For white South Africans, the country is a democracy, but for Indians, Coloreds, and most decisively blacks, one could persuasively argue that it remains a totalitarian government, even with recent constitutional "reforms." Consider the following situations, which show the impact of *apartheid* on racial minorities.

Since Afrikaners took control of the South African government in 1948, there has been an effort to limit the migration of blacks to cities and their environs—a clear illustration of internal colonialism's principle of restricting racial minorities' activity. In Cape Town this policy has been sufficiently successful that by 1970 black men in the area of that major South African city outnumbered black women by three to one, and in the African township of Langa, where thousands of workers were kept in barracks, the ratio was 11 to one.

Many men who were driven to the cities because it was the only place to find work felt that living without their families was wrong. One worker who had brought in his family illegally complained bitterly, saying that the construction firm which employed him and was about to build a first-class hostel for single men was failing to acknowledge the importance of the family in a country's development. He said, "That is why I am critical of its approach. Because it neglects the very core of nation building" (Badsha, 1986: 42).

This man lived in Crossroads, a squatter settlement outside of Cape Town. Blacks resided illegally in this area for a number of reasons. Some, like the man quoted above, refused to live in single housing provided by their companies, risking the wrath of the law to be with their families. Others had been forced out of the city as the economy expanded and the legal areas for black residence became hopelessly overcrowded. Still others streamed into the area from outlying black areas looking both for jobs and a place to live. During the 1970s thousands of shacks and modest houses were built.

Authorities reacted harshly. The infamous pass law, which required blacks to have passes to enter so-called white areas, were reinstated, employers were threatened with huge fines if they hired "illegal" blacks, and, finally, the flimsy cottages and shacks of about 25,000 people living nearby were destroyed. The word was out that Crossroads would be bulldozed shortly afterward.

But Crossroads had become a community. Despite the absence of all modern conveniences and effective housing, life was better there than any place else in the vicinity in which blacks were permitted to reside. Crime rates were low, work was fairly plentiful, and the nutritional status of children was considerably better than that of children living in the countryside.

Eventually in 1979 the people of Crossroads won a stay of execution from the government, but the situation remained uncertain as officials refused to make a long-term commitment. Then in 1985 there was a battle between stone-throwing youngsters and police that left 22 people dead. In 1985 the government finally declared that Crossroads would remain and be upgraded (Badsha, 1986: 110). For the present, at least, the residents of the community had won a substantial victory.

Difficult as it is, life in urban areas tends to be much better than in the homelands and independent territories restricted to blacks under *apartheid.* In the Qwa Qwa reserve, for instance, a government commission reported that by 1920 the area was already overcrowded with 5000 inhabitants; by 1970 the number had risen to 24,000.

The level of impoverishment is apparent in the following family history. The Serote family arrived in Qwa Qwa from a nearby white-owned farm in 1974. Since then Mr. Serote worked at a variety of jobs, but in 1982 tuberculosis made him too ill to continue. In that same year, Mr. Serote's eldest son obtained a job some distance away in the gold-mining town of Welcom. He too became ill but clung to the job because it was the family's only source of income. The second son was removed from school halfway through that year; he would have gone to work but he was too young to apply for a job as a migrant worker and could find nothing within the territory.

By the middle of the year, the family faced a severe crisis. Mrs. Serote and her youngest daughter were both diagnosed as suffering from pellagra, an extreme form of malnutrition, and a younger child was sent home from school because he was fainting from hunger in class. Drought and exhaustion meant that even the small vegetable garden near the house no longer received care. Begging or borrowing from neighbors was no longer possible, and because of the impersonal system of blacks' relocation, neither Mr. nor Mrs. Serote had relatives in the vicinity. When interviewed both parents spoke of their anxiety for and guilt about their children, confessing that they had failed as parents. "I cannot sleep at night any longer," said Mrs. Serote, "because my son was so ill when he last came home, but I sent him back to work [in Welcom] because his is the only income we have. I am forced to kill one child in order to feed the others" (Badsha, 1986: 15). Neighbors were "appalled and ashamed" by the horrible sight of a family literally starving to death before their eyes while, besieged by their own poverty, they could do little to help.

Blacks are the poorest, most victimized racial group in South Africa, but other racial minorities are also poor and exploited by racism. In Durban, for instance, blacks, Indians, Coloreds, and whites once shared neighborhoods, but *apartheid* laws have forced all but whites out of the choice areas, compelling minority-group members to move elsewhere. Indians were ordered to leave prime locations close to the Indian Ocean, and in the vacated areas, real-estate speculators cashed in on high-rise apartments and shopping-centers restricted to whites. In the middle 1980s, an irate Indian leader explained, "They don't need their laws anymore! They've done it! Whoever comes into power will not be able to change *this*" (Lelyveld, 1985: 26–27). Racial minorities' displacement, in short, has been accomplished: *Apartheid* had triumphed.

A recent study of racial minorities' residential location in South African cities confirmed this conclusion, indicating that racial segregation has expanded through the twentieth century, with a marked increase since the 1960s when urban segregation laws were most strongly enforced. The highest level of racial segregation has been among blacks, followed by Indians, and then Coloreds. While there is not total racial segregation, *apartheid* generally prevails in South African cities. As a result even with official elimination of *apartheid,* prospects for urban integration are remote (Christopher, 1990).

In South Africa, blacks live in a police state. The significance of that statement is apparent in the following section.

Being Black in South Africa: Living in a Police State

While racism continues to exist in the United States, its victims often have the opportunity to confront it—with an appeal to the appropriate agency, some type of legal action, or public protest.

In South Africa few blacks have had such opportunities. Under *apartheid* they have known that they are considered racially inferior and that the best they can expect is the opportunity to make a modest living and, away from work, to be left alone by whites. Often, however, black South Africans have been subjected to the stringent controls described by internal-colonialist theory.

In his autobiography Mark Mathabane, a black South African who was born in 1960, described the experience of growing up in Alexandra, a black ghetto near Johannesburg. Both then and now, violence has been an intimate part of residents' daily lives.

As internal-colonialist theory emphasizes, the white power structure has controlled blacks' physical activity—in this case through police action. Once a year in Alexandra they designated "Operation Clean-up Month," during which black policemen led by white officers would comb the ghetto searching for gangsters, prostitutes, people whose passbooks (which indicated that they were permitted to live and work in the city) were not in order, or families living illegally in the area.

One winter in the middle of the night, the police raided the shack rented by the Mathabane family. Twice they banged at the kitchen door, yelling that if it weren't opened immediately, they would break it down. Five-year-old Mark was sleeping on a piece of cardboard close to the door, and he was so frightened that he urinated, soaking himself and the blanket in which he was wrapped. From the bedroom his mother whispered not to open the door until she and Mark's father had a chance to hide themselves.

When Mark opened the door, two tall black policemen in starched brown uniforms rushed into the room and shined a flashlight in his eyes. One kicked the young boy in the side, sending him crashing into a crate in the corner. Mark tried to stand up, but another kick flattened him. "What took you so long to open the bloody door?" the policeman shouted. He was about to kick the boy again when his partner stopped him.

They began searching for Mark's parents. The bedroom door was locked from the inside, and when no one responded to the policemen's demand to open it, they knocked it down.

Looking under the bed, they spotted Mr. Mathabane, who was naked, and ordered him out. "I'm coming, *nkosi* [lord]," Mark's father whimpered. They asked him where his wife was, and he said she was sleeping at the residence where she was employed as a kitchen girl. Apparently the policemen believed him.

One interrogator demanded to see Mr. Mathabane's passbook, quickly noting that several taxes were unpaid and that one entry indicated that Mrs. Mathabane was expected to sleep at home. How could he account for his wife's absence, the policeman asked, and playfully began prodding Mr. Mathabane's penis with his nightstick. Mark's father offered an excuse for his wife.

Why, the policeman continued, did an old man want to remain in the city. Mr. Mathabane, who was only in his thirties but was prematurely aged by an impoverished life, replied that there were no jobs in the reserves.

The policeman said that the statement was wrong—that until recently he had been living in the reserves and that people like his own father continued to lead comfortable, productive lives there. In Alexandra and other black ghetto areas, residents knew that the white leadership preferred black policemen with a rural background. Such recruits resented the less poverty-stricken, more sophisticated urban blacks and enjoyed acting as cruel instruments of the white power structure.

The policeman summarized the offenses displayed in Mr. Mathabane's passbook and asked whether he could figure out a solution. Looking up for a moment from the floor, Mr. Mathabane forced a smile—not a spontaneous smile but "a begging smile, a passive acceptance of the policeman's authority. After smiling my father again dropped his eyes to the floor" (Mathabane, 1986: 22). The policeman whispered in Mr. Mathabane's ear, giving him the chance to buy his way out of the predicament with a bribe. But Mark's father had no money, and so he was forced to serve two months of hard labor on a white man's potato farm.

In 1966 the raids increased, and frequently they occurred in daytime. Children became adept at observing and analyzing police actions and would rush home to warn their parents. But Mark was unable to do so. He wrote:

> That brutal encounter with the police had left indelible scars. The mere sight of police vans now had the power of blanking my mind, making me forget all I had learned, making me rely on my instincts, which invariably told me to flee, to cower, lest I end up face-to-face with a policeman and get flogged. I became a useless sentry. (Mathabane, 1986: 28)

Many black South Africans have grown to maturity with similar experiences. They have found that living under *apartheid,* where the brutalities of oppressed status is a constant reality, has been a continuous nightmare.

THE FUTURE OF SOUTH AFRICAN RACE RELATIONS

Nobody has the crystal ball that forecasts South Africa's future, but some people are making predictions. Roughly speaking, there seem to be three camps, whose predictions about that country's future racial policy are probably closely allied to their hopes. While representatives of all three camps exist in South Africa, each has its supporters outside the country, too.

First, there are the white racists, who believe that *apartheid* can survive indefinitely with little or no moderation. Some difference of opinion exists within this group, but its members are staunch supporters of the racial and political status quo.

Second, one finds the moderates, who hope that the current racial policy can be reformed to permit a decent, pleasant life for all residents of the country. In November 1987 the proponents of this position felt that the release from prison of Govan Mbeki, a leading black anti*apartheid* activist, was an indication of government leaders' willingness to discuss sharing power with blacks. But the likelihood of such a change sharply declined three months later when the government banned political activities of 17 leading anti*apartheid* groups (Crooks, 1988).

Third, many South Africans, Americans, and other observers of South African race relations believe that *apartheid* simply can't be reformed—that it must be eliminated by either peaceful or violent means. Oliver Tambo, a prominent official of the African National Congress, which is the leading organization for black majority rule in South Africa, expressed this view when he stated that "reform of *apartheid* is a meaningless concept." He went on to explain that white politicians pursuing such a course were trying to give the impression that change would occur but were scrupulously avoiding any fundamental change. Tambo concluded, "The bottom line of this strategem can be summed up as a sharing power while retaining control over the destiny of our people in the hands of the white minority" (Tambo, 1987: 9).

In February 1990 F. W. de Klerk, the new president of South Africa, legalized the African National Congress and released Nelson Mandela, its celebrated leader who had been in prison for 27 years. Three months later Mandela and de Klerk negotiated an agreement that called for a committee on the release of political prisoners, most of whom are black; immunity for politically motivated crimes; and a common commitment to eliminating a national climate of tension and violence.

When the statement was released, the two leaders seemed at ease with each other, smiling and shaking hands for photographers but also courteously disagreeing on specific issues. Yes, the situation was encouraging, Mandela conceded, but when asked whether *apartheid* was dying, he indicated that when he had been sent to prison in 1963, he could not vote. Mandela added, "Twenty-seven years later, I still have no vote and that is due to the color of my skin. You can then decide whether *apartheid* is alive or not" (Wren, 1990: 6).

About two years later, a major step toward ending *apartheid* occurred. On March 18, 1992, 68.7 percent of South Africa's whites approved the idea that all adult citizens of the country be permitted to vote. Contributing to the decisive result, which surprised most experts, were fears about renewed black rebellion and concern about revived international economic sanctions (Wren, 1992). In spite of the importance of the referendum, immediate benefits for blacks and other racial minorities remain questionable. With institutional racism firmly entrenched, their long-term inequality seems likely to continue.

Meanwhile struggles for power involve more than simply blacks against whites. Mandela has hoped to build the African National Congress into a strong, disciplined, multiracial political party of blacks, Coloreds, Indians, and whites. But the group has contained members of diverse backgrounds—prisoners, exiles, trade unionists, and community-organization personnel, with varied, sometimes opposing ideologies and goals. In addition, other black-rights organizations exist. Most powerful is the Pan Africanist Congress, whose leaders claim that Mandela and the African National Congress will sell out blacks' interest during negotiations with the government. In some areas, notably poverty-stricken portions of the province of Natal, violence has been widespread. As long as violence has stayed out of white residential areas, police have been tolerant of the members of different black organizations killing each other in a struggle for territorial control. In fact, many observers suspect that Natal police have supplied ammunition to the most powerful terrorist organization. Between 1987 and 1990, a virtual civil war existed in Natal; over 3500 people were killed and another 70,000 made homeless (Thompson, 1990).

About the only thing certain about the future of South Africa is that the society will continue to change—drastically. Some changes in race relations are occurring that even the most optimistic anti*apartheid* opponents would not have predicted just a few years ago. At the same time, it seems unrealistic to expect the absence of violence. Many whites want *apartheid* or are comfortable with it. They will not simply accept the loss of their privileged positions. For many of them, violence against blacks has always been a readily used option. Blacks, demanding power and equitable economic distribution, are increasingly unwilling to settle for second-class citizenship. Scarred by 300 years of extreme racist oppression, some are willing to strike out violently against any group blocking their efforts for advancement.

In a six-week span in August and September 1990, nearly 800 blacks were killed in what on the surface appeared to be confrontations restricted to blacks—between Zulu tribal members of the Inkatha organization and Xhosa tribal people belonging to the African National Congress. But while struggles between these two groups were real, Nelson Mandela and other black leaders were convinced that white supporters of *apartheid* were the "hidden hand" behind much of the violence. According to Mandela, white extremist groups hired black mercenaries who by violent acts sowed fear and dissension among blacks. On September 13, 1990, a gang of young black men boarded a commuter train near Johannesburg and then methodically attacked black passengers with shotguns, knives, and machetes, killing 26 and wounding over 100 (Wren, 1990a).

Will the South African leadership, white and black, receive sufficient support from their respective constituencies to negotiate a largely peaceful dismantlement of the *apartheid* system? We must wait and see.

Race relations in Brazil offer a contrasting picture.

THE BRAZILIAN CASE

Since the emancipation of slaves a century ago, Brazil has had the international reputation of being a racial paradise, or at least close to it. In recent years, however, that image has begun to tarnish. In 1978 and 1979, for instance, Brazil's leading television network, *Rede Globo,* presented a series for children adapted from stories written by Monteiro Loboto, a well-known Brazilian author, and the series was widely acclaimed. In 1979 the African country of Angola, which is also Portuguese speaking, decided to show the series. After seven installments, however, Angolan television abruptly cancelled the series, charging that it was racist, depicting blacks only in inferior positions. Most offensive to Angolan viewers was the role of Tia [Aunt] Nastácia, an elderly, black cook whom the Angolans considered to be a racial caricature. Brazilians were surprised and asked many questions. Were the Angolans justified? How should blacks be represented in the media? (Skidmore, 1985: 15). If this had been an isolated incident, then concern about racism probably would have soon passed. But it was only one situation drawing widespread criticism.

In the following pages, we briefly examine the racial history of Brazil, then analyze current racial inequalities, and consider future race relations.

The History of Brazilian Race Relations

Predominantly three groups have produced the current racial composition of Brazil—European, initially Portuguese whites, Native Americans, and blacks from Africa.

In the sixteenth century, Portuguese colonists, primarily men, began immigrating to Brazil, and in many cases these men fathered numerous children whose descendents are currently found both among whites and racial minorities. Some of these early immigrants became sugar plantation farmers while others, former Jews known as "new Christians," settled in small ports along the sea coast and engaged in skilled trade, skilled labor, and the professions and became moneylenders to the sugar planters, who were often heavily in their debt. In the nineteenth century, immigrants from other European countries began to come to Brazil. At first Germans and Swiss arrived, followed later by Italians, Poles, and Spaniards.

To supply laborers for the first sugar plantations, early Portuguese colonists hunted down and enslaved Native Americans—substantial numbers of them, since each large sugar plantation required about 200 workers. Early settlers had a few black slaves and found them more manageable than Native Americans since they had been subdued by the slavery system. However, because of wars with Holland during the colony's first two centuries, whites were unable to add appreciably to the number of black slaves. When the wars with Holland finally ended, African slaves replaced Native Americans in agricultural work; Native Americans were often used to care for livestock (Smith, 1972: 52–55).

For about a century, the slave trade occurred in Brazil. While the number of slaves brought to Brazil is unknown, it certainly was significant. In 1819 the population of the country was about 3.6 million people, with about 80 percent—2.9 million—blacks or mulattoes (people of mixed blood). In contrast, in the United States, the ratio was reversed, with whites forming about 80 percent of the population, and racial minorities—blacks and Native Americans—comprising the remaining 20 percent. Even in the American South, where blacks most heavily concentrated, they never represented more than 38 percent of the population.

The different proportions are significant because, unlike the United States, nineteenth-century Brazil simply did not have enough whites to fill key positions in a commercially expanding country, and so blacks and mulattoes could become skilled tradesmen, cowboys, small food growers, and boatmen (Drimmer, 1979: 102). Out of economic necessity, in short, the colonial-labor principle applied less drastically to Brazil than to the United States.

Most slaves, however, remained unskilled agricultural workers. When blacks were freed in 1888, they found few jobs available. At that point they had to compete for agricultural jobs with Native-American laborers now willing to work for wages and with a steady stream of European workers better prepared to function in the postslavery economic system. Many blacks could not find jobs and quickly slipped into terrible poverty (Fernandes, 1969: 1–3). For many Brazilian blacks, that poverty has carried into the present era.

Thus historically racial minorities in Brazil have had diverse economic opportunities. Socially Brazilian society gives the impression of being racially liberated. In modern times racial intermarriage is common, and explicit racial segregation is both unusual and illegal (Webster and Dwyer, 1988). Overall racial practice in Brazil has been fairly progressive, certainly more progressive than in either South Africa or the United States.

But many Brazilians have not been content with such modest claims. Since about 1950 governmental officials and other leading citizens have vocally asserted that Brazil is a racial democracy. They have emphasized two themes—that under no circumstances should people admit that racism occurs in Brazil and that any claim that racism does exist should be attacked as "un-Brazilian" (Smith, 1972: 59).

In the 1970s such attacks were extensive. For instance, when a major newspaper ran a feature story describing the "black is beautiful" movement in Rio de Janeiro, powerful whites sharply criticized the paper, claiming that publicizing such "un-Brazilian" groups was itself "un-Brazilian." But the white elite went much further to protect the country's racially democratic image: In particular, prominent faculty members at the University of São Paulo were forced to retire. While ideologically these men varied, they all were involved in race-relations research where they raised questions that members of the white elite found troubling. In addition, the federal government confiscated a modern journal of opinion, *Argumento*, which featured a hard-headed analysis of Brazil's racial situation. But an even more significant action occurred. Government officials decided to omit the topic of race from the census of 1970, thereby preventing researchers' access to a potentially revealing data source. Without this information or any other large studies on race in Brazil, meaningful analysis and discussion of the issue was impossible. Thus supporters of the doctrine of racial democracy temporarily defeated a potential major threat (Skidmore, 1985: 15–17).

By the late 1970s, however, the tone of the times had changed, and as we see, a major study of race in Brazil produced some important, interesting findings.

Racism in Modern Brazil

A twelve-year-old black boy reached through a car window and snatched a woman's necklace. As he fled, four white men grabbed him and started beating his face and ribs. A black woman intervened, and she too was beaten. Eventually the police arrived and carried off the badly bruised boy. In such situations angry crowds often lynch young thieves on the spot.

Currently there are about 36 million Brazilians under 18, with about 60 percent of them needy and about seven million of them maintaining few or no links with their families (Riding, 1985). The most desperate poor in Brazil—abandoned children, youths who live from muggings, robberies, and other crimes, and families who must remove children from school to perform menial jobs contributing to the family's survival—are overwhelmingly black (Sundiata, 1987: 68).

About 44 percent of Brazil's population is black or mulatto (Christmas, 1988), and many Brazilian minority-group members suffer life-threatening poverty. Two factors contribute significantly to making poor racial minorities' situation in Brazil worse than in the United States. One major difference is that since Franklin Roosevelt's New Deal in the 1930s, the American government has been willing to supply a welfare "safety net," albeit a flimsy one, for the nation's poor, and Brazil offers the poor no similar support.

The second major advantage in the United States has been the strength of the black professional class, whose members, unlike blacks and mulattoes in Brazil, have historically been denied full participatory rights in society. As a result American black professionals have developed a race consciousness that has extended concern to all members of their race, even the poorest (Sundiata, 1987: 68). The irony is that in Brazil the relatively open racial situation has tended to discourage a sense of black consciousness, including a systematic concern by affluent blacks for poor members of their race.

The relative openness of race relations in Brazil does not imply that blacks have been spared diverse effects of racism. Using data from the large 1976 National Household Sample Research, investigators revealed clear indications that racism in Brazil has occurred and continues to occur.

As in the United States, educational attainment in Brazil links to occupational success. Among whites about 27 percent reported no schooling or less than a year while the comparable figure for racial minorities was 46 percent. As the amount of education increased, the gap between whites and racial minorities expanded. Thus while 19 percent of whites and 12 percent of minority-group members completed five to eight years of school, 11 percent of whites and only 3 percent of racial minorities obtained nine or more years of education. For the five-to-eight-year bracket, whites had a 1.55 greater chance of completion, but at the nine-year-and-more level, their chance was 3.15 times greater.

Income differences were equally distinct. Among racial minorities 54 percent received the minimum wage or less while a considerably smaller percentage of whites—23 percent—fell into this category. At the affluent end of the income distribution, 24 percent of whites and 15 percent of minority-group members had an income two to five times the minimum wage, and 16 percent of whites and 4 percent of minority-group individuals received over five times the minimum wage. Overall whites' income was about twice the minority-group members'.

For both education and income, the gap between Brazilian racial

minorities and whites increases when one evaluates higher status categories. Data on these topics indicate racial inequality, but what needs more
analysis is whether racial minorities' inferior job attainments occurred
simply because they started from disadvantaged positions, or, in addition,
because they encountered racism. Research on social mobility provides
clues.

Social mobility is the movement of a person from one social class or
status level to another, either upward or downward with accompanying
gains or losses in wealth, power, and prestige. The following analysis of
social mobility involves people in three broad occupational levels—manual, nonmanual, and upper; the manual and nonmanual categories are also
subdivided.

Among people born into families where the father was employed at
the lower-manual level (workers in domestic services, traditional industries, and local trade), 49 percent of minority-group members compared
to 36 percent of whites remained at the same occupational level while just
21 percent of minority-group individuals and 38 percent of whites rose to
nonmanual positions. Among those coming from the high-manual level
(workers in modern industries and unskilled workers in services), 29 percent of minority-group members and 41 percent of whites obtained nonmanual occupations. Among those born into the nonmanual category, 64
percent of whites and 53 percent of minority-group people in the lower-
nonmanual level (lower-level clerical workers and small owners in commerce and services) achieved positions equal to or higher than their fathers', and in the higher-nonmanual category (high-level clerical workers
and small farmers), the proportions were 44 percent for whites and 26
percent for racial minorities. At the upper level (professionals, managers,
and big-business owners), 47 percent of whites and 24 percent of minority-
group individuals stayed in this highest occupational category; or, revers-
ing the focus, one sees that 76 percent of minority-group people compared
to 53 percent of whites at the upper level were downwardly mobile from
their fathers' upper-level occupations.

These data involve situations where racial minorities and whites origi-
nated from families with about equal socioeconomic status, and yet whites'
upward social mobility or sustained high status was consistently greater
than minority-group members'. Since no other factors influencing these
outcomes are readily apparent, it is hard to avoid concluding that racism
plays a significant role.

In brief, racial inequality persists in Brazil's occupational structure.
There are two major processes. First, racial minorities obtain less education, and as a result they enter the labor market with fewer qualifications.
Second, racial discrimination affects workers' hiring and promotion. Because of these processes, racial minorities suffer "a cycle of cumulative
disadvantage" in their quest for status attainment (Hasenbalg, 1985; Silva,
1985).

These are harsh, important facts that might strike some readers as somewhat abstract. If that is the case, the following illustration should help clarify how racial discrimination can occur in Brazil. José (a pseudonym), a well-known black lawyer and legal scholar, tried in 1970 to pass a set of examinations to receive an appointment to the Law Faculty of the University of Bahia. In a competition organized within the university, José received the highest score on the written examination but failed on the oral examination, which could be attended only by candidates and their examiners. In the following four years, José continued to fail the oral examination, and while he was reluctant to conclude that racism was involved, he saw no alternative explanation. Then in 1974 the oral examinations were opened to the public. José invited friends and legal colleagues to attend, and this time he not only received the highest score on the written examination but also passed the oral (Turner, 1985: 76). He had triumphed but not without extensive exposure to racist treatment.

Besides blacks and mulattoes, Native Americans also suffer racial oppression in Brazil. In the state of Roraima, the government has failed to take active steps to prevent illegal gold-mining and drug-smuggling on Native-American reserves. In Roraima and the nearby state of Acre, forest Indians' traditional way of life is rapidly disappearing as poor people from the rest of Brazil move in and clear the forests (*Economist,* 1987).

The following situation illustrates some complexities of blacks' discrimination in modern Brazil.

The African Connection: An Uncomfortable Policy

During a major holiday in Rio de Janeiro, ambassadors from Ghana and Nigeria appeared in a street celebration, singing in the Yoruba language and dancing with a well-known Brazilian dance troop. Many onlookers were confused about their identity, and in his column a journalist asked, "Who are these two personalities with complicated names?" (Dzidzienyo, 1985: 135). We can consider why African ambassadors' public appearance was a distinctly incongruous event in Brazilian society.

Throughout the book we have noted that racial oppression involves restrictive norms imposed on a racial minority, particularly, limited access to the prized economic, political, and social rewards within the society.

Suppose, however, the nation's dominant group—in this case Brazil's white power structure—wants to establish close, mutually beneficial economic and political relations with groups racially and culturally linked to their own oppressed racial group—in this instance African nations. Let's consider how Brazil's African connection has developed in the past three decades.

Since the early 1960s, Brazilian leaders have encouraged increased relations between their country and independent African countries. Such connections interest many Brazilian groups, including political leaders seeking to increase the nation's stature through broader political alliances, white business people wanting to develop new markets for their products, and black Brazilian groups trying to establish a variety of political, economic, and cultural ties to citizens in African countries.

During the 1960s the all-white Brazilian leadership acted efficiently to advance the African connection—condemning *apartheid* while maintaining political and economic ties to South Africa; encouraging an increasing number of African leaders to make official visits to Brazil; and giving repeated affirmations of historical and cultural links between Africa and Brazil.

But from the African viewpoint, something critical was usually missing—visible involvement of black Brazilians in the official relations between Brazil and African nations. For instance, many black Africans consider the city of Bahia the place where black culture thrives in Brazil. However, when the *Asantehene,* the monarch of the Ashantis of Ghana, visited Bahia, he was not officially introduced to any black Bahians during his two-day stay. In contrast, in São Paulo, his party met a large number of black Brazilians, including federal and state politicians, professionals, journalists, and students. The reason for the difference was that in São Paulo, Adalberto Camargo, a black elected official, played a major role in planning the *Asantehene*'s schedule.

Sometimes the African connection produces controversy among black Brazilians. For instance, Abdias do Nascimento, a well-known writer, painter, and activist, criticized black organizations in Bahia for failure to promote black Brazilians' involvement in relations with African officials. Nascimento's critics, in turn, accused him of being argumentative and antiwhite.

At present black Brazilians are minimally involved in their nation's official relations with African countries. The white political and economic leadership in Brazil, the oppressing group for black Brazilians, would like the involvement to remain modest. Black Brazilians and many African officials take an opposing view. How this situation unfolds will affect not only the African connection but also many black Brazilians' political, economic, and social status in their own society.

The Future of Brazilian Race Relations

Recently an upsurge of black consciousness has occurred in Brazil. Groups involved have differed in style and goals but have shared the strongly held belief that the myth of racial democracy has been harmful for blacks and mulattoes and must be destroyed (Turner, 1985). Yet it is doubtful that such a movement can significantly change racial minorities' plight in Brazil.

Certainly racism thrives in that society. While internal-colonialist policies are toned down in Brazil, whites hold minority groups in check. A larger if related problem is that in this society dire poverty exists for an enormous number of people, primarily members of racial minorities whose plight results principally from historical racial oppression, not explicit racist practice today. Elimination of current racist practices would do little to benefit most of them. To significantly change their lives, the government would need to enact drastic economic reforms, beginning with a "safety net" welfare program.

But such a policy is not likely to develop soon. In 1990 Fernando Collor de Mello was elected president, campaigning as a champion of the "shirtless and shoeless" and an enemy of the "corrupt elite." Once in office, however, his policies reversed these priorities: Brazil's poor racial minorities faced new rounds of layoffs and income cuts while the Collor government protected elites' economic interests (Silverstein, 1990).

CONCLUSION

The material in this chapter offers distinct contrast to the American racial picture, and at the end we find ourselves with three quite different pictures. Runaway winner of the blue ribbon for racial oppression is South Africa, where in spite of recent developments, the dominant white group still maintains an explicitly racist policy of white political, economic, and social superiority and racial minorities' subjugation and misery. Neither the United States nor Brazil so blatantly establishes the racist supremacy of a dominant group. In South Africa internal colonialism continues to thrive even though it is under attack. The American experience reported in this book suggests that even if *apartheid* is officially dismantled, its negative impact in politics, work, housing, education, and the family will persist indefinitely.

In the United States, the mainstream ideology involving race has been changing, showing signs of lessened racism. Survey data suggest that most white Americans don't like to think of themselves as racist, don't wish to assert a sense of racial superiority. Nonetheless ample evidence of racism exists. One might conclude that the American racial picture is somewhat like Brazil's. In both cases current ideology differs from the present reality of sustained racism.

Furthermore another parallel between the two societies might be growing. Earlier we noted that because of more pronounced historical racism in the United States than in Brazil, the black professional class has maintained closer ties to poor blacks than their affluent counterparts in Brazil. That connection, however, is starting to change. Perhaps 10 to 15 percent of young American blacks are completely removed from any contact with poor people (Clark, 1979), and thus like successful Brazilian blacks, they are developing an insensitivity to the combined impact of poverty and racism.

What is unique about Brazil is that for decades there has been an ideology of racial democracy, which the elite has strongly supported and even defended. If a Brazilian makes the claim that racism occurs in their country, they are unpatriotic—un-Brazilian.

In all three countries, notable parallels occur: In each of these societies, minority-group members are considerably poorer and more deprived educationally, economically, and politically than whites; in addition, all three societies offer explicit illustrations of recent racial discrimination. Unfortunately we have found cross-cultural evidence from three very different societies indicating that race continues to be a remarkably "persistent category of advantage and privilege."

REFERENCES

Badsha, Omar (ed.). 1986. *South Africa: The Cordoned Heart.* Cape Town, South Africa: Gallery Press.

Christmas, Rachel Jackson. 1988. "In Harmony with Brazil's African Pulse." *New York Times* (November 20): 43.

Christopher, A. J. 1990. "*Apartheid* and Urban Segregation Levels in South Africa." *Urban Studies* 27 (June): 421–440.

Clark, Alisha. 1979. "African-American College Students' Attitudes." *Journal of Black Studies* 10 (July): 243–248.

Crooks, Kai. 1988. "Peaceful Paths to Change Are Being Closed One by One." *Black Enterprise* 18 (May): 36.

Drimmer, Melvin. 1979. "Neither Black Nor White: Carl Degler's Study of Slavery in Two Societies." *Phylon* 40 (March): 94–105.

Dzidzienyo, Anani. 1985. "The African Connection and the Afro-Brazilian Condition," pp. 135–153 in Pierre-Michel Fontaine (ed.), *Race, Class, and Power in Brazil.* University of California, Los Angeles: Center for Afro-American Studies.

Economist. 1987. "An Amazonian Tragedy." *Economist* 305 (October 17): 52.

Fernandes, Florestan. 1969. *The Negro in Brazilian Society.* New York: Columbia University Press.

Hasenbalg, Carlos A. 1985. "Race and Socioeconomic Inequalities in Brazil," pp. 25–41 in Pierre-Michel Fontaine (ed.), *Race, Class, and Power in Brazil.* University of California, Los Angeles: Center for Afro-American Studies.

Lelyveld, Joseph. 1985. *Move Your Shadow: South Africa, Black and White.* New York: Times Books.

Mathabane, Mark. 1986. *Kaffir Boy.* New York: Macmillan.

Oberholster, A. G. 1988. "Evolution of South African Society," pp. 39–58 in H. C. Marais (ed.), *South Africa: Perspective on the Future.* Pinetown, South Africa: Owen Burgess Publishers.

Riding, Alan. 1985. "Brazil's Time Bomb: Poor Children by the Millions." *New York Times* (October 23): 2.

Silva, Nelson do Valle. 1985. "Updating the Cost of Not Being White in Brazil," pp. 42–55 in Pierre-Michel Fontaine (ed.), *Race, Class, and Power in Brazil.* University of California, Los Angeles: Center for Afro-American Studies.

Silverstein, Ken. 1990. "Collor's 'New Brazil': Shock Treatment for the Poor." *Nation* 251 (November 12): 554–557.

Skidmore, Thomas E. 1985. "Race and Class in Brazil: Historical Perspectives," pp. 11–24 in Pierre-Michel Fontaine (ed.), *Race, Class, and Power in Brazil.* University of California, Los Angeles: Center for Afro-American Studies.

Smith, T. Lynn. 1972. *Brazilian Society.* Albuquerque: University of New Mexico Press.

South African Foundation. 1988. *1988 Information Digest.* Johannesburg, South Africa: South African Foundation.

Sundiata, I. K. 1987. "Late Twentieth Century Patterns of Race Relations in Brazil and the United States." *Phylon* 48 (March): 62–76.

Tambo, Oliver. 1987. "Strategic Options for International Companies." *Black Scholar* 18 (November/December): 8–13.

Thompson, Leonard. 1990. "South Africa: The Fire This Time?" *New York Review of Books* 37 (June 14): 12+.

Turner, J. Michael. 1985. "Brown into Black: Changing Racial Attitudes of Afro-Brazilian University Students," pp. 73–94 in Pierre-Michel Fontaine (ed.), *Race, Class, and Power in Brazil.* University of California, Los Angeles: Center for Afro-American Studies.

Webster, Peggy Lovell, and Jeffrey W. Dwyer. 1988. "The Cost of Being Nonwhite in Brazil." *Sociology and Social Research* 72 (January): 136–138.

Wren, Christopher S. 1992. "South African Whites Ratify De Klerk Effort to Negotiate a Move Toward Majority Rule." *New York Times* (March 19): A1.

Wren, Christopher S. 1990. "South African Talks Yield Outlines on an Agreement on Basic Political Changes." *New York Times* (May 5): 1.

Wren, Christopher S. 1990a. "Mandela Says De Klerk Concedes 'Hidden Hand' in Recent Killings." *New York Times* (September 15): 1.

Chapter
10

Racism in the Land of Dreams

*I*t was a popular talk show in a medium-size American city. Some whites accused Estelle Powers, the African-American hostess, of reverse racism, but a recent poll revealed that 72 percent of a representative sample of the local public considered her tough but fair.

On this particular evening, Powers's guest was Jack Baker, a successful white businessman. Baker had taken his father's small real-estate business, turned it into a corporate force that extended into three neighboring states, and diversified into construction, radio, and television.

Powers thanked Baker for appearing on her show. "My staff took a vote," she said with a quick smile, "and four out of five predicted you'd turn us down."

"I've nothing to hide," Baker replied.

Powers quickly reviewed major events in Baker's life—well-publicized delinquent activities in his early teens, attendance at military school, entrance into the family firm, and his subsequent business expansion.

Then Powers turned to her guest and said, "Mr Baker, recently you were interviewed by Frank Cobbs of the *Herald Eagle.*" Powers glanced at a newspaper article pinned to her clipboard. "You said, and I quote, 'If I were just starting out, I'd definitely want to be black. That would give me a step up on the white competition.' " She stared at him. "Do you really believe that?"

Baker folded his hands and looked intently into the camera. "Absolutely."

"What about racism?"

"It has been eliminated, or close to it."

"How do you figure that?"

"As a business man, I talk to people all day long. The racial slurs, the innuendos, they aren't there anymore, or, at any rate, when they do occur, it's just harmless fun."

"Harmless fun?!" I . . ." Powers interrupted herself. "I doubt that you and I could resolve that point. So consider this." She thumbed through a half-dozen sheets on the clipboard. "On these pages are the results of many reputable studies showing that racism persists in all major activities of modern society."

Baker smiled broadly and turned up his hands in mock dispair. "I have great respect for the academic world, Ms. Powers, but professors who do these studies are ruled by their liberal biases."

"You mean to tell me, Mr. Baker, that these well-documented accounts of racism are, in reality, nothing but false liberal claims?"

"That puts it well. But there's another critical point." Powers raised his right hand and shook the index finger emphatically. "By focusing on racism, liberals have avoided the heart of the issue—the true cause of poverty among minority poor in this country."

"What would that be?"

"The inability to cope." Baker explained that in his view illegitimacy, broken families, and crime occurred because poor blacks, Puerto Ricans, Native Americans, and some other racial minorities lacked discipline.

Powers interrupted. "You yourself lacked discipline at one time. You broke the law, got into trouble . . ."

"But the difference was that I got the discipline, pursued my dream, and captured it."

"How did you get discipline?"

"By going to military school."

"But what about some black or Puerto Rican kid whose parents are too poor to send him or her to military school, a private drug-treatment program, or whatever facility the child desperately needs?"

"That, Ms. Powers, is when Uncle Sammy steps in. For 60 years now, your liberal friends have been developing federally financed programs for every social problem under the sun. Even with racism no longer a viable excuse, the programs go on."

"If you are correct that the federal government is always ready to assist minority-group members, then perhaps you, especially with your expertise in inner-city real estate, can clarify a point: Why are there so many homeless minority individuals and families?"

Baker beamed. "People like sports terminology, and often I've found in inspirational talks to young people that it helps clarify issues. In a sentence, Ms. Powers, a homeless family is a graphic example of a social unit without a game plan."

Powers slammed down her clipboard. "What about the role played by developers like you who have virtually eliminated low-cost housing in the inner city?!"

On and on they go. This is a hypothetical dialogue, but there is nothing hypothetical about the positions presented here. When many Americans assess people's actions, they, like Jack Baker, focus on what they consider individuals' strengths and weaknesses: They claim that failure to achieve one's dreams is the result of personal and cultural deficiency. Structural conditions lying outside individuals, including racism, play little or no role in such analyses. Like Baker some people argue this position tirelessly, offering arguments that can seem convincing if the listener knows little about the sociological perspective on racism. In a culture stressing individualism and competition, widespread support for Baker's position is probably inevitable.

In contrast, Estelle Powers's position is implicitly sociological, looking beyond individuals and their respective successes and failures to consider conditions that have promoted or restricted their opportunities.

Racism, we have seen, can significantly limit people's chances for success and happiness. This book was launched with Troy Duster's claim that throughout the nation's history race has been "the most persistent category of advantage." From this position it was a reasonable step to introduce internal colonialism, which emphasizes that since whites' earliest occupation of this land, they have systematically controlled racial minorities in governance, physical activity, and work, and condemned their traditional cultures. These points in the internal-colonialist theory help us to see that while racism has toned down in modern times, it remains healthy.

We have learned that racism persists in all the substantive areas we have examined. At times, perhaps, some of you might have been surprised how widespread racism is. Professional sports has long been considered an area where a person of ability can find success, regardless of race. Yet research has shown clearly that racial discrimination exists in professional football, basketball, and baseball. It might seem apparent that if a family can afford a certain house, then they can buy it. But if the family is African-American or Puerto Rican, then residential discrimination has been prevalent.

Racism persists, and so as we draw toward the end of the book, we can briefly consider measures to eliminate or restrict it.

COMBATING RACISM

Public-service announcements, sermons, and classroom lectures often stress that racism is wrong. But in spite of many notable efforts to condemn racism, the impact is limited. The problem is that such efforts do not alter structures supporting the problem.

Public officials often either fail to appreciate or simply deny that reality. When a major racial incident occurs in a city or at a college or university, authorities are likely to call meetings and create task forces, which issue reports but make few meaningful changes.

Nor can one hold the mayor of a city or the president of a college or university mainly responsible for failing to eliminate racism. As we have seen throughout this book, racism permeates American society: The steps to restrict it significantly go well beyond the capacities of political or university officials. Let's consider what needs to be done.

To begin, we must keep the internal-colonialist perspective firmly in mind. What is the significance of that focus in this context? It seems to be twofold. First, internal colonialism suggests that racism has been relentless and widespread throughout the history of American society. Second, the implication of this conclusion is that measures to eliminate or even restrict racism require major efforts. Inexpensive, painless solutions to racism won't work.

Thinking along these lines, Stephen Steinberg (1989) contended that an effective policy to eradicate the historical impact of racism must address fundamental problems. The following discussion includes several of Steinberg's issues, along with an additional point:

First, there must be a national commitment to eliminating ghettos. Poverty inherited from the days of slavery along with discrimination in housing have produced and maintained ghettos, and ghetto residence restricts a person's educational and occupational opportunities. Yet on television news and in textbooks, ghettos are discussed with the same neutrality shown to suburbs. That shouldn't be: Ghettos are among the most stark representations of internal colonialism's emphasis on the restriction of racial minorities' physical movement.

Steinberg pointed out that to implement such a multibillion-dollar program effectively, organizers would need to keep a vigilant watch on its activities, making certain that it did not become simply another scandal-ridden opportunity for construction, real-estate, and political interests. In addition, it would be essential to enlist the participation of local individuals and groups, whose perspective on ghetto dwellers' needs and interests emerge out of daily experience, not from some removed, possibly misguided, or even racist viewpoint.

We should consider one cautionary idea. A clear distinction exists between eliminating negative aspects of ghetto life and destroying vital if poor inner-city communities. Herbert Gans (1962) and Jane Jacobs (1961) produced classic studies stressing that most city planners tend to view poor, urban neighborhoods negatively, simply assuming that they are destructive to their residents and the city at large. As a result their orders are to bulldoze indiscriminately, with the frequent tragic result that vital communities developed over long periods of time are destroyed. Eliminating ghettos, in short, should not mean destroying vital communities. Before determining appropriate alterations, each area must be examined carefully to assess its strengths and weaknesses.

A second issue in Steinberg's discussion is that affirmative action needs continued support and growth; it represents a direct attack on the colonial-labor principle. Historically racial minorities were restricted in education and work, limited to training and jobs that would directly benefit white controllers. Affirmative-action programs attempt to address historical wrongs.

Consider some impressive successes. American Telephone and Telegraph Company, one of the largest private employers in the United States, established an agreement in 1973 with the Equal Employment Opportunities Commission to redress past discriminatory hiring practices. By 1982 the percentage of minority craft workers had increased from 8.4 percent to 14 percent of the work force, and among management the proportion of minority-group members had risen from 4.6 percent to 13.1 percent. Between 1962 and 1968, the number of black employees at IBM rose nearly tenfold—from 750 to 7251—and then in 1980 more than doubled to 16,546. Under threat of court orders, government agencies have aggressively pursued affirmative-action policies, and the results have been decisive. One result has been that since the late 1960s, the number of black police officers has increased by 20,000 (Steinberg, 1989).

The opening years of the affirmative-action period yielded modest results. In general, research found that between 1966 and 1973, companies forced to establish affirmative-action programs because they were doing business with the federal government increased their percentage of black workers more than companies not required to meet affirmative-action standards. Between 1974 and 1980, the number of African-Americans receiving jobs because of affirmative action increased even more than in the previous seven-year period; in addition, at this time as a result of affirmative action, blacks were often able to obtain better paying, more prestigious positions (Jaynes and Williams, 1989: 316–317; Leonard, 1985). Reviewing investigations on the topic, a team of researchers concluded that "affirmative action seems to have effected educational and occupational gains for women and for racial minorities" (Crosby and Clayton, 1990: 65).

A criticism frequently directed against affirmative action is that it has promoted racial minorities' opportunities for white-collar positions and ignored their involvement in blue-collar jobs. But this has not been the case. The focus of many affirmative-action initiatives has been law enforcement, construction work, and craft and production positions in large companies.

Another criticism is that giving minority-group members a hand up undermines their morale and self-confidence. Certainly each affirmative-action program needs to be examined and reexamined for its impact on participants, and if clear indications of destructive effect appear, then alterations are necessary. Often, however, this position claiming favoritism toward minorities simply serves to praise the value of individualism while conveniently forgetting structural factors underlying racism and poverty. A significantly greater concern seems to be that the vicious cycle of poverty enveloping so many minority-group members continues to expand. To prevent that, affirmative action must proceed with all deliberate speed.

With the groundwork for affirmative action now established, it appears just and reasonable to extend its programs into all educational and work areas. Inevitably resistance will continue, but if this society truly is dedicated to the elimination of racism, this policy must persist.

A third issue also relates to jobs and additionally involves immigration policy. In the past quarter-century, this nation has lost 3 million industrial jobs and also absorbed over 11 million legal immigrants, along with countless millions of illegal arrivals. Frequently immigrants have taken jobs for which Americans, particularly minority Americans could be trained.

Consider the area of nursing. To meet a critical shortage of nurses, the United States has been importing tens of thousands of foreign nurses. At the same time, nursing schools throughout the country have been closed. A program oriented to the needs and interests of American minorities would emphasize that the nursing shortage could be met with a radically different approach—expand nursing schools, publicize and promote the opportunities for nursing throughout the public-school system, especially in areas where there are large numbers of minority students, and, ultimately, stop importing large numbers of foreign nurses (Steinberg, 1989: 51–54).

So far we have covered two major issues addressed by internal colonialism: The first point relates to the restriction of physical activity and the last two address problems associated with the colonial-labor principle. The fourth and final issue relates to the tenet declaring minority cultures inferior and the dominant culture superior.

In this chapter's opening dialogue, Jack Baker indicated that some racial slurs might be considered harmless fun. But a comment or joke that might seem funny and harmless to a white person can be insulting and painful to a minority-group individual. For many Americans it is often easy to overlook comments and situations that are distinctly racist.

Even specialists on racial issues find themselves contributing to racism. Stephen Steinberg raised this point with his analysis of the term "underclass," which became popular in the early 1980s. The term focuses on individuals' and groups' failures to attain conventional rewards, thus keeping them "under" the established class system. It is a vague term, lumping together diverse ethnic and racial groups and failing to single out specific conditions, especially racism for racial minorities, that have played a crucial role in limiting their opportunities (Steinberg, 1989: 43–44). This term has racist, blame-the-victim overtones, implying minorities' cultural inferiority; and it is used widely. That is because even experts on race relations sometimes fail to see that their analysis of racial situations is simplistic.

The previous discussion might seem inconsistent with the book's emphasis on the overriding importance of institutional structures producing racism. Why emphasize the importance of individuals' attitudes? While altering institutional structures producing racism must be the priority, perhaps an individual or group's starting point should be the recognition that successful steps must be modest but concrete, located in immediate realities. Eliminating the term "underclass" is a good case in point.

As this book draws to a close, we analyze one last episode about race and oppressed status.

A Student Effort to Combat Racism

It is hardly surprising that in a society where norms supporting racial conflict and separation prevail, race relations in high schools will mirror the larger social pattern.

In 1988 in a high school in Ann Arbor, Michigan, a science teacher reprimanded several African-American students for their "rowdy behavior." In the course of his reprimand, he asked, "Do you want to grow up to be dumb niggers?" The question launched a controversy that involved public confrontations between parents, teachers, and administrators. But throughout all this activity, student input was not sought.

A number of local high-school students decided to become involved. They initiated a survey, assessing students' feelings about racism in the Ann Arbor high schools and took several actions based on their findings. Two of the students—Shael Polakow-Suransky and Neda Ulaby—wrote up the highlights in an article.

In October 1987 these students took over a largely dormant organization called Student Advocates to the School Board (SASB). Members convened a meeting of students from each of Ann Arbor's four high schools. Representatives of all three racial groups in the schools—African-Americans, Asian-Americans, and whites—participated. In the first meeting, students discussed their personal experiences and began to develop a group approach. In subsequent meetings SASB students conducted brainstorming sessions in which they reworked questions for their survey until reaching a consensus. Ultimately, SASB members realized, they would need their administrations' approval for the final questionnaire, but they were determined to keep the survey's development a wholly student effort.

By January the students completed a working copy of the question-naire. English-class members in one of the larger high schools served as guinea pigs, and as a result of this initial testing, some questions were reworded and the survey was shortened.

The district administration agreed to print up the questionnaires, and 3500 copies of the three-page instrument were produced. Two thousand and six students (57.4 percent of those surveyed) filled it out. Those who didn't either were absent the day the survey was given, or teachers in a given class chose not to administer it. Responses to demographic questions indicated that those who answered the questionnaire provided a racial and social-class cross-section of the district.

When asked about segregation at school, most students indicated that it occurred both academically and socially and that minorities often felt that they were objects of discrimination. One respondent indicated that because of segregated classes, minorities don't consider whites to be peers. Another student claimed that segregation was voluntary, with each racial group claiming to be superior. Ninety-two percent of the students indi-cated that social segregation existed to some degree, but most felt that it was not bad and, in fact, was natural.

Reading the questionnaire commentaries on segregation, the re-searchers were impressed by clear linguistic indications of racial segrega-tion. Polakow-Suransky and Ulaby indicated that the pronouns *we* and *us* were often opposed to the pronouns *they* and *them*, producing psycholog-ical barriers between student racial groups.

Tracking was another topic in the questionnaire. When asked to choose from a list of alternatives one or more reasons why minority-group students were more likely to be tracked into lower classes, 52 percent said it was because minority-group students had lower scores on standardized achievement tests, 51 percent indicated it was because they didn't try as hard, 46 percent said it was because they had been labeled troublemakers, and 44 percent concluded it was because of their grades from elementary and junior high school. Often students were unaware that because of institutional racism, many members of racial minorities had suffered edu-cational disadvantages since early childhood, making their likelihood of ending up in lower classes much greater than it would be for whites. Some students did recognize the destructive, self-fulfilling impact of tracking. One wrote, "If you've been treated like a dumb black child all your life, you begin to actually believe it."

Many students had strong emotional responses to members of other racial groups. Some whites felt that blacks engaged in reverse discrimina-tion—that black organizations were segregationist and represented just another form of racism. Frequently whites were deeply resentful of the anger and bitterness encountered in daily interactions with African-Amer-ican students. Some white students felt that teachers set lower standards for black students and that blacks took advantage of minority status when pursuing college admissions and scholarships. On the other hand, African-

American students felt that they often encountered racism, and that little effort occurred to right wrongs of historical oppression. In addition, student responses indicated that highly negative stereotypes of black students continued to thrive in the Ann Arbor high schools.

SASB members analyzed their data and wrote up a report, which they presented to the school board. They included a list of recommendations, such as developing workshops and class discussions about the race-related issues contained in the survey; reevaluating local policies on tracking, with the aim of eliminating the practice; requiring all students to take a course exposing them to issues involving American racial oppression; and creating a task force both to evaluate the entire high-school curriculum from a multicultural perspective and to develop guidelines for handling racial incidents in the high schools.

In the next several months, SASB students organized follow-up activities for the last weeks before the end of the school year. They felt that for the first time, they were beginning to confront structures supporting racism and racial isolation. At that point students started to encounter resistance from school administrators. Two school principals backed out of earlier commitments to support students' efforts. Polakow-Suransky and Ulaby indicated that they were unhappy to discover that "the resistance to change at this level was more powerful than the district's stated policy of pursuing excellence and equity" (Polakow-Suransky and Ulaby, 1990: 606).

However, SASB members were able to schedule successful class discussions and workshops in the two smaller high schools, and they presented a proposal to the school board asking that each school be required to spend 15 hours the following year on multicultural educational activities.

During the next spring semester, SASB members decided to pursue a suggestion repeatedly made in students' questionnaires—follow up on younger students. They designed a curriculum, using simulated games, cooperative learning activities, and group discussions in which sixth graders would interact with high-school students. The SASB efforts received sufficient administrative support to make it likely that by the middle of the 1990–1991 school year, five middle schools would be participating in it.

Two years later it was difficult to gauge the impact students' efforts to dismantle racist structures produced on the Ann Arbor high schools. Currently the history curriculum is being reevaluated with the intent to present a multicultural perspective. In the 1989–1990 school year, there was a new required course on human behavior, containing a large component on racism. Members of the student group met with counselors to discuss ways of dealing with tracking, but little change has occurred in that area.

Looking back on a couple of years of hard work, Polakow-Suransky and Ulaby indicated that SASB efforts had made a difference but that schools, like all American organizations, are conservative and will only change slowly. The authors concluded that the impact of racism is so pervasive in people's thoughts and actions that the struggle to find new ways to eliminate it must be unrelenting.

This group of high-school students produced impressive results. What steps would be necessary to implement such a program at your college? It might be interesting and productive to discuss this issue in class.

CONCLUSION

In the years ahead, Americans will be forced to make tough decisions about race. What programs will most effectively curtail or eliminate the legacy of racism? Throughout this book we have examined the inhumanity of racism. Certainly it is fitting to do everything to be humane—to give all citizens an opportunity to participate fully in the bounty of our great nation.

But the issue goes beyond such altruism. It has become painfully apparent that a great shadow has spread across our society—fear of the ever-expanding violence of primarily minority citizens who have been denied access to valued opportunities and rewards. It is now painfully apparent that no token measures are going to buy them off. If the United States doesn't make a frontal attack on the combined forces of racism and poverty, then those formidable foes are going to grow in strength and in the terror they produce. Reviewing race relations in the 1990s, sociologist Lewis Killian concluded that new taxes and a more equitable distribution of wealth are necessary. He warned that without such measures "the new enemy will be our own underclass" (Killian, 1990: 13).

At the moment American culture is a racist culture. This condition is undeniable, regrettable, but potentially changeable. Collectively Americans should do what those addicted to alcohol or hard drugs are required to do: Look hard and long at themselves and face their problem head on, in this case saying, "We are racist." A heartfelt realization can be a first step toward effective action.

REFERENCES

Crosby, Faye, and Susan Clayton. 1990. "Affirmative Action and the Issue of Expectancies." *Journal of Social Issues* 46: 61–79.

Gans, Herbert J. 1962. *The Urban Villagers.* New York: Free Press.

Jacobs, Jane. 1961. *The Death and Life of Great American Cities.* New York: Vintage Books.

Jaynes, Gerald David, and Robin M. Williams, Jr. (eds.). 1989. *A Common Destiny: Blacks and American Society.* Washington, DC: National Academy Press.

Killian, Lewis M. 1990. "Race Relations and the Nineties: Where Are the Dreams of the Sixties?" *Social Forces* 69 (September): 1–13.

Leonard, Jonathan. 1985. "The Effectiveness of Equal Employment and Affirmative Action Regulation." Report to the Subcommittee on Civil and Constitutional Rights of the Judiciary Committee, U.S. Congress. Berkeley, CA: School of Business Administration, University of California, Berkeley.

Polakow-Suransky, Shael, and Neda Ulaby. 1990. "Students Take Action to Combat Racism." *Phi Delta Kappan* 71 (April): 601–606.

Steinberg, Stephen. 1989. "The Underclass: A Case of Color Blindness." *New Politics* 2 (Summer): 42–60.

Glossary

apartheid South African government policy involving racial segregation of major facilities—residential areas, hotels, restaurants, buses, work locations, and even staircases and toilets

authority power that people generally recognize as rightfully maintained by those who use it

caste system a socially legitimate arrangement of groups in which the ranking of the different groups is clearly designated, members' expected behavior is specified, and movement of individuals from one group to another is prohibited

conflict theory a perspective contending that the struggle for power and wealth in society should be the central concern of sociology

discrimination the behavior by which one group prevents or restricts a minority group's access to scarce resources

ethnocentrism the automatic tendency to evaluate other cultures by outsiders' cultural standards

frustration-aggression theory a perspective emphasizing that people blocked from achieving a goal are sometimes unable or unwilling to focus their frustration on the true source, and so they direct the aggression produced by frustration toward an accessible individual or group

index of dissimilarity a calculation indicating the proportion of a particular racial group that would need to change residential areas in order to achieve racial balance; a condition in which that group's percentage in a given census district would be similar to its percentage in that city

individual racism an action performed by one person or group that produces racial abuse

institutional racism discriminatory racial practices built into such prominent structures as the political, economic, and educational systems

internal colonialism a theory emphasizing that the control imposed on indigenous racial minorities passes from whites in the home country to whites living within a newly independent nation

looking-glass self individuals' understanding that the sort of person they are is based on how they think they appear to others

lynching one group's use of mob action to kill a member of an oppressed group, thereby warning other members of that oppressed group either to accept an even more lowly status or to forsake any developing plans to rise above their subordinated position

macro level the large-scale structures and activities that exist within societies and between one society and another

mass media the instruments of communication that reach a large audience without any personal contact between senders and receivers

mentoring a process by which people of higher rank and achievement instruct and guide the intellectual or career development of less-experienced individuals outside of classrooms

micro level the structure and activities of small groups

minority group any category of people with recognizable racial or ethnic traits that place it in a position of restricted power and inferior status so that its members suffer limited opportunities and reward

norm standard of desirable behavior

normification behavior that gives the impression that an individual widely considered inferior is trying to deny being different

pluralism a theory emphasizing that a dispersion of power exists in government or other structures within American society

political incorporation inclusion of racial minority-group members as significant players in political coalitions that contain some whites and successfully challenge established white conservative groups for control over a city's political activity

political institution the system of norms and roles that concerns the use and distribution of authority within a given society

power the ability of an individual or group to implement wishes or policies, with or without the cooperation of others

prejudice a highly negative judgment toward a minority group, focusing on one or more characteristics that are supposedly uniformly shared by all group members

race a classification of people into categories falsely claimed to be derived from a distinct set of biological traits

racism the ideology contending that actual or alleged differences among different racial groups assert the superiority of one racial group

self-fulfilling prophecy an incorrect definition of a situation that comes to pass because people accept the incorrect definition and act on it to make it become true

social mobility the movement of a person from one social class or status level to another, either upward or downward, with accompanying gains or losses in wealth, power, and prestige

stereotype exaggerated, oversimplified image maintained by prejudiced people of the characteristics of the group members against whom they are prejudiced

structural-functional theory a perspective suggesting that interacting groups tend to influence and adjust to each other in a fairly stable, conflict-free pattern

vicious cycle of poverty a pattern in which parents' minimal income significantly limits children's educational and occupational pursuits, thereby keeping them locked into the same low economic status

Index